THE
RE-USE
ATLAS

A DESIGNER'S GUIDE TOWARDS A CIRCULAR ECONOMY

RIBA Publishing

DUNCAN BAKER-BROWN

To Kate and Molly who help keep me sane and informed.

To Professor Anne Boddington who has supported me and most of my hare-brained ideas for over 15 years.

To Nick Gant, Tony Roberts and Ian McKay for the ongoing conversations.

© RIBA Publishing, 2017

Reprinted 2019

Published by RIBA Publishing, 66 Portland Place, London W1B 1AD

ISBN: 978 1 85946 644 5

The right of Duncan Baker-Brown to be identified as the Author of this Work has been asserted in accordance with the Copyright, Design and Patents Act 1988.

All rights reserved. No part of this publication may be reproduced, stored in a retrieval system, or transmitted, in any form or by any means, electronic, mechanical, photocopying, recording or otherwise, without prior permission of the copyright owner.

British Library Cataloguing-in-Publications Data
A catalogue record for this book is available from the British Library.

Commissioning Editor: Elizabeth Webster
Copy Editor: Kathryn Glendenning
Production: Phil Handley
Designed and typeset by Mercer Design, London
Printed and bound by W&G Baird Ltd, Great Britain

While every effort has been made to check the accuracy and quality of the information given in this publication, neither the Author nor the Publisher accept any responsibility for the subsequent use of this information, for any errors or omissions that it may contain, or for any misunderstandings arising from it.

www.ribapublishing.com

This book is printed on Cocoon Silk, FSC certified, 100% recycled paper. Cocoon papers meet the same performance standards as non-recycled papers with excellent printability and whiteness (CIE 124), and a high quality surface which helps bring out the best in printed images.

ABOUT THE AUTHOR

Duncan Baker-Brown RIBA FRSA

DUNCAN BAKER-BROWN is an architect, writer, academic and environmental activist, based in Lewes, near Brighton, on the south coast of England, where he lives with his wife and daughter. Born next to a farm near Epping Forest in Essex, Duncan soon became aware of the fragility of the natural environment as he witnessed first the M11 and then the M25 motorways cut through countryside he had grown very fond of.

For nearly 25 years Duncan has been at the forefront of teaching, researching and practising sustainable design, working on projects as varied as exhibitions and symposiums, new houses and schools, as well as whole urban districts such as London's Greenwich Millennium Village with Ralph Erskine. While working for Rick Mather Architects he set up BBM Sustainable Design with his business partner Ian McKay after they had won the RIBA 'House of the Future' competition. In 1994 Duncan started his teaching career at the University of Brighton's School of Architecture, where he and Ian had met as postgraduate students. They quickly began to work on research projects, such as 'CityVision' in 1997, which considered ways people could live in beautiful, sustainable cities.

More recently Duncan has become well known as the architect behind a series of experimental off-grid 'sustainable house' projects, such as Channel 4's 'The House that Kevin Built' with Kevin McCloud. This was the first house in the UK with an A+ energy certificate, as well as the first one made from 90% organic material. It was followed by 'The Brighton Waste House', which was designed and constructed in collaboration with more than 360 students at the University of Brighton. It was Europe's first permanent building made from waste.

Duncan is a passionate and informed public speaker on many issues pertaining to sustainable development and the circular economy.

For further information:

http://arts.brighton.ac.uk/staff/duncan-baker-brown

http://bbm-architects.co.uk

Search for 'Can Architecture Matter?' on the TEDx Talks channel on YouTube

ACKNOWLEDGEMENTS

OVER THE LAST FIVE YEARS I have had hundreds, if not thousands, of conversations with many people who have helped me formulate questions and opinions that have coloured the direction and content of this publication. I would like to start by thanking everybody who contributed to the content and design of this book, including my commissioning editor, Liz Webster, and design and production manager, Phil Handley, Professor Anne Boddington, Professor Graeme Brooker, Professor Jonathan Chapman, Nick Gant, Dr David Greenfield, Cat Fletcher, Nitesh Magdani, Stuart Smith, Professor Dr Walter Stahel and Dr Ryan Woodard. In addition I have been having informal conversations with my good friend of more than 20 years, Tony (Anthony) Roberts. Thank you Tony for your many suggestions for case studies that could be included in this Atlas.

I completed more than 60 interviews with inspiring people from nearly every continent around the world, many of which are ongoing conversations today. Of course a number of these are captured in the interviews and case studies that are included within Part 2 of my book, so I won't list them here. However, I would like to take the opportunity to thank the following people who have offered me advice and knowledge over the past couple of years (and longer): Dr Ben Croxford, Professor Martin Charter, Oliver Heath, Sophie Thomas, Michael Moradiellos del Molino, Jeremy Sumeray, Munish Datta, Lydia Dutton, Gereon Uerz, Fran Ford, Annabelle Cox, Stephen Bayley, Mike Pitts, Steven Cross, Professor David Robson, Hattie Hartman, Professor Joan Farrer, Jon Khoo, Professor Jo-Anne Bichard, Daniel Pan, Nick Hayhurst, Caroline O'Donnell, Professor Alan Tomlinson, Jonathan Essex, Bruce McClelland, Catherine Joce, Kate Cheyne, Glenn Longden-Thurgood, Professor Andre Viljoen, Kirsty Sutherland, Dr Ryan Southall, Keir Black, Ian Bailey, Jeff Turko, Michelle Wright, Ben Sweeting, Gareth Lawrence, Luiz Dias, Gemma Barton, Professor Peter Lloyd, Professor Andrew Lloyd, Michele Field, Professor Dr Michael Braungart, Bryn Thomas, Alistair Boyd, Tom Hammick and Professor Jonathan Woodham.

I would like to thank the following people who helped enable and deliver the Brighton Waste House (named unless already acknowledged above): Professor Catherine Harper, Dianne Lock, Francesca Iliffe, Martin Randall, John Ritson, Isobel Creed, Jacob Browne, Mike Sansom, Gary Lester, David Pendegrass, James Cryer, Tom Dowds, Dr Caroline Lucas MP, Kevin McCloud, plus

Mears apprentices, as well as more than 360 design and construction students from the University of Brighton and City College Brighton and Hove.

I couldn't have entertained the idea of writing this book without the support of the University of Brighton, which granted me a four-month sabbatical from teaching in the School of Architecture and Design. For that I am very thankful. My colleagues from BBM Sustainable Design also supported me enormously during the year I have been working on this book. They have, of course, also helped me work on numerous fascinating projects over the years. So I would like to thank Daniel Harding, James Rae, Tom Cuthbert, Stuart Paine, Rebecca Kinneavy and Magali McKay, and of course my amazing partner Ian McKay, who for many years has been my primary collaborator.

Finally, I would like to thank my mother and two brothers, Stuart and Byron, for their constant encouragement, and, of course, my gorgeous wife Kate and my lovely daughter Molly-Rose, who have been a constant inspiration and support.

CONTENTS

iii   ABOUT THE AUTHOR

iv   ACKNOWLEDGEMENTS

ix   FOREWORD
Graeme Brooker

xiii   PREFACE
Professor Walter Stahel

1   INTRODUCTION
Duncan Baker-Brown

PART 1

5   **Setting the Waste Scene**

7   CHAPTER 1
Resource Matters
Duncan Baker-Brown

16   CHAPTER 2
What a Waste!
Cat Fletcher

21   CHAPTER 3
The Political Narrative
Dr David Greenfield

PART 2

29 Circular Inspirations
Duncan Baker-Brown

31 INTRODUCTION

33 STEP 1
Recycling Waste

55 STEP 2
Reusing Waste

81 STEP 3
Reducing the Amount of Material Used

109 STEP 4
The Circular Economy

PART 3

143 The Waste House Story
Duncan Baker-Brown

PART 4

159 Looking Forward

161 CHAPTER 1
Product Moments, Material Eternities
Professor Jonathan Chapman

166 CHAPTER 2
Educating the Circular Economy (or Learning in Circles)
Professor Anne Boddington

173 CHAPTER 3
How are Closed-Loop Systems Relevant?
Duncan Baker-Brown

183 ENDNOTES

188 INDEX

190 PICTURE CREDITS

FOREWORD

Tabula Plena

Professor Graeme Brooker
Head of Interior Design, Royal College of Art

IT IS A PRIVILEGE TO BE INVITED to contribute the foreword to this book and be given the opportunity to contextualise its unique contents. *The Re-Use Atlas* is a timely book, overflowing with projects and ideas, work that is suffused with the compelling enthusiasm of its author and contributors. *Atlas* is the ideal term to use in the depiction of *reuse*, a process that describes the durability of things and the tenacity of the people undertaking their extended existence. The Greek myth of Atlas symbolised a feat of endurance: as the son of Zeus, the Titan god was condemned to hold up the sky in perpetuity. Obstinacy, persistence and the enduring qualities of something or someone are entirely apt to be implied in the title of a book about the intensified durability of things and places.

Upon the first reading of this Atlas, my initial reaction was how reliant all aspects of the book were on the abundance and also the scarcity of existing matter. It is this variability in the sources of the raw material for reuse that has led to the development and description of numerous, clever, engaged strategies of *contingency*. These strategies are conditional approaches that are based on the provisional understanding of not just working with what is already there, but which are methods that explore what might be exposed during the transformational processes of their reuse. The approaches to extant matter made me think of how this *Re-Use Atlas* demonstrates the requirement of a very specific sensibility: one that is prepared to rely on what was either already in situ, or what was about to be found or exposed during the processes of change. This sensibility denotes the inclination to understand and accept the qualities of extant materials, in order to transform them. It is an approach that is significantly distinguished from the idea of design as unfettered origination, or, of the conjuring up of ideas out of the ether.

Instead, *The Re-Use Atlas* brings this sensibility into sharp focus, through the numerous ideas and people that it contains, and the exemplary projects that it meticulously depicts.

In the Oxford English Dictionary, *contingency* is described as 'an event conceived as of a possible occurrence in the future'[1]. Its etymology is rooted in the Latin for *touching* or *coming into contact with*. The active, or *hands-on* dimension of the word is exemplified in the very root of its meaning. On this basis, I would suggest that this Atlas is an advocate for a *hands-on* attitude, or, at

FIG. 0.1 (OPPOSITE) Some of the waste material investigations undertaken by students on the Sustainable Design MA at the University of Brighton

the very least, it examines ways of actively rethinking and remodelling what surrounds us. In other words, in this book, *matter*, such as materials, objects and spaces, are found, repurposed, transformed, and adapted in an *applied* manner. Each idea in this Atlas, each case study, each agent engaged in the processes of 'closed-looping', are turning the linear circular in a *hands-on* manner. By doing this, their work epitomises the activation of significant behavioural change. The Atlas charts the processes of how they are turning a linear economy, based on the scarcity and abundance of matter, circular, and effectively reusing and making products, services, energy, materials, buildings, cities, behave in a more resilient and enduring manner. It is an *applied* approach; one that values existing entities, extant matter, objects that are already in circulation and which have become the site for mediation and transformation into something they were often never intended to be.

Therefore, this *Re-Use Atlas* is a vital component in the understanding of how to reprocess matter and obsolete material into something that is put back into the cycles of use. It is focussed on the consideration that in all of the exemplars and ideas that are mentioned in this book, the redundant or adapted materials that were examined were not only a site of depredation, but also provide a condition for mediation. In other words, reusing materials foregrounds the enactment of research and design processes that will ensure that not only meaningful change will take place but that they originate new and unique processes of research, thinking and knowledge that is just not the same as the usual design processes that often focus on starting from scratch.

I have summarised these observations under the heading *Tabula Plena*. *Tabula rasa* is often understood as starting with a blank slate. Its etymology is derived from the rubbing smooth of wax tablets, literally a scraping away of existing writing in order to start again from an erased or empty surface. Conversely, *tabula plena* refers to working with what is already in situ, and refers to an abundance of existing material and buildings, stuff that is already there and which is ready for reconfiguration.[2] One of the key aspects of a *tabula plena* approach is how the processes of reuse foreground trans-disciplinary activities: a process that promotes a future way of thinking regarding all creative disciplines. It is one where no form of creative endeavour is exempt from circular thinking. In this Atlas, I was struck by how artists, architects, designers, educators, writers and policymakers transcended normative boundaries of creative work through collapsing distinctions between objects, environments and processes, particularly as stuff gets reconfigured into new spheres of production and use. Arguably, the processes of reuse collapses agendas, redistributes values, and can render traditional built environment processes and languages as obsolescent. This is an enduring part of the activities of reuse: as use and value is changed, matter is diminished or enhanced. As *stuff* is made redundant, revalued and subsequently reconfigured, disciplinary-specific approaches can become inconsequential and superseded.

My discipline of interior design is usually named as a serial offender in the production of waste. This is usually because it is regarded as primarily driven by fashion and rapid change. This is partly true, but I consider that all aspects of interior space, whether regarded as architectured, designed or decorated environments, are originated through working with the existing. What I mean by this is that I always consider that one of the defining characteristics of making interior space to be the processes of designing, constructing, educating and thinking – all processes based on working with the extant. Regardless of whether a line on a page of a space yet to be built, or the enclosure of an existing building, the design of interior space requires the development of strategies and tactics for working with the found and the already there. This is as opposed to a *tabula rasa* approach. Instead interior space origination also begins with the *tabula plena:* the analysis of the existing entities of a place or set of ideas. I find it fascinating that many of the projects and work in this book are innovative interior spaces, created from existing environments, and originated primarily around forms of human occupation and substantive thinking about spacial identities, all of which are fundamental principles of the design of the interior.

I thoroughly recommend this book to you. I would suggest you read it in a variety of ways; front to back, in sections, or dip into it when it's needed. Try reading it in different locations and spaces, or when not on the move and at home. As you do, look around you. View your context and environment and consider it and its *legacy*. The objects, elements and environments that we use and inhabit, are all just stockpiles of matter, stuff that will eventually need to be reconfigured. This is the legacy of this book, to make you aware of how one day we will no longer start making our world from scratch anymore, but instead will only be able to repurpose what is already here and with us already. It is the *tabula plena* approach. The legacy of *The Re-use Atlas* is to ensure that its reader will view their surrounds as a supply of matter, stuff to be reused and reconfigured, things to be remade again and again. This is the challenge of the 21st century. It is the challenge of the *tabula plena*, to understand it, and develop sensibilities around it, making the linear circular through the reconfiguring of the existing to make new places and environments. *The Re-use Atlas* is one of the first books to explicitly document and chart these processes. I hope you enjoy reading it as much as I have.

PREFACE

Professor Walter R Stahel,
Architect and Founder-Director of the Product-Life Institute, Geneva

Reuse and the Circular Economy

I AM FORTUNATE TO LIVE in a house that was built in 1756 – at least that is the age of the purlins, small trees that were cut and immediately put on the roof in those days. So the reuse and repair of building stock, with periodic remanufacturing and technological upgrading of key components, is something I have been familiar with for 40 years. As with any old building, the house has a 'soul', a unique character, which first had to be discovered and then protected in any refurbishment – a continued challenge as the legal environment changes.

The term 'use', and the optimisation of the use or utilisation of manufactured objects, is at the core of the circular economy, not the term 'cycle' as one might have expected. This distinguishes the circular economy from the linear industrial economy, which optimises the production of the same objects up to the point of sale.

The term 'reuse' implies a change in utilisation, ownership or location; armed forces are among the reuse champions as they heavily depend on mobility in using most of their equipment. The Bailey bridges[1] and inflatable pontoon bridges are typical examples of military reuse inventions. Reusable inflatable structures are common today for such temporary applications as funfairs, sports events and temporary bridges on remote construction sites, but also as seasonal structures such as tennis halls or to store cars during the winter.

Reuse associated with fixed permanent structures offers multiple opportunities: the structure itself, its components or its materials. It involves the 'factor time' and defines a new type of sustainable quality, combining technology, risk and sustainability management (see Figure 0.3 overleaf).

For designers, the factor time implies adaptability, flexibility, even humbleness – we do not know the future, but we can prepare for it. Durability as quality of an object is not created by its solidity (witness the German bunkers on the French Atlantic coast) but by its desirability (witness Europe's Gothic cathedrals).

The circular economy has been part of human development since the beginning as a strategy to overcome poverty and scarcity: 'use it up, wear it out, make it do or do without'. The building waste of the past included timber beams, dimension stone and bricks, components which could be reused to build new structures: castles were destroyed and their material reused; German *Trümmerfrauen* (debris women) cleaned the bricks on World War II bombsites for reuse to build new houses.

FIG. 0.2 (OPPOSITE) The Hy-Fi Tower by The Living, New York, constructed of organic bricks grown from mycelium

xiii

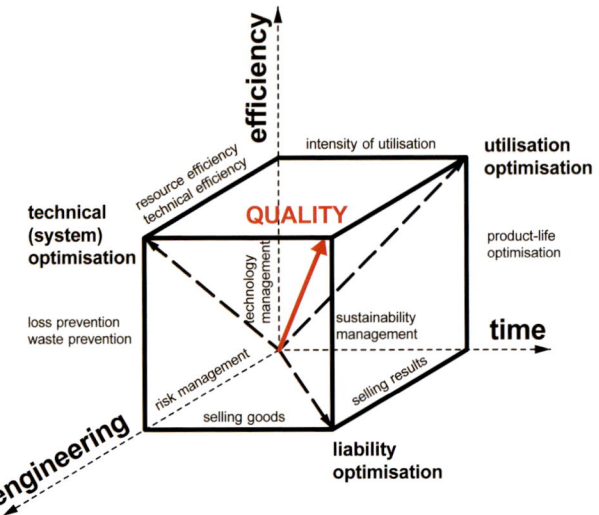

FIG. 0.3 Performance Economy: introducing time in the economy.

But the modern circular economy is based on overcoming saturated markets and abundance, not scarcity. The linear industrial revolution, focused on increasingly efficient manufacturing processes, has enabled mankind to overcome scarcities of food, goods and shelter, but its success increasingly creates situations of saturated markets, unmanageable waste (such as space waste and plastic objects accumulating in the oceans) and overconsumption of natural resources, which are incompatible with the limited carrying capacity of Planet Earth. Paris authorities have started to study the refurbishment of buildings as a new policy mainly because it has run out of landfill sites for building waste.

Shelter and clothing are among the most basic requirements for survival of humans, according to Abraham Maslow, followed by safety, belongingness and love, esteem and self-fulfilment.[2] To put it crudely, architecture has followed Maslow's evolution from adopting caves for shelter to building ego – monuments of cultural identity.

With regards to resource consumption, the building and construction industry is the industrial economy's biggest consumer of material resources, and the biggest producer of waste. As most of this waste comes in the form of inert materials, the problem is one of mass and volume rather than toxicology.

The actors of the linear industrial economy manage the resource consumption up to the point of sale, where ownership and liability are passed on to the buyer. The use and operation of buildings, another major consumer of resources, principally energy for heating and cooling, are managed by the owner-occupier, not the builder. Solving the problem of waste is left to local authorities.

The actors of the circular economy are managing manufactured capital (stock) in time, by (re)using goods, components and materials with the objective of preserving the stock's economic value, based on a philosophy of caring and stewardship and considering the whole life cycle of goods, with a focus on the (re)use phase.

A recent example of component reuse is the deep retrofit of New York's Empire State Building in 2010. It included the onsite remanufacturing of its 6,514 windows into triple-glazed super-windows.

> **Cutting winter heat loss by two-thirds and summer heat gain by half, the advanced glazing, along with improved lighting and office equipment, will cut the building's peak cooling load by one-third. This load reduction allowed the renovation of the old chiller plant, slated for replacement and expansion, saving more than US$17 million in budgeted capital expenditure.[3]**

When Nestlé renovated its headquarter building in Vevey, Switzerland, in the late 1990s, it developed a reuse strategy for the same problem. The existing windows were donated to Bosnia, where many school buildings had been heavily affected during the Bosnian War, and where the windows from Vevey – in perfect working condition – could be directly reused.

Reusing materials for the same application is becoming the norm in some European countries in road resurfacing and demolition–rebuilding projects. 'Ceramic waste' can be reused as aggregate in new concrete structures, but needs the establishment of new material standards and testing methods. The stock of buildings is a strategic resource base for future use, if we learn to sustainably deconstruct buildings at the highest level of value preservation. Urban mining is one of the new terms for the recovery of waste materials for reuse.

Yet the reuse of materials to prevent waste is also a management option in new infrastructure projects. In Switzerland, construction of the new Gotthard rail tunnel – the world's longest – produced the equivalent of five Giza pyramids of mining waste,[4] which was used as raw material to build the new (infra)structure of the project, including spray-concrete for the tunnel itself. Of the 28 million tonnes of rock excavated, 15kg was delivered to the Swiss post office, ground into fine powder and, using a special paint, integrated into a special issue of postage stamps named 'Gottardo 2016'.

For society, the circular challenge of the existing built environment is two-fold: how to finance the operation, maintenance and replacement of our ageing infrastructure, and how to best adapt building stocks to changes in demand and technological progress. Changes in demand come both from markets – churches are transformed into residential or commercial property, for instance – and society – energy needs have to be decoupled from CO_2 emissions, through energy savings or substitution; and urban planning may set priorities for the future that differ from the past. And some buildings become part of the national heritage, our cultural capital, and need to be preserved accordingly.

Why is the circular economy more sustainable than the industrial one? The activities of the circular economy are ecological because they are regional and low-carbon, use few resources and preserve the water, energy and material embodied in the goods. And these activities are labour intensive, on a micro- and a macro-economic level. A 2015 Club of Rome study of seven EU countries found that a shift to a circular economy would reduce a nation's greenhouse gas emissions by up to 70% and grow its workforce by about 4% – the ultimate low-carbon economy.[5] The solutions with the highest preservation of monetary value are normally also the most environmentally friendly and most labour-intensive ones: reuse, repair, remanufacture. Despite the higher labour input, these activities are economically viable because material resource inputs are greatly reduced, compared to the industrial economy.

A circular economy manages and reuses manufactured capital – infrastructure, equipment, goods, components and materials – in loops, taking into account that time is a key factor: doubling the service life of goods halves the resource consumption in manufacturing and halves end-of-life waste volumes. But while building waste in the past consisted of components such as dimension stone and bricks that could be reused as such, modern constructions use composite materials such as steel-reinforced concrete, welded structures and plastics which cannot be 'undone'.

Today's building industry thus faces a triple challenge of:

- developing efficient and waste-free construction methods, enabling a later reuse of components and materials
- designing buildings for minimum resource consumption during operation and maintenance, which includes flexibility and adaptability to changes in use
- developing methods enabling the deconstruction of buildings and infrastructure while preserving the highest value.

Emergent nearly-waste-free reusable construction methods include modular system buildings: for instance, temporary multistorey structures for office and residential space using purpose-fitted ISO shipping containers now exist in a number of countries. Examples of modular construction systems using standardised steel beams and panels of corrugated steel sheet have been around for a long time, especially for industrial and agricultural halls in the USA. Prefabricated elements made of timber panels have started to be developed for multistorey hotels and schools since fire legislations have been changed in countries such as Switzerland.

Designing buildings for minimum resource consumption during use is becoming mandatory in a number of European countries with regard to energy use. However, their efficiency may be reduced in residential buildings because they impose restrictions on inhabitants' behaviour (sleeping with closed windows; preference for warmer room temperatures than planned). Plus-energy buildings – which produce more energy than they use and thus are autonomous – were a favourite with former New York City mayor Michael Bloomberg because of their social contributions: they provide lighting to their surroundings and prevent people getting trapped in lifts during power cuts (blackouts), which have become more common in recent years for a number of reasons. Buildings thus will increasingly have to be designed as urban systems solutions.

The development of methods to deconstruct high-rise buildings has recently started in Japan. The ANA Intercontinental Hotel was probably the first attempt to deconstruct a high-rise structure using an eco-friendly and resource-saving process. The building was demolished top down in 2014 beneath a turban that was lowered hydraulically floor by floor to minimise noise and dust emissions; a vertical shaft with a goods lift in the middle of the building allowed the deconstructors to recover components and sorted materials, while generating energy from the downward lift transports. A future task could be the deconstruction of nuclear power stations in Germany, which will be shut down as part of the *Energiewende*, the political decision to rely entirely on wind and photovoltaic energy for the future electricity supply.

Can appropriate design, such as eco-design, at least partly solve this problem? Let us look at the 12 Principles of Design for Environment (Eco-Design), defined by IDSA, the Industrial Designer Society of America, in 1992.

The 12 IDSA Principles of Design for Environment [6]

- Make it durable.
- Make it easy to repair.
- Design it so it can be remanufactured.
- Design it so it can be reused.
- Use recycled materials.
- Use commonly recyclable materials.
- Make it simple to separate the recyclable components of a product from the non-recyclable components.
- Eliminate the toxic/problematic components of a product or make them easy to replace or remove before disposal.
- Make products more energy/resource efficient.
- Use product design to educate on the environment.
- Work towards designing source reduction-inducing products (ie products that eliminate the need for subsequent waste).
- Adjust product design to reduce packaging.

Many products of modern technology – IT, photovoltaic panels, windmills – violate the fifth and sixth of these principles: their production cannot use recycled materials, and some of the materials, such as components using nanotechnology or carbon fibre laminates, cannot be recycled. The Internet of Things (IoT) will probably increase the number of components of modern technology in future buildings, multiplying the problems posed by construction waste.

But a more concrete danger is that the construction industry will be regarded as an elegant way to 'eliminate' the bulk of this waste, namely components made of fibre laminates, the volume of which is rapidly increasing. Carbon laminates today are extensively used in mass-produced goods such as aircraft, cars and windmills. Some French researchers study ways to cut carbon laminates into small cubes and use them as 'eco-friendly' aggregate in reinforced concrete – 'eco-friendly' because they replace natural sand and gravel and thus reduce the environmental impairment of concrete production.

But – and this is a huge but – what goes in will come out when the buildings are demolished, many decades later. We would simply displace the waste problem in time, leaving an undesired heritage to our children – certainly not a sustainable solution.

Reuse poses new challenges, both risks and opportunities, to designers, architects and engineers. Architecture is thinking in systems to create systems solutions. And architecture is about time. A lighthouse on such a forlorn rock as Fastnet Rock is timeless functionality: form follows function. But it is not only about architecture, it is primarily about shipping safety, improving our quality of life.

Built structures are moments of history frozen in stone, the durability of which depends on their desirability over time more than the materials chosen. So architecture is about culture. Besides reuse, there are other strategies to achieve higher resource efficiency, such as dematerialisation through technological progress – witness pneumatic structures in construction and transport – which can offer solutions, as well as sufficiency.

In the late 1960s, I worked as a young architect for John R Bicknell and Paul A Hamilton, two chartered architects in London, on the Paddington Maintenance Depot (PMD), near Little Venice. Built to maintain the lorries of British Rail, it fits into a triangle between the Grand Union Canal, Harrow Road and West Way, and consists of a low-level oval building and an office block, separated by a road, making optimal use of a then urban wasteland – a singular building, which received a Concrete Award distinction. When British Rail later abandoned its lorry fleet, the building became redundant and was only saved from demolition after having been awarded a Grade II* listing. After a long period of neglect, this landmark has finally been reused, with some interior transformation, as the headquarters of the Monsoon fashion label. It is now, a long time after the death of Messrs Bicknell and Hamilton, a jewel in the new fashionable pedestrian zone between Paddington and Little Venice, along the Grand Union Canal.

Reuse is nature's principle: waste is food in a cascading chain to bacteria. All waste is therefore made by 'industrial man', be it in space, water or on land. Extending the use phase of built structures through reuse is not only a strategy to achieve higher resource efficiency, it is a conscious decision by people – planners, owners, politicians and architects – on how we shape our future.

INTRODUCTION

Duncan Baker-Brown

How to read this book … and why you should

How can designers and architects respond to the huge challenges that the circular economy presents? There are many books that have been published over the last ten years that have attempted to define the concepts of a circular economy and speculate upon the benefits, whether they be financial, environmental or social. There are also a few books that look at the challenges facing the people who design the stuff that will need to become a material resource for the future.

This book considers many of the issues that present themselves when considering what steps we need to take to turn our 'throwaway, linear culture' into a 'circular system' similar to the ecosystems found in the natural world. We demonstrate, via exemplar projects from around the world, various strategies that, crucially, take one on a transformative route *towards* a circular economy: a route that acknowledges there are other issues to consider, not least that of clearing up the mess humankind has created over the last 1,000 years. So we will also look at projects that encourage the first phase of this process and will include the cleaning up of our oceans and landfill sites, working with existing buildings

and neighbourhoods, etc. Therefore, I have included upcyclers and hackers (they take artefacts, products, buildings even, and adapt them instead of throwing them away), retrofitters and super-users, as well as the emergent closed-loopers.

While I want this book to be read at length, I suspect that more often it will be dipped into as a reference. In addition to the 'prequel' and 'sequel' essays, I have focused on the series of short case studies. All are based on interviews with the main protagonists, and all have 'key words' below the titles so that readers can see the main issues addressed by each project. I have also written a short opinion piece at the end of each case study, by way of a summary but also to encourage further debate.

The case studies are divided into four chapters, or 'steps', each one taking you nearer the concept of the circular economy. Each step is supplemented by an in-depth interview with someone whose work exemplifies the concept discussed, giving an idea of the challenges and opportunities that present themselves as one navigates a route towards circularity.

It was important to have the word 'atlas' in the title, as the book is intended to act as a guide for designers, architects, clients and students, to help them negotiate the often-confusing language and rhetoric that

FIG. 0.4 Rusting drum on a beach in Sicily

surrounds this latest response to the challenge of protecting our planet. All interviewees were asked *why* they were pursuing their particular interests, and most particularly *how* they were going about their 'circular' work within the linear economy that prevails today.

This book also offers an overview of what is actually happening in the second decade of the 21st century in the worlds of sustainable design and architecture. Originally I considered writing a book that just focused on emerging attempts to design in a completely closed-loop, circular way. Professor Dr Michael Braungart, co-author of the seminal text *Cradle to Cradle*,[1] is often quoted as saying that sustainable development promotes the idea of being 'less bad'. 'Recycling and reusing stuff is not worth the effort. It is merely slowing down the inevitable.'[2] *Cradle to Cradle* promotes the wholesale behaviour change required to live in a circular economy, in harmony with Planet Earth. This is, in my opinion, correct. However, we are not starting with a clean, fresh and vibrant planet. Humankind has literally wrapped the surface of Planet Earth with the detritus associated with our day-to-day lives. This has occurred to such an extent that many scientists consider that we have entered a new human-made geological era, the 'Anthropocene'. This has been occurring at an ever-increasing rate since we abandoned the idea of being hunter-gatherers and started cutting down forests to plant crops for food.

Although I sympathise with Braungart's position, I cannot ignore the need to deal with what could be called 'the great clean-up' – that is the clearing up of ocean plastic, the mining of landfill sites, and the reuse of existing materials and structures residing in our cities, towns and villages. This book includes inspiring projects that aim to turn traditionally linear systems, which result in the pollution of our oceans and landscapes, into mini circular systems that begin to clean up our environment while producing new products, employment and, in some cases, social empowerment. During this challenging process, the simple techniques of 'recycling', 'reusing' and 'using less' material are elevated in status because of the benefits to the natural world of clearing up new material flows that are normally ignored, and putting them back into circulation.

This may sound like 'being less bad' and, even, being naive or hopelessly optimistic. However, we cannot simply clear up the difficult waste material that wraps the surface of our planet and bury or burn it. We need to put it back into the emergent circular economy via cleverly designed products and buildings that allow for easy disassembly, facilitating reuse until we can find a way of safely disposing of synthetic, toxic materials.

Like many architects, I also teach in a school of architecture. Combining academia with everyday building sites has led to the idea of testing concepts through a series of 'live' construction projects that have also been a pedagogic vehicle involving students. With this in mind, the choice of case studies has been informed for the most part by a requirement that products and buildings should adhere to current performance regulations.

For me, it is the interviewees' answers to my questions *'Why?'* and *'How?'* that make the case studies most useful for assessing the potential for introducing concepts around circular metabolisms and the circular economy in particular.

FIG. 0.5 (OVERLEAF) Calf on a rubbish dump in Malkhoutfontein, South Africa

The Re-Use Atlas is divided into four parts. Part 1, 'Setting the Waste Scene', includes a chapter written by a co-founder of Freegle UK, Cat Fletcher, who takes a careful look at the challenges of reducing the waste associated with our lifestyle choices. Dr David Greenfield then examines the bureaucracy and legislation that hinders the flourishing of a circular economy, as well as considering what legislation is needed to help things along. Part 2 is dedicated to 'Circular Inspirations' – that is the aforementioned case studies. Part 3 focuses on 'The Story of the Waste House', which was the project that got me completely immersed in this subject area. Finally, Part 4 is a collection of essays from experts considering issues that will enable a successful circular economy. Professor Jonathan Chapman discusses the concept of 'emotional longevity' in relation to the design of products. What is it that makes us not want to throw something away? Professor Anne Boddington looks at how teaching and learning methods need to adapt to be relevant to a circular economy. The final chapter considers the big challenges that may hinder the uptake of circular systems in large commercial developments. It is inspired by numerous interviews I have had with people involved in promoting the concept of the circular economy within the design and construction industries.

I hope you enjoy my Atlas.

PART 1

Setting the Waste Scene

7   CHAPTER 1
Resource Matters
Duncan Baker-Brown

16   CHAPTER 2
What a Waste!
Cat Fletcher

21   CHAPTER 3
The Political Narrative
Dr David Greenfield

CHAPTER 1

Resource Matters

Duncan Baker-Brown

> It's all about 'managing resources', and humankind has never been good at that.

Ever since our hunter-gatherer ancestors began to try alternative lifestyles around 10,000 years ago, humans have had ever-increasing problems finding resources. Although exhausting and dangerous, the hunter-gatherer technique followed the route of accessible resources. Settling down and relying on one place to provide everything required to satisfy human needs has always proved to be a big challenge. On occasion it has resulted in hunger and localised extinction of whole societies.

There are, however, many examples of long-established communities that have lived in harmony with their natural environments. Some of these still exist. Herbert Girardet in his book *The Gaia Atlas of Cities*[1] states that as late as the 1980s, 13 of China's major cities functioned as what many would define as sustainable cities, that is the city fed the hinterland and the hinterland fed the city. For some, that all changed when China embraced elements of the Western free market economy and broke away from its established closed-loop systems in search of linear consumerism.

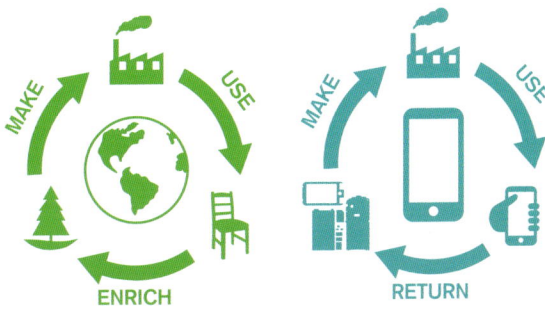

BIO-SPHERE

TECH-SPHERE

It is, of course, a lot easier to find examples of humankind's rampant consumption of resources. Our appetite for stuff is insatiable. There is a famous photograph by LA Hoffman which shows the last group of 23 North American bison in what is now Yellowstone National Park. In the 16th century there were between 25 and 30 million buffalo in North America.[2] North American bison escaped extinction, just. Now a little over a century later there are about 15,000 of these (with many more cross-bred with domestic cattle), which are descended from those last 23 survivors. Humans do not know when to stop consuming resources. Acting in a measured, balanced and sustainable way does not come easily to human societies. That is why we are in the middle of a mass extinction of species and some resources are scarce, while even plentiful resources are difficult to access.

Many people just don't believe there is a different way of existing. However, my colleague at the University of Brighton, Dr Ryan Woodard, cites the precise year when the UK 'invented the concept of waste': 1861. In that year, plundered resources from the British Empire made the country so resource wealthy that it could afford to make bricks solely out of new material. Up until that point rubbish was reused whenever possible. Perhaps one could conclude, therefore, that the idea of a linear economy has only been prevalent for around 150 years.

In the meantime, while pledging commitment to the United Nations climate change agreement COP21 (obviously good news) and with the EU publishing its own Circular Economy Package, governments around the world are nonetheless looking towards the most controversial method of extracting fossil fuels – 'fracking'. Oil-rich countries flex their muscles defending their land or grabbing that of others. In addition, there is the very real problem of resource security. Even if you don't have concerns about the destruction of natural environments due to the mining of minerals and the felling or burning of hardwood forests for palm oil plantations, there are just too many conflicts around the world to make the sourcing of raw materials safe and reliable. Still the UK government appears to want its citizens to burn their way out of the recent recession by dropping green energy incentives in favour of sponsoring the aforementioned 'fracking'. There is precedent for this type of initiative. Immediately after World War II my London-based grandparents were encouraged to burn their coal fires through the night, simply to kick-start the bankrupt UK economy and get the coal mines busy again.

Despite this I am convinced that we are at the beginning of another Industrial Revolution: one that can take best advantage of 'big data', hyper-fast communication networks and, critically, a greater understanding of our host planet, to enable humankind to make well-informed decisions when considering which resource streams to tap into. It is well understood that many large corporations, academic institutions, NGOs and governments are considering ways of functioning in a more intelligent way that works with healthy natural circular systems. The stupidity of digging down for carbon in the ground while the sun burns your back is not lost on many people. *Cradle to Cradle*[3] threw down the gauntlet to humankind, to stop beating itself up about the environment; to stop being 'less bad'; to design circular systems instead of linear ones, and be positive while you do it, because this has the potential to improve the lives of many more people than our current linear system does – and it will do so while allowing Planet Earth to recover and heal. However, the most exciting bit of the *Cradle to Cradle* challenge for me is that it can only happen if we *design* new systems, materials, products and places that allow for circular systems to flourish. I also believe, as Freegle UK co-founder Cat Fletcher and many others do, that design will save the world, or at least be the catalyst that allows huge populations of humans to live in harmony with it. Sophie Thomas, the former director of circular economy at the RSA,[4] underlined this point. During her time at the RSA, Thomas oversaw the 'Great Recovery' programme. In the paper 'Rearranging the Future'[5] Thomas states:

PART 1   SETTING THE WASTE SCENE

> Research has shown that over 80 per cent of the environmental impact of products we use every day is built in at the concept design stage, and that very little account is currently taken of the end-of-life implications of these designs. Moreover, if the system has not been designed to take account of the actual products, materials and behaviours that flow through it, there is very little point in merely changing the design of a single product. A keyboard designed for disassembly will still end up being shredded and put into the e-waste furnace unless a logistical system has been designed to divert it out of the existing infrastructure.

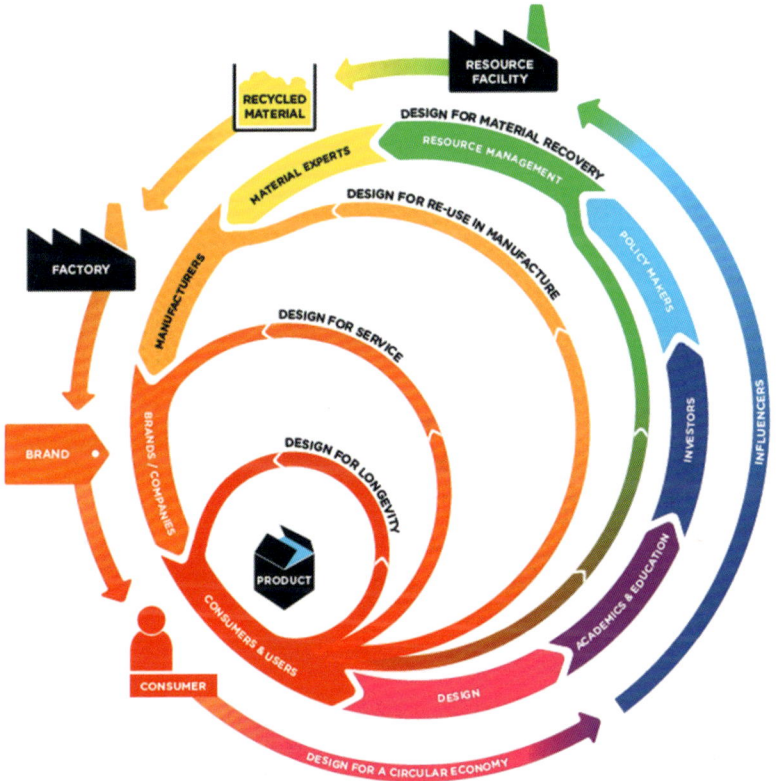

As part of its 'Great Recovery' programme, and in effect in response to their own research, the RSA developed four design models for a circular economy, shown in Figure 1.1.

FIG. 1.1 Four design models developed by the RSA as part of its 'Great Recovery' programme, June 2013

RESOURCE MATTERS CHAPTER 1 9

So are we progressing towards a circular economy?

Things are changing. More people – individuals, as well as multinational corporations – are concerned about where the materials that go towards manufacturing their products come from. More and more companies, large and small, are not prepared to put up with the negative PR associated with illegally mining the raw materials for their products, or the displacement of indigenous communities. Some of the largest companies supplying the construction industry are doing positive things to clean up the environment and promote equitable trade. The issue of ethics is now being taken seriously, and that huge topic is the subject of numerous books, exhibitions, conferences and symposia. At the same time, dropping the well-intentioned but much maligned and misunderstood word 'sustainable' from the environmental debate could be helping matters. The concept of the circular economy is more easily comprehended as a positive way of living in a smarter way that emulates natural systems and will give increased benefits to everyone.

As stated earlier, many human cultures have worked in harmony with their immediate

ORIGINS OF THE CIRCULAR ECONOMY

So where did the concept of the circular economy, or 'economy in loops' as it was initially explained, come from? In 1976 Professor Walter Stahel, architect and industrial analyst, presented preliminary ideas on this to the European Commission. Entitled 'The potential for substituting manpower for energy', it was co-authored by Genevieve Reday and described a future of an economy in loops, with its positive impact on job creation, economic competitiveness, reduced dependence on natural resources and the prevention of waste. Many people credit Stahel with coining the expression 'Cradle to Cradle' in the late 1970s. By 1981 he had synthesised his ideas in his award-winning paper 'The product-life factor',[6] which identified a number of concepts that practitioners featured in this Atlas are putting to the test. For example, Stahel identified that the ultimate sustainable business model in a closed-loop economy would be 'selling utilisation' instead of products.

During the 1980s much work was being done by Stahel and also by Professor Dr Michael Braungart, including the Product-Life Institute in Geneva and Braungart's Environmental Protection Encouragement Agency (nicknamed 'the cradle of cradle to cradle'). Today there are a number of independent think tanks and academic institutes around the world doing fine work developing ideas, providing training schemes, and even certifying products, including the Ellen MacArthur Foundation,[7] formed in 2010 by the solo long-distance yachtswoman Dame Ellen MacArthur with the specific aim of accelerating the transition to a regenerative circular economy. Combining thought, leadership and education with big business, this foundation has quickly become an influential think tank, a catalyst for discussion and a publisher of papers and books. In the summer of 2016 the University of Bradford awarded the world's first Circular Economy MBA to Gin Tidridge,[8] who completed the course while working as a sustainability specialist for B&Q. There is momentum behind this concept.

PART 1   SETTING THE WASTE SCENE

environment. However, since the beginning of the Industrial Revolution, the consumption of natural resources has grown exponentially, and unsustainably. Today you can expect nearly 90% of the raw materials used in manufacturing to become waste before the product leaves the factory, while 80% of products get thrown away within the first six months of their life.[9] However, material flow analysis conducted in 2010 by WRAP (Waste and Resources Action Programme) concluded that nearly 20% of the UK economy is already operating in a circular fashion.[10] It went on to predict that this could rise to nearly 30% by 2020. The EU Circular Economy Package[11] adopted in December 2015 outlined an Action Plan and included an annex with a detailed timetable for implementation. The document focuses on the number of new jobs and wealth generated by a circular economy. In the same year, WRAP published data predicting that an expansion of the circular economy could generate as many as 3 million new jobs and reduce unemployment by 520,000 across the EU by 2030.[12]

My personal journey towards a circular economy

Since working on the 'RIBA House of the Future' in 1994 (see Figure 1.2), I have been interested in the numerous ingredients that go towards making truly sustainable developments. Over the years I have become more and more interested in unpacking the supply chain associated with construction projects, and trying out different material sources with the aim of CO_2 reduction, the preservation of ecosystems and the creation of work. Many architects and

FIG. 1.2 BBM's RIBA House of the Future, 1994

FIG. 1.3 Sketch of Romney Marsh Visitor Centre, explaining how it is designed for remanufacture

designers clearly understand the principles of designing buildings that require little or no traditional energy sources to perform properly. The greater challenge it seemed, to both my partner (Ian McKay) and I, was the reduction of the carbon and 'ecological footprints' associated with the actual design, construction and occupation of said low-energy buildings: whole life costing, in other words. So, naturally, re-examining material sources and construction systems, in addition to issues of programme (what goes on in the buildings we design and what type of lifestyles they encourage), have been two of our main pursuits over the two decades (and counting) of practice and teaching that we have enjoyed.

During the first decade of the 21st century my practice, BBM, was one of a number considering the potentials of designing buildings using locally sourced, non-toxic, organic and replenishable materials. This countered a rush to burn timber due to UK government 'green' incentives encouraging the burning of biomass.

We wanted to prove that most timber and other biobase materials could be used in high-performance building: to literally 'lock' CO_2 rather than release it back into the atmosphere.

In 2001 we constructed the first public building utilising straw bales, Romney Marsh Visitor Centre (see Figure 1.3). It was also 'built for demolition' using mainly local materials that could easily be pulled apart; the building is a simple material store for the future. The first residential building in the UK using locally sourced sweet chestnut cladding in 2005 followed this. We felt that chestnut had great potential as it is extremely durable but also because of the ancient 'working' forests that still survive in Sussex, where our practice is based, and could support even greater levels of biodiversity if worked again. The potentials for our landscape to supply and inform the aesthetic of contemporary building became apparent.

PART 1 SETTING THE WASTE SCENE

By 2007 we felt able to curate an exhibition that toured the south-east of England, entitled 'Built Ecologies: translating landscape into architecture'.[13] It considered how our landscapes could inform the aesthetic of buildings if they supplied them with material, as well as the potentials for genuinely low carbon developments, employment and perhaps a renewed 'sense of place' and a local identity once commonplace in the UK.

In 2008 BBM was contacted by Talkback Thames, the production company behind Channel 4's 'Grand Designs', who were keen to do a live version of the programme (Kevin McCloud was the presenter of the six-part TV programme entitled 'Grand Designs Live' which covered the construction of 'The House that Kevin Built' over six consecutive days.). We were asked to test our ideas and prove that a prefabricated dwelling made from over 90% organic, replenishable material could be constructed live on television in only six days. This we did, and our team also created the UK's first dwelling with an A+ Energy Performance Certificate. The building was constructed with zero waste on site and it was then disassembled, with the ground floor forming part of a research project at the University of Bath. The rest of the building parts were sent back to suppliers. Perhaps what was most interesting about this project was the fact that it could be built in the first place. At the time, a number of UK practices (Architype, Fielden Clegg Bradley Studios and White Design among them) were developing a suite of materials, and even inventing construction systems, that could meet this challenge. It reminded me of another point in architectural history, when emergent 'high tech' architects developed, and even invested in, the companies supplying the prefabricated construction systems to deliver their futuristic visions. Was there an embryonic architectural movement developing here?

Although 'Grand Designs Live' attracted over 5 million viewers a night, 'The House that Kevin Built'[14] (THTKB; see Figure 1.4) was up, down and gone in a week. Quite a strange project to work on when you consider how slow architecture normally is. The speed of the project also meant that the knowledge gained by our team was not exchanged at all. So I was keen to repeat the process of building THTKB again, but to slow it down to about six months, in order to offer it as a teaching tool involving design and construction students, and to properly capture and share the knowledge gained in the process.

FIG. 1.4 'The House that Kevin Built', completed after only six days

FIG. 1.5 A new country house made from materials found on the surrounding private rural estate

The rebuilding of THTKB didn't happen. However, the idea captured many people's imaginations, including Professor Anne Boddington, Dean of the College of Arts and Humanities at the University of Brighton, who was able to persuade her colleagues in the estates department to provide land for the project. However, by 2011, I began to realise there were new emergent themes that our THTKB rebuild project could, or even should, address, i.e. the idea that natural, organic, replenishable materials, that were sourced locally to the development site, could provide high quality, durable and, crucially, affordable material for the construction industry. These natural resources absorb CO_2 and release oxygen while they are growing, and in effect, store CO_2 until they are either burnt or composted. So proving that they are more valuable as building materials rather than fuel for fires is a big deal from an environmental point of view. Projects such as THTKB, and later on, a series of buildings we did for private clients in the Sussex Weald which were made almost entirely of these low-value materials (see Figure 1.5, image of Little

PART 1   SETTING THE WASTE SCENE

England Farm House), started to propose that this idea was feasible: and therefore begin to add value to materials that the UK government was encouraging us to burn in so-called 'renewable' biomass boilers and stoves.

In April 2012 I met with Diana Lock, from the environmental management consultancy Remade South East (ceased trading in 2014). Lock was insistent that many large corporations only had one big theme on their minds, and that was how to continue to make their products and deal with the very real challenges of 'resource security'. Whether due to war, unreliable governments or environmental despoliation due to mining and forest clearing, manufacturers were looking at alternatives to relying on raw materials. The other pressing issue was the emerging tough legislation on the safe and proper management of waste generated in manufacturing, as well as other legislation on the need to reduce the amount of waste generated. Corporate responsibility throughout the whole process was another big issue. Lock claimed that old-fashioned 'linear systems' would be gradually replaced by 'circular systems': sensible companies were looking at strategies to reduce their dependence on raw materials, as well as their capacity to create waste. In other words, companies were looking at how to redesign their products, systems and contracts to create a circular, 'closed-loop' process, giving greater security and profitability to the business. I soon found out that many companies were indeed looking at unpacking the way they produced their products. Apple, for example, became keener to lease their products as they had invested in the physical and virtual infrastructure to accept products back from their customers, clean them up and literally re-lease them.

Where are we today?

The construction industry, despite recent efforts, is still the largest source of waste generated annually in Europe, producing 33% (821 million tonnes).[15] It is closely followed by mining and quarrying (29% or 734 million tonnes). If the construction and manufacturing industries could alter the way they practise, it could have a hugely beneficial effect on the environment. In the UK, 50% of all waste generated comes from the construction industry.[16] Looking at the whole of the planet, the construction and inhabitation of buildings consumes nearly 40% of annual raw materials.[17] The UK construction industry throws away about 20% of all material arriving on site. In other words, for every five dwellings built in the UK, one dwelling's worth of stuff goes to landfill or even incineration. Those hard-nosed developers aren't so tight with their money after all. Since the 1960s it has been cheaper to throw materials at a construction site rather than let the labour force run out of things to do. That situation is changing as the cost of raw materials and the products they are processed into goes up. Also rising is the cost of sending stuff to landfill or incineration – or 'energy from waste' as some people call that particular disposal process.

The projects covered in Part 2 are taking advantage of the opportunities available to people prepared to mine the Anthropocene.[18] They prove that there are different ways of developing that can create new business opportunities and models without destroying our natural resources. Perhaps it will be the new 'hunter-gatherer' who will make the most of the new epoch.

CHAPTER 2

What a Waste!

Cat Fletcher, co-founder of Freegle UK and a Waste House partner

IT IS TIME TO TRULY UNDERSTAND the shocking impact of our consumption on the planet's ecosystems. Globally we have around $100 trillion of economic activity[1] ($100 billion of that is online via Amazon alone every year[2]) which is reliant on the extraction, harvesting and processing of 62 billion tonnes of materials every year.[3] Around 60% of goods produced from this vast quantity of raw materials was privately consumed by only 12% of the world's population (in 2002) whereas 33% of the world's population in South-east Asia got to consume only 3.2% of all goods[4] – a truly unfair distribution of global resources and wealth.

All this human consumption is also responsible for almost 2 billion tonnes of waste[5] annually, with increases year on year as populations and urbanisation grow in all corners of the planet. Shockingly, 3.5 billion people have no or very poor waste management infrastructure, which leads to further poisoning of their soil, air and water, especially because increasingly discards are petroleum-based products – plastics. So the people who consume the least, with little hope of basic material wealth, bear the brunt of the impacts of the minority who consume the most.

Turning the ship around

Our 7.13 billion world population is set to rise by 41% by 2050.[6] But we do not have enough natural and replenishable resources to endlessly sustain current extraction, production, use and waste because we only have one planet with finite materials to fulfil our demands.[7] So we need to alter our demands rather than trying to endlessly manipulate solutions to problems that could simply be avoided in the first place: by changing how we make, distribute, use and discard things.

Prevention is better than cure, which is why design really *can* save the world. But it may take some time.

Reassuringly, people across the globe are experimenting and changing the way we make and consume things and this book features some interesting actors (professionals, companies, organisations, researchers and individuals) who dare to design and build things differently and better.

Just a decade and a bit into the 21st century, while we can or might redesign all systems, products and processes, and rethink our relationship with stuff, enough to properly address the unsustainable situation we find ourselves in, we need to acknowledge that we are in the midst of a messy transitional state. We need to turn the ship around. Some of the crew know that, but are yet to convince the captain that we will never arrive or survive the journey unless we re-navigate the route.

Population growth combined with excessive developed-world lifestyles and the ever expanding 'consumer class' in emerging economies is straining our reliance on natural resources to breaking point. It is directly responsible for often irreversible environmental degradation, threatening future environmental, economic and social stability for everyone. Australia's Great Barrier Reef is a fair indicator of this point[8] – only 7% of the world's largest living organism remains unbleached and that will lead to a massive downturn in tourist revenue in the future. Visionaries of the circular economy (like Cradle to Cradle founder Michael Braungart[9]) argue vehemently that we need to stop doing bad things better and instead focus entirely on changing the design of products, the means of production and distribution, and our models of consumption in order to reduce waste and save ourselves from sacrificing earthly pleasures and all our finite resources. But in my opinion I think it is up to governments and corporations to stop doing bad things better and change the way they operate. In the meantime consumers have no choice but to do bad things better as they are trapped in a broken system that encourages them to consume more and forces them to have to discard so much (as products are bad, waste infrastructure is inadequate, advertising and capitalism requires over-consumption….). There is simply too much stuff already in circulation to leap straight to the new shiny, perfected model of material sustainability. Even IKEA agrees there is a 'peak stuff' issue.[10]

For starters, a lot of reuse needs to be facilitated if we are to keep materials within existing goods from being destroyed forever (burnt and buried), where their value is unlikely to ever be recovered. Recycling extracts materials out of discarded products to be used again to make new products, but much of what we discard is not recyclable or fails to enter that process – globally we are not very good at recycling. Reuse substitutes the demand for new products, so challenging our current excessive model of consumption. This speeds up the journey to a more circular economy by simply reducing demand for new products. The facilitation of reuse creates localised employment and enterprise and requires less energy and transport than recycling, recovery or disposal.

Every day around 5 million tonnes of waste is generated globally. Around 30% is uncollected and of the 70% accounted for, only 19% is recycled, 11% is burnt (incineration, now euphemistically labelled 'energy from waste recovery' and incorrectly described by some as a renewable energy) and 70% is still sent to landfill sites.[11] These horrific figures come about because half of the world's population does not have access to waste management infrastructure and, in countries where we do, we have over-invested at the bottom of the waste hierarchy (recycling, recovery and disposal; see Figure 1.6). It is challenging to promote and develop activity at the top of the waste hierarchy (reduction, prevention, reuse–repair and upcycling) because that is counter to our linear economic model which relies on the never-ending consumption of new stuff (the polar opposite of reduce, prevent and reuse!). This is despite analysis, research, policy and anecdotal reflection that prevention is better than cure and should be pursued. The EU

FIG. 1.6 The 'waste hierarchy' ranks waste management options according to what is best for the environment. It gives top priority to preventing waste in the first place.

insisted that all Member States produce a waste prevention programme back in 2013[12] yet England's waste prevention programme[13] is generally unknown to most. It clearly states all the reasons why we should act at the top of the waste hierarchy and how to do that but is not enabled in any clear way, not seriously funded[14] and is on a voluntary basis.

We know we are travelling in the wrong direction, but the fact that we do not prioritise changing direction is what's confounding and frustrating.

Too much 'stuff'

Oceans are intrinsic to the cycles of life – playing a key role in our food chain, weather patterns, transport and leisure. And we have filled them with detritus – the stuff we probably didn't need in the first place; the packaging; the stuff we used once and discarded; the stuff we forgot to pass on for reuse; the stuff that slipped through waste management systems and didn't get recycled, burnt or buried; and the stuff not managed elsewhere. We are awash with the end result of our addiction to owning stuff. The rise of the 'sharing economy' is a call to share individually owned, under-used assets and make them available for collective use; thus in theory eliminating the need to individually own what you need to use. In reality it is unfortunately mimicking old business models and encouraging more consumption, but that's another story.[15] This does, however, reflect the difficulty we face when trying to reduce our seemingly inbred postmodern desire to 'have stuff' or 'make more money'. Perpetually. We don't seem to know when to stop. We don't naturally identify when we have enough. We are all busy. Too busy to stop consuming. Busy spending time, energy and money so we can save time, energy and money. It's all a bit bonkers.

Stuff. Objects. Things. Goods. Materials. Bits and bobs. Gadgets. Effects. Gear.

18 PART 1 SETTING THE WASTE SCENE

Possessions. Gizmos. Thingamajigs. Bits and pieces. Kit. Equipment. Impedimenta. Matter. Trappings. Belongings. Let's make sure we design new things and buildings with a whole life cycle in mind that does not burden the future with unnecessary waste.

Research tells us that any income over £70k does not increase our wellbeing.[16] Over and above that level, the increased purchasing power to own more and 'better' stuff actually leads to higher levels of misery and stress in spite of all those lovely and many things. As it turns out, it isn't *just* stuff that makes us happy, but challenging that belief is tricky and goes against the grain. What does make us happy is a connection with people and/or a community, access to open spaces, education and health services ... and options (but not 63 zillion options – that's just overwhelming). But we do have a world with 63 zillion options! Most of these choices are about what, how or when to consume something. We are now actively encouraging the same consumer aspirations in BRICS (Brazil, Russia, India, China and South Africa) – the global emerging economies. The entire world economy is based on buying stuff, as are most of our still local economies. So any suggestion of buying *less* new stuff is met with haughty disregard from commerce, ignored by the economic-growth fanatics, is seen as marginal and eccentric socially, and is generally way too disruptive to all of our comfort zones – but we need to adapt.

It is easy to enter the 'reuse revolution': opportunities to partake in reuse vary wildly, from Sotheby's or Christie's to charity shops, eBay, auctions, architectural salvage, vintage markets, classifieds, Freegle in the UK, Freecycle elsewhere, swishing, shwopping, boot markets, upcycled products, garage sales or hand-me-downs – we need to value the reconsumption of our existing stuff and we need a retail sector that can embrace that change of gear. Diversify! Retailers should be offering repair, bring-back schemes, upcycled products and reuse incentives, and should diminish their reliance on sales of new goods. Go! There are big retailers already hedging their bets by offering take-back / reuse schemes and other arrangements, like Apple's Renew, Marks & Spencer's schwopping scheme, H&M, Unilever, Lush, B&Q and Caterpillar, with Patagonia blazing a noble trail and newcomers like Buy Me Once.[17] Let's embed circular thinking into all new design, production and marketplace models so the next generations are not swimming in (bad) stuff but can consume enough good stuff and still have a good life. Designing out waste can, in the process, eliminate greedy consumption patterns, prevent untold pollution, lower carbon emissions and enable greater equality locally and globally.

Good stuff is durable, made from locally sourced, sustainable materials,[18] is repairable, fit for purpose and dismantle-able (thus easily upcycled or recycled). It has a valued purpose (not just a fantasy-advertising-based, flash-fashionable appeal). Let's make stuff remarkable again. Meaningful. Special. Let's have a global deep breath and learn to say 'enough' and be happy with less.

Even in the past seven years of so-called austerity in the UK, the self-storage industry has grown to £350 million a year.[19] Ironically in a period when many cannot buy enough food, heat their homes or contemplate a holiday, there are others who have *so* much stuff that they rent space external to their homes and offices just to store it. This is considered quite normal. There are now reality

TV shows following the adventures of the people who buy unknown goods at auctions of abandoned rental storage units around the world and try to make a buck. Waste is a result of misappropriated scientific and business ingenuity that's focused on product creation and has not been held responsible for long-term impacts of all those products, of six-plus decades of instant gratification, of an advertising industry heralding the ownership of more stuff as a barometer of status and pride. We suffer political weakness where decisions are swayed by the need for short-term economic growth to be re-elected and political cycles that cannot deliver long-term sustainable visions (because they are nebulous and not immediately rewarding); and by short-term financial systems that do not reward nature preservation nor wellbeing but are obsessed with quick wins, by numbers on a screen and shareholders' bank balances.

Since World War II we have focused on reducing the cost of goods – a well-meaning ambition to enable everyone to have a better standard of living after years of rationing and make-doing-and-mending. Yet this desire for cheap and cheaper over time moved production to faraway lands where labour was cheap. So most of the world's manufacturing now occurs in China. Most of the world's recycling takes place there too, because the cheapest shipping in the world is from any Western port *back* to China. The largest freight-carrying ship in the world was launched in December 2014; it can carry 57 million pairs of shoes. It is so large that only six ports around the globe have the capacity to dock it.[20] But as incomes increase in emerging economies, giving populations the opportunity to consume like us, they are unlikely to be a source of cheap labour for too much longer.

Maybe that's when the consumer bubble will burst: when we have run out of people to exploit to make all this stuff.

The role of construction

The UK generated 200 million tonnes of waste in 2012. Around 50% of this was generated by construction. Commercial and industrial activities generated almost a quarter (24%), with households responsible for a further 14%.[21] In the UK we consume around 600 million tonnes of new products annually.[22] Of all that stuff, the construction industry, along with the operation of the built environment, consumes 60% of all these materials and accounts for 45% of CO_2e emissions in the UK. So, tackling the impacts associated with buildings and infrastructure – from design through in-use to demolition – is critical for meeting the UK government's 2050 greenhouse gas targets.[23] We throw away 400,000 tonnes of carpet to landfill annually.[24] Some 8 million tonnes of wood is thrown out every year, yet 80% is reusable. The UK's Wood Recycling Network diverted 8,500 tonnes of wood from the waste stream in 2012.[25] But why don't we do more of this instead of engineering new facilities to recycle, recover and destroy materials (which unintentionally increases demand for waste and disincentivises the very prevention, infrastructure, practice and innovation we could all benefit from)?[26]

We really do need to rethink our human and material relationships.

We need products and buildings that are designed to be useful forever, in many guises.

So may this book inspire you to reassess why, how and what you make, use and discard and thus accelerate our collective journey to a less wasteful culture, attitude and economy.

CHAPTER 3

The Political Narrative

Dr David Greenfield, Managing Director of SOENECS Ltd

The stagnation of circular economy policy in the 20th and 21st centuries

ONE OF THE GREAT POLITICIANS of the early 20th century, Theodore Roosevelt, had views that would today be lauded as forward-thinking and circular in their context. He started his seventh annual message to Congress on 3 December 1907 with the claim: 'The conservation of our natural resources and their proper use constitute the fundamental problem which underlies almost every other problem of our national life.' He went on to state: 'To waste, to destroy our natural resources, to skin and exhaust the land instead of using it so as to increase its usefulness, will result in undermining in the days of our children, the very prosperity which we ought, by right, to hand down to them amplified and developed.'[1] These are profound words that today would be applauded as progressive at any of the numerous conferences, exhibitions and debates on the circular economy.

Fast-forward over a century and on 2 December 2015, Frans Timmermans, the European Commission's First Vice-President, echoed Roosevelt's views when he launched the new EU Circular Economy Package, saying: 'We need to retain precious resources and fully exploit all the economic value within them. The circular economy is about reducing waste and protecting the environment, but it is also about a profound transformation of the way our entire economy works. By rethinking the way we produce, work and buy we can generate new opportunities and create new jobs.'[2]

The European Commission adopted the new Circular Economy Package to forward plan to 2030 with an ambition of boosting 'the EU's competitiveness by protecting businesses against scarcity of resources and volatile prices, helping to create new business opportunities and innovative, more efficient ways of producing and consuming'.[3] Many observers would suggest that we have lost a century in trying to regain the momentum of the early 20th century. However, while historical retrospect is quite interesting and indeed ammunition for moaning about what could have been, we are where we are and now have to look forward, learning the lessons of the last century.

Where did it all go wrong?

So how have we got to this position? Will.i.am, one of the biggest names in the music industry and an eco-entrepreneur, explains in an interview for the launch of his collaboration with Coca-Cola and Harrods EkoCycle: 'The reason why you have waste is because companies purposefully made things to break. It's called "planned obsolescence", and it started in the 1950s when governments gave incentives to companies to make shit to break to boost our economy.'[4] The rationale behind the strategy is to generate long-term sales volume by reducing the time between repeat purchases (referred to as 'shortening the replacement cycle').[5]

According to Rosie Spink in the Guardian, 'It's standard practice for companies to plan obsolescence into their products – including by introducing software upgrades that aren't compatible with existing hardware – and they simultaneously profit from the fact that the average laptop has a high likelihood of breaking within 3–4 years.'[6] The concept is something that can be both beneficial and problematic – on the one hand efficiency in technology can be improved over time, while on the other hand it encourages rampant consumerism and wastefulness.

The concept of built-in obsolescence is not just confined to consumer goods, it's also entirely applicable to new buildings and the fittings that are contained within them. One of the principal questions we need to ask is 'How can policy change the way designers approach use of materials and products to avoid obsolescence, and encourage design so that maintenance is easy and feasible?' Sophie Thomas, former director of circular economy at the RSA, summed up the new thinking well: 'Gone are the days of sustainable design; now we have to learn to think about life cycles, and designers have a key role to play.'[7]

The concept of the circular economy is not new. It has simply gained a momentum that hitherto has not been seen. It mainly concerns structuring the economy in a sustainable way, with the priority being to use materials efficiently and reduce and ultimately eliminate waste flows. The materials cycle is the central issue.

The aim of the circular economy is to maximise the circularity of materials within an industrial society, by designing products and buildings that can be dismantled and refurbished and reused, avoiding the creation of waste. This reuse concept is at the top of the traditional hierarchy, but has been seen by many as 'too difficult'. The circular economy suggests that extending the lifespan, or reuse, of products can be achieved in various ways – repair, upgrading, remanufacture or remarketing of the same product – and the more the design is focused on this and the more valuable the product is, the faster this happens.

Origins of circular economy policies

An article on The Guardian website says that the circular economy is touted as a practical solution to the planet's emerging resource crunch. It highlights that reserves of key resources such as rare earth metals and minerals are diminishing, while exploration and material extraction costs are rising.[8]

Many schools of thought have been subsumed into the worldwide phenomenon that is the circular economy; while the name is new, the influences aren't. The Ellen MacArthur Foundation suggests the following influences:[9]

- Cradle to Cradle
- performance economy
- biomimicry
- industrial ecology
- blue economy
- regenerative design.

The practical applications of the circular economy concept to modern economic systems and industrial processes, however, have gained momentum since the late 1970s, led by a small number of academics, thought leaders and businesses. One of the fundamental claims of the circular economy movement is recognised by the House of Commons Environmental Audit Committee (EAC) – that a 'circular' approach of reusing resources, maximising their value over time, makes environmental and economic sense.[10] This recognition by the EAC gives proponents of the circular economy reassurance that the government understands the merits of moving to a circular approach, but doesn't guarantee that it will succeed. Indeed, weight-based material-flow analysis conducted in 2010 by the Waste and Resources Action Programme (WRAP) estimated that one-fifth of the UK economy is already operating in a circular fashion. Are we doing well enough to not need a policy lever?

Using policy to dictate change

The circular economy instigates a robustness to reuse, which considers the practicalities of material management, rather than waste management. One of the bastions of resource and waste management policies is the waste hierarchy that was introduced in 1975, as part of the European Union's Waste Framework Directive (1975/442/EEC).[11] The waste hierarchy emphasised the importance of waste minimisation, and the protection of the environment and human health. As a policy mechanism it is one of the best known in Europe and demonstrates that the right policies can be highly influential.

Over time, the hierarchy has been adopted by Member States as a central plank of policy. In trying to invigorate the concept within the existing policy framework, a revised resource management hierarchy was created in 2013 to include the concepts of circularity (see Figure 1.7).[12]

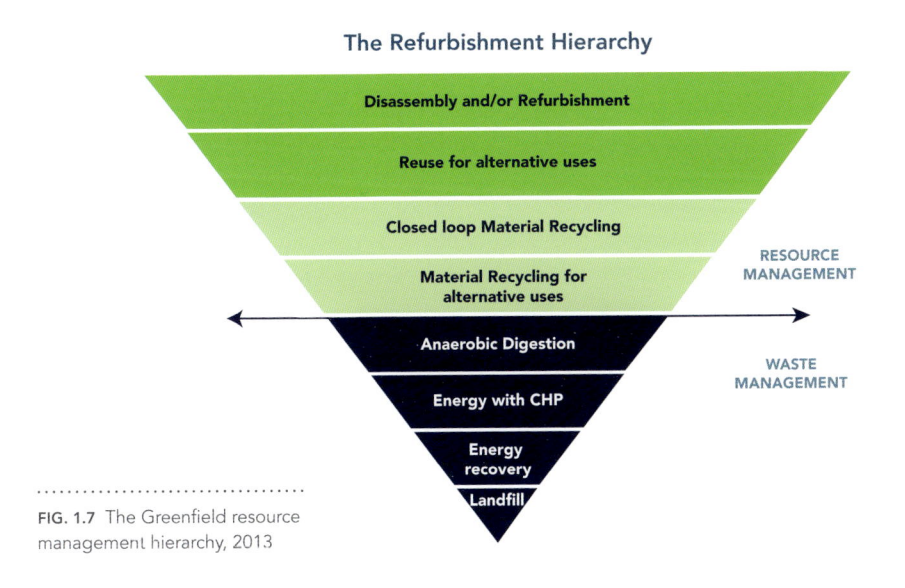

The Refurbishment Hierarchy

- Disassembly and/or Refurbishment
- Reuse for alternative uses
- Closed loop Material Recycling
- Material Recycling for alternative uses

RESOURCE MANAGEMENT

- Anaerobic Digestion
- Energy with CHP
- Energy recovery
- Landfill

WASTE MANAGEMENT

FIG. 1.7 The Greenfield resource management hierarchy, 2013

In the new resource management hierarchy, the aim is to maximise and clarify the solutions available through the circular economy. In essence this has meant the hierarchy has grown up, with new layers added at the top for dismantling and refurbishment, reuse for alternative uses, closed-loop material recycling and material recycling.

While this new hierarchy may give much guidance to many people, unless it is adopted as a policy it seldom has the reach to impact on a national scale. One of the key challenges is how advisors will influence civil servants to push the boundaries of policy.

Existing UK policy and approach

Depending on your political leaning, photographer and environmentalist Ansel Adams' view on politics – 'It is horrifying that we have to fight our own government to save the environment' – is either far-fetched or accurate. He has been proved right in certain short-term cases, such as the way the change to the Feed-In Tariffs (FITs) occurred in 2015, but in many ways inaccurate in the long term, where legislation such as the Environmental Protection Act 1990 has had a positive impact.

The UK government describes a circular economy as 'moving away from our current linear economy (make–use–dispose) towards one where our products, and the materials they contain, are valued differently; creating a more robust economy in the process'.[13] In itself this is a very accurate portrayal of the concept as identified by the Ellen MacArthur Foundation, but it does not go into the detail identified by the EMF, which states: 'A circular economy is restorative and regenerative by design, and aims to keep products, components and materials at their highest utility and value at all times. The concept distinguishes between technical and biological cycles.'[14] Should we be worried by this mismatch? Probably not. Having a definition that recognises the concept is a far-reaching step, but needs to be backed up by actions.

One of the main criticisms is that the UK's devolved governments have different approaches; indeed, as seen in the Scottish government consultation of 2015, Scotland recognises that circular economy matters because of the significant potential benefits:

- to the economy – improving productivity, opening up new markets and improving resilience
- to the environment – cutting waste and carbon emissions
- to communities – more, lower-cost options to access the goods we need.[15]

Whereas, according to the Green Alliance Circular Economy Taskforce, 'support in the English Government has focused more on encouragement than legislation'.[16] Does this mean that government intervention is not required? The case for government adoption is summed up by the Environmental Services Association, who suggest that the prize of a circular economy – 50,000 new jobs with £10 billion investment, boosting GDP by £3 billion[17] – is too big an opportunity for UK PLC to miss.

UK performance in the circular economy

The UK has some of the most progressive environmental laws, and in 2014 was ranked 12th best in the world for Environmental Performance Index (EPI; see Figure 1.8).[18]

FIG. 1.8 The EPI categories

While many people will be surprised at the UK's ranking, the score does mask some variances, such as biodiversity and habitat and climate and energy, where the UK ranks 70th and 85th, respectively. Dismissing the variances for the moment, the rank does indicate that perhaps many of the government's laws and policies, albeit adopted through the EU in many cases, have set the right political framework for change.

The question is: can this recent history be transferred to the new kid on the block, the circular economy? According to the chair of WRAP, Dr Julie Hill, what started as a theoretical construct is gradually becoming an idea accepted by businesses and some policymakers as conveying an important aspiration for the future, namely to keep resources in economic use for as long as possible.[19] If this acceptance continues, then perhaps policy will make the change. However, adoption by the sector is still the challenge.

THE POLITICAL NARRATIVE · CHAPTER 3 · 25

The 2015 EU Circular Economy Package

The EU's Circular Economy Package has been many years in coming; proposed new recycling targets were originally put forward in July 2014 alongside a series of circular economy proposals by the former Environment Commissioner Janez Potocnik. These were scrapped by the new Commission in early 2015, in order to develop a 'more ambitious' policy package, which resulted in a consultation in May 2015, leading to the European Commission adopting a new Circular Economy Package. This package is designed to stimulate Europe's transition towards a circular economy, boosting global competitiveness, fostering sustainable economic growth and generating new jobs.

The ambition of the package is huge; however, the ambition may be tempered by the detailed proposals. One of the leading influencers of the circular economy phenomenon, Walter Stahel, suggests the 'package falls short on future proofing, by failing to plan for impacts as a result of the circular economy'.[20]

The package is split. The first part focuses on managing waste better. The second proposes an action plan for the circular economy, setting out measures to 'close the loop' and tackle all phases in the life cycle of a product: from production and consumption to waste management and the market for secondary raw materials.

The scrapped package included a 75% recycling target, which has now been reduced to:

- a common EU target for recycling 65% of municipal waste by 2030
- a common EU target for recycling 75% of packaging waste by 2030
- a binding landfill target to reduce landfill to a maximum of 10% of all waste by 2030.

The aim of the package is to move to a global circular economy market where 'the value of products and materials is maintained for as long as possible; waste and resource use are minimised, and resources are kept within the economy when a product has reached the end of its life, to be used again and again to create further value.' As a policy instrument, will this have an impact on how construction and design is undertaken?

The package recognises that construction and demolition waste is among the biggest sources of waste in terms of volume. As a result, the Commission will develop targeted guidelines to be used on demolition sites for the purpose of recovering valuable materials, and also focusing on the treatment of hazardous waste. The Commission is also proposing sorting systems for construction and demolition waste in the revised proposals on waste. The Commission will also develop indicators to assess environmental performance throughout the life cycle of a building and encourage design improvements that will reduce the environmental impacts.

These three policies could dictate construction of tomorrow. However, is much of this already happening in major construction sites across the UK? The planned 'Brexit' of the UK could have huge implications for the adoption of the circular economy in Britain. It is too early to predict what may happen; it would, however, be prudent to suggest that the concepts of the circular economy will be adopted into UK law, if adopted by the EU.

Opportunities for design and construction

The 21st century has already seen a huge amount of major new construction and redevelopment, and will continue to do so. The rising skyline in London, which seems to be getting a few new skyscrapers every year, highlights this. In July 2014, the Mayor of London published the London Infrastructure Plan. This articulates the Mayor's ambition that London becomes a world leader in the development of the circular economy so that it is best placed to reap the rewards of this transition. The Plan projects that by 2036 there will be an additional one million households living within the Greater London area.[21]

How do we build one million new homes within a circular economy?

Circular economy policy and BIM

The requirement for a well-designed waste management system should form a fundamental part of the design and planning process because 80% of all environmental costs are predetermined during the conception and design phase of a project.[22]

The UK government has put in place policy that has the potential to deliver this: the Digital Built Britain plan. Launched in February 2015, this deals with Level 3 BIM – Strategic Plan.[23]

The starting point of the BIM model is very similar to that of the circular economy; they are both of a circular nature and see demolition and waste as the least desirable option. However they vary in how much effort is put into design and testing. This is crucial as it gives the opportunity for all stakeholders to consider the operation and maintenance stage of the building.

Using BIM concepts and the rhetoric around waste management, the definition of circular economic development might be understanding the supply chain for that project: the architects, material purchasers, developers, facility managers, operators, financiers, electrical, mechanical and civil engineers and potential users need to be involved in the final design of the programme. This may mean longer lead-in times to begin with, but will allow for consideration of circular concepts such as leasing of materials rather than purchase, fittings that allow for dismantling and reuse, flexible spaces that will extend the lifetime of the development and design that will allow for maintenance.

Policy failures and solutions

Policy needs to influence best practice; it's all well and good everyone considering the operation phase and meeting current standards, but do those standards allow for circular design at that stage? As an example, in April 2015, LWARB and LEDNET launched Waste Management Planning Advice for New Flatted Properties. The consultants SOENECS Ltd and BPP LLP were tasked with looking at how policy could change the practice of designing flats in London so that they met the requirement of the BSI for bin stores. In particular, British Standard BS5906: 2005 focuses on operational requirements for the location of waste storage within buildings, for the benefit of residents and waste collection crews, for example:

- that residents should have to carry their waste no more than 30m from their units to waste storage areas
- that containers must be placed within a maximum of 20m from the refuse vehicle access point to reduce the distance needed to pull bins.

What the BSI failed to do was show the impact of complying. In the case of many new buildings in London, the space for residents to separate recycling in their homes, store and then deposit it were foregone in favour of compliance with the BSI (or at least compliance with an interpretation of the BSI). This resulted in many developers situating bins in the basement of a multistorey building and meeting the BSI as residents were no more than 30m *horizontally* from a bin. In many cases, as residents were well over 30m in practice, the impact might be for residents to just 'bin' rather than recycle.

The recommendations from SOENECS and BPP included the following:

- Authorities need clear planning policy that provides certainty over waste management requirements for consideration by developers and has teeth in determining applications.
- Development management planning policies will set out requirements in greater detail rather than strategic planning policies.
- Supplementary Planning Documents (SPDs) that include more detail on requirements of planning policies have weight but need clear policy on which to be based, and can take time and resources to prepare – various alternative options exist that may be more appropriate to different authorities.[24]

This resulted in the creation of a new template strategy for developers to use, but most importantly coupled with a planning policy that required a strategy at master-planning stage. Thus when presented with a new policy, a solution of how to accomplish that requirement was provided.

Conclusion

This chapter has explored the history of the circular economy and the politics surrounding it, as well as some of the challenges associated with construction in the 21st century. It demonstrates that in many cases policy can influence, but as has been shown can be used by developers to distort the intent of the policy. In reality, the challenge of getting the construction sector to change isn't about encouraging policymakers to introduce policies, it's about getting architects, material purchasers, developers, facility managers, operators, financiers, electrical, mechanical and civil engineers and potential users to buy into the circular economy and understand the benefits. New European targets will point the direction, but it is essential the sector refocuses and moves towards new methods of designing, planning, constructing and dismantling, with an understanding of circularity at the heart of all decisions, regardless of Brexit.

PART 2

Circular Inspirations
Duncan Baker-Brown

31 INTRODUCTION

33 **STEP 1** Recycling Waste

55 **STEP 2** Reusing Waste

81 **STEP 3** Reducing the Amount of Material Used

109 **STEP 4** The Circular Economy

INTRODUCTION

Duncan Baker-Brown

THIS PART OF *THE RE-USE ATLAS* is a series of 'steps' towards the reality of a circular economy. Many people are busy visioning what this will look like. However, these visions are a long way from the linear way most people currently exist on the planet – finding stuff, processing, utilising and casting it aside. The idea of designing things in such a way as to ensure they are always a useful resource for either the natural or synthetic worlds is quite alien.

In the meantime, many ideas and concepts that consider living in harmony with natural ecosystems have gained in popularity. Green/eco/low-energy/Passivhaus/hacking/reuse cafes/upcycling/ designing for demolition, etc. are all words and ideas that more and more people are getting to grips with.

While considering the idea of this book, I was concerned that there are many different interpretations of what it means to be a 'green' designer. I am also aware that many 'reuse' and 'being less harmful to the environment' ideas are dismissed within *Cradle to Cradle*[1] philosophy as simply slowing down the inevitable – for example recycling plastic cups into fleeces to wear simply prevents that plastic from being toxic ocean waste for a couple of years. I feel that this over-simplifies some initiatives that are positively influencing behavioural change.

The ideal of a circular economy is clear, but I am concerned that it appears to be such a big leap from where we currently stand that there is a need for some clearly defined stepping stones to help us along our way to a more circular existence.

One of the biggest challenges that faces humankind is how to exist without damaging so much of our planet's natural resources. This is done as we mine for resources, as we refine them, utilise them and then when we throw them away. In one way or another, humankind has managed to practically wrap the landscape with our cities, roads, flight paths and landfill sites, while oceans are filling up with plastic waste: a pretty gloomy state of affairs.

However, most of that development has only happened over the last 150 years or so, and it should be noted that we have only been manufacturing plastic for a little over 100 years. Until biodegradable options are commonly available, there needs to be an emphasis on cleaning up the vast areas of oceans and landscape that are currently contaminated by dangerous waste. This 'big clean-up' will create a huge amount of material that in theory could be put to good use, or reuse.

Part 2 of my Atlas is divided into four chapters, taking the reader on a step-by-step route towards closed-loop systems. Each 'step' contains a number of case studies that capture some of my first-hand research, gleaned from interviewing over fifty people involved in inspiring projects from around the world that tackle recycling, reuse, the reduction of resource use, and finally closed-loop systems. These case studies are supplemented with one longer interview with a significant protagonist from each of the aforementioned steps. Therefore, unless stated otherwise, any comments quoted from people in the case studies have been taken directly from interviews I have had personally with them.

FIG. 2.1 Adidas FC Bayern Munich Parley Jersey made from reclaimed ocean waste

PART 2 CIRCULAR INSPIRATIONS

STEP 1 Recycling Waste

[DEFINITION]

STEP 1 PROJECTS recycle waste into a new product or material. The case studies presented here should be seen as the first step towards reducing humankind's negative impact on Earth. Reprocessing waste is not a particularly sophisticated approach as waste material is recycled by being ground down, melted, pulped, etc, often into a less useful and second-rate 'new' material. The processes can also involve waste and mixing materials together that will make future disposal even more difficult. Recycling processes also consume valuable energy and water. However, recycling does identify 'waste' as a valuable 'resource' and reduces (or at least delays) the amount of material being burnt or going to landfill. This is a basic step towards 'circularity' and one that organisations such as Parley for the Oceans are taking seriously. Parley's position (which is one I share) is that we have to clean up the oceans and shorelines to save marine wildlife and to take plastic out of the food chain. Its approach is clear and explained via its 'AIR' initiative (AVOID/ INTERCEPT/ REDESIGN).

A quote from its website sums up why recycling forms an integral part of our route towards circularity.

Awareness campaigns, clean-up operations and recycling initiatives allow us to help alleviate immediate threats to marine wildlife and reduce the use of virgin plastics in product design, manufacturing and distribution. In close collaboration with major brands, we also work to reduce overall plastic use. But we can only end ocean plastic pollution in the long run if we invent smarter materials and synchronise the economic system of mankind with the ecosystem of nature. Therefore Parley with its global expert network is operating an extensive research and development program to invent alternatives and to establish new industry standards.[1]

RECYCLING WASTE | STEP 1 | 33

STEP 1 CASE STUDY No.1

Adidas training shoe, developed in partnership with Parley for the Oceans

awareness-raisers | environmental extivists | designers | brand developers

[**THE STORY**]

' When I started Parley in 2012, the forecast was that by the year 2048 the oceans will die, leading to irreversible damage to our planet. Turns out, this was too optimistic: we actually have 10 years to spin things around.'[2]

CYRILL GUTSCH

German-born Cyrill Gutsch set up New-York-based Parley for the Oceans in 2012 (his story is recounted at the end of Step 1; see page 49). By April 2015 Parley announced its first commercial partnership – with sportswear giant Adidas, initially making training shoes out of ocean plastic waste. Why was this significant? Gutsch states that the fashion, sports and tech industries can create trends, and 'trends have the power to shift thinking and behaviour – sometimes even overnight. Technology and fashion are perhaps the fastest change agents there are.'

If we only have a decade to clean up our oceans, Gutsch believes that we have to effect behaviour change, and do it quickly. Marrying major brands, their huge marketing budgets and customer demographics with the environmental challenges is Gutsch's method of doing just this. He aims to focus on the 'consumables' and brands that are helping to create the environmental problems in our oceans in the first place. Gutsch hopes that people buying products made of ocean plastic waste will be fascinated by the stories associated with them and then start behaving differently as a consequence.

Parley has attempted to 'take ownership of the supply chain' with Adidas. In June 2015 Parley held an 'Oceans. Climate. Life' launch event at the United Nations in New York. Gutsch and his Adidas partners could have shown images of the destruction that 100 years of plastic production has caused. However, instead they presented the first training shoe made entirely from ocean waste. The shoe upper was made with nylon, salvaged by Parley partner organisation The Sea Shepherd, who had chased down a deep sea fishing trawler for 110 days because it had been poaching rare fish off the coast of West Africa. The Sea Shepherd then salvaged the trawler's 75km of illegal gill nets and took them back to port. The story caught the attention of the press and social media to such an extent that 18 months later Adidas and Parley had 500,000 of the 'Ultraboost Uncaged Parley' in production. This shoe is made from ocean plastic collected from the Maldives. The first commercial shoe was produced in November 2016, and they expect to produce one million of these shoes made from ocean waste by the end of 2017.

PART 2 CIRCULAR INSPIRATIONS

CLOCKWISE FROM TOP

FIG. 2.2 Adidas x Parley running shoe, only available in limited numbers

FIG. 2.3 The Sea Shepherd unloading its cargo of 75km of illegal gillnets

FIG. 2.4 Yarn for Adidas x Parley running shoes, made from ocean waste plastic

FIG. 2.5 Close-up detail of Adidas x Parley running shoe showing green fishing net

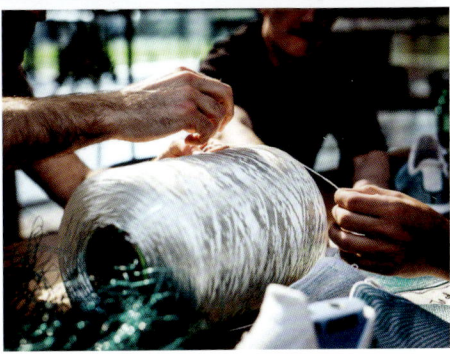

RECYCLING WASTE STEP 1

This has only happened because of the hard work of all elements of the Adidas product and material research team, as well as their desire to unpack and change elements of their supply chain. Adidas used the chemistry and innovative manufacturing processes of 'tailored fibre technology' (TFP), which allows a more flexible combination of yarns, fibres and threads. This enabled shoes to be made of material previously ignored – waste plastics from our oceans.

The idea is actually pretty straightforward. By marketing popular products made from materials that have interesting narratives, companies will encourage consumers to learn about the problems associated with the materials used (for example, ocean plastic waste) and, crucially, to feel part of a positive response. Consumers will hopefully change their behaviour and return their shoes back to Adidas to reprocess, and avoid the product becoming waste.

This is only the first step. Parley for the Oceans is also investing in the teaching and research required to replace 'dumb' 20th-century plastics with bio-plastics and other materials that will eventually turn to compost – that is nutrients that feed ecosystems rather than simply polluting and destroying them.

[OPINION]

Parley creates products with a clear narrative; a story to tell that is enticing and intriguing. Its products allow consumers to learn as much as they care to (or not) about the environmental issues associated with the consumable, while knowing that they are 'doing their bit' for the environment by choosing (for example) Adidas and Parley training shoes over 'normal' ones. Whether consumers will dwell on this long enough to remember to return the worn-out training shoes to Adidas is one of the big questions that will need answering if this is to be seen as a successful programme.

In the meantime, Parley will continue with its support and research into the materials and products humankind needs to begin to live in harmony with the planet, while raising awareness among the huge corporations it works with, as well as with their customers. Only time will tell if it is successful – and we don't have too much of that.

FIG. 2.6 The Adidas x Parley Ultraboost Uncaged shoe, made from waste ocean plastic

PART 2   CIRCULAR INSPIRATIONS

STEP 1 CASE STUDY No.2

Gumdrop Bins

designer | inventor | entrepreneur | behaviour-change enabler

[THE STORY]

UK councils spend over £150 million a year removing chewing gum from pavements and other surfaces. Chewing gum is humankind's most common habit, with over 3.74 trillion sticks of the stuff made every year. This equates to over 100,000 tonnes of gum manufactured annually. The negative outcome from all this chewing is that most of the gum ends up on our pavements. The removal of this waste is an expense most local authorities would rather not have and many cannot afford.

In 2009 Anna Bullus was studying design when she had an idea to create bins specifically designed to deal with the problem of collecting chewing gum. Bullus discovered that waste gum could be reprocessed into a range of plastic-type compounds that could then be used as a resource in the rubber and plastics industry. It took only eight months to prove the concept. However, it took another five years to commercialise and scale up the process to recycle chewing gum into marketable Gum-tec compounds that can be infinitely reprocessed without losing any of their first-generation qualities. Recycling often renders a material less effective than the first time it is processed, but not in this case.

What Bullus proposed to do through her London-based company was hugely ambitious.

FIG. 2.7 The original Gumdrop Bin, fixed to a lamp post

She wanted to create a genuinely closed-loop recycling process that added value to an environmentally destructive material. By designing a chewing gum bin that was actually made of waste chewing gum, Bullus has simultaneously reduced the environmental burden of chewing gum while creating a clever product that requires this material to enable further production of Gumdrop Bins. By collecting bins when they are full and reprocessing them again into more gum bins, Bullus has created her own closed-loop system. She has plans to utilise these recycled plastic compounds as a material source for other products, such as 'Gum Boots'.

RECYCLING WASTE | STEP 1

CLOCKWISE

FIG. 2.8 A Gumdrop Bin key ring

FIG. 2.9 Wellington boots made from old chewing gum

FIG. 2.10 A selection of products made from old chewing gum

[OPINION]

Anna Bullus has had a brilliant idea that completely understands the problems associated with the waste product we know as chewing gum. The Gumdrop Bin relies on being an eye-catching object. If it succeeds in enticing you to throw away your old chewing gum responsibly (and apparently if these bins are installed, over 46% of gum normally thrown on the floor ends up in them) then it has also allowed you, the end user, to participate in a genuinely circular, closed-loop production process.

As with all 'Step 1' case studies, the Gumdrop Bin can be criticised by Cradle to Cradle experts as perpetuating the production of one of an expanding family of unintelligent plastic materials: unintelligent because it is toxic, it cannot or is hardly ever reused (although in this particular case it can be recycled), and it doesn't biodegrade. It therefore creates huge environmental problems if left to be simply thrown away. Bullus has skilfully turned this linear life cycle of chewing gum (made, chewed, stuck on a pavement) into a circular one involving the potential for perpetual reprocessing, which in turn reduces the environmental burden.

Getting involved in the synthetic plastics business is complex, and environmentalists will often state that by recycling you are justifying the manufacture of more virgin plastic. However, plastics are omnipresent, covering huge areas of the world's landscapes, shorelines and, of course, our oceans. They are now part of our food chain and even our geology, and they have only been around for about 100 years. The Gumdrop Bin is an excellent case study proving that intelligent design could make the big clean-up of Planet Earth viable and affordable.

38 **PART 2** CIRCULAR INSPIRATIONS

STEP 1 CASE STUDY No.3

Re-worked

designer | inventor | entrepreneur

[THE STORY]

Re-worked was set up in 2005 by Adam Fairweather as a non-profit business investing in green and social enterprise. This approach originated from Fairweather's research at the University of Brighton in 2003–4, where his lead project considered waste streams from within the coffee industry that could be recycled within a circular economic model. In 2003 cafe culture was growing rapidly, along with the 'grab and go' fast-food culture that requires large amounts of packaging. Fairweather saw a huge opportunity to recycle coffee grounds into high-value products that could challenge perceptions around waste and hopefully encourage reuse and recycling.

By 2004 Fairweather had developed a biodegradable polymer material made from waste coffee grounds. This material can be moulded into a robust and, crucially, reusable coffee cup to replace the ubiquitous paper/plastic throwaway cup. Re-worked received several grants to develop the material and subsequently to create a working supply chain model. Although the coffee cup was never commercialised, it led to a spate of interesting new products and collaborations.

Re-worked soon began a collaboration with recycling pioneer Smile Plastics Ltd, a producer of decorative recycled plastic panels. Founded in 1994, its products have been used around the world in spaces such as the V&A, Design Museum, Wellcome Collection and Selfridges. Fairweather explored additional ways that businesses could engage with the idea of reusing coffee through making flat panel materials from recycled coffee and plastics. The finished product, 'Çurface', is a dense and durable material originating from recycled coffee grounds. The panels have been used for a wide range of applications, including furniture. A key application for Çurface is within coffee shops, where the source material comes from in the first place. It is used as surfaces in furniture and countertops and has become a powerful way of engaging consumers and commerce with the issue of socio and environmental sustainability (note Çurface is no longer produced for retail purposes).

After trials running a coffee collection service in central London, Re-worked started a new collaboration and partnership with a coffee supply company called Redcup. They developed a new business concept known as 'Greencup', offering commercial catering establishments a full service of coffee supply, servicing and collection: a closed-loop system. The initial model was set up for urban hubs where the coffee could be collected by the delivery driver, or service engineers,

PART 2 CIRCULAR INSPIRATIONS

CLOCKWISE FROM TOP (OPPOSITE)

FIG. 2.11 Waste coffee grounds

FIG. 2.12 Loading waste coffee grounds for reprocessing

FIG. 2.13 Reprocessing old coffee grounds into Çurface sheet material

FIG. 2.14 Çurface material made from 70% coffee grounds and 30% bioresins by Re-worked

FIG. 2.15 Çurface bespoke recycled coffee panels for Sanremo coffee machine manufacture

while on site for other jobs. Now that the business has expanded to a national level, the delivery and collections are managed by third parties. Greencup is the first company in this sector to take responsibility for its full supply chain, offering full closed-loop services to its customers. Re-worked also developed a soil conditioner made from coffee grounds that could be sold back within its customers' establishments. The Greencup proposition has been taken up by many garden centres around the UK, including Wyevale Garden Centres, whose Coffee Ground cafes send their coffee grounds for recycling and sell the resulting soil conditioner.

Partnerships with Google (2010–2014) and the Italian espresso machine manufacturer Sanremo Srl followed. Google had its coffee collected and made into furniture for its own self-service café in its London headquarters, and Sanremo included a variation of the Çurface material as panels on its green espresso machine 'Verde'.

[**OPINION**]

This study proves just how vibrant and creative the UK design industry is. It also shows how determined individuals need to be to make a success of their ideas. Fairweather has had to reassess the whole supply chain, as well as the production methodologies within it, to enable his designs to be realised. He has also never allowed a brilliant design idea that was perhaps ahead of its time and not destined for mass production (his coffee cups) to become a vanity project. He learnt from that experience and then moved on to other circular economy-focused projects.

It is perhaps the challenges presented by the 'closed-loop' concept that interest Fairweather most, not a particular solution.

FIG. 2.16 Garden fertiliser made from used coffee grounds

RECYCLING WASTE | STEP 1 | 41

STEP 1 CASE STUDY No.4

Bureo Skateboards

environmental | social activists | inclusive entrepreneurs

[THE STORY]

Bureo designs and manufactures skateboards using discarded fishing nets, which is good news for shorelines and oceans. The founders, mechanical engineers and keen surfers and skaters Ben Kneppers, Dave Stover and Kevin Ahearn, met in 2011 in Sydney. During his time as an environmental consultant in Chile, Kneppers noticed the huge amount of plastic that was having a detrimental effect on the coastline and ecosystems. He also realised that, as with many coastlines that surfers inhabit, there was limited or no waste management provision; pollution just built up.

The trio quickly realised that they could marry their passion for surfing and skating with their concern for the environment. They needed to change people's perception of waste. People needed to stop avoiding waste (literally averting their eyes from the sight of it) and start respecting it as the dangerous matter it is. The first move was to look at ways in which waste material could have added value. This became a straightforward combination of their passion for the environment and their passion for skating: a sustainable skateboard company.

Once they got accepted onto Boston's Northeastern University Business Accelerator programme in 2013 they were able to develop the mechanical processes required to turn ocean plastic into a material appropriate for a skateboard. They then partnered with a company in Santiago, Chile, that could carry out the material processing on a commercial level. They stuck with the idea that the actual source material, ocean plastic, would originate from Chile. To achieve this they had to set up systems to collect, clean, recycle and reprocess the waste plastic. For example, Bureo encouraged fishermen to dispose of their fishing nets in a responsible way by providing them with purpose-built collection points. They used Kneppers' links with the World Wildlife Fund to develop these and set up an initiative called 'Net Positiva'. However, to really change

....

CLOCKWISE FROM TOP LEFT (OPPOSITE)

FIG. 2.17 Discarded nets on a beach in Chile

FIG. 2.18 This is the amount of discarded fishing net required to make one skateboard

FIG. 2.19 Collected nets are shredded to process into skateboards

FIG. 2.20 Shredded fishing nets are processed into nylon pellets

FIG. 2.21 Aluminium mould for skateboard

FIG. 2.22 The skateboard processing factory

FIG. 2.23 A Bureo skateboard made primarily of salvaged fishing nets and vegetable oils

PART 2 CIRCULAR INSPIRATIONS

RECYCLING WASTE STEP 1   43

decades of wasteful behaviour, Bureo had to meet with the fishing communities and explain to them the long-term mission to clean up the oceans and shorelines (fishing supplies make up only 10% of ocean plastic pollution, but it tends to be the most harmful to marine mammals, fish and birds). As Ahearn points out, 'a normal skate company would just be buying the raw pallet; we had to set up an entire supply chain down here in Chile'.

In 2014 Bureo produced its first commercially available boards for retail. Currently its boards 'consume' between 3m^2 and 5m^2 of fishing nets, depending on the design. The boards were not the only unusual part of the product.

The wheels were sourced from Satori Wheels (http://satoriwheels.org/) because they are made from 30% vegetable oil with 100% recycled plastic cores.

[OPINION]

Being this particular about the supply chain and specification of the skateboards has slowed down the development of the business and the products. However, the medium- and long-term benefits to the fishing (and other) communities and the environment they live and work in could be profound. The founders of Bureo plan to hand over many of the responsibilities for collecting and supplying material to new start-up community-based companies. These are all good measures that will hopefully begin to change destructive linear processes, such as the fishing industry, into something a bit more like a closed-loop system.

FIG. 2.24 Close up of skateboard wheels made from 30% vegetable oil

44   PART 2   CIRCULAR INSPIRATIONS

STEP 1 CASE STUDY No.5

Building materials made entirely from waste products

inventors | scientists | new material flows | bio-base | construction waste

[THE STORY]

In the last 25 years, sustainable innovations in construction materials have often focused on insulation products: for example, insulation made from sheep's wool. Initially this material was made from surplus and waste processed wool from the carpet and textile industries. Although a good 'reuse' product, the first version was imported all the way from New Zealand, which meant it had a big carbon footprint. Later versions were made in the UK. The issue of embedded 'carbon footprint' has gradually been addressed to a point where UK-based designers can now specify insulation made of waste wool from British sheep. There are numerous variations of this product, including one where the wool is reinforced with waste plastic to give it added rigidity, and for me it is a great alternative to 'traditional' high (embodied) energy products. It performs well and because of the oils naturally occurring in the wool the product is water resistant, which is a great benefit when the woollen insulation batts are hanging around a wet building site.

It is also possible to get insulation made from waste cotton, hemp, flax, denim and, of course, recycled newspaper cellulose. However, today there is a new generation of construction products utilising waste materials, both organic and synthetic. These materials are beginning to emerge from the laboratories and help our buildings turn waste into a valuable resource.

'Newspaper Wood' is from Norway, where over one million tonnes of paper and cardboard are recycled every year. Newspaper is rolled up and stuck together with solvent-free glue to create a material like a timber log. It is cut into sealed, waterproof planks which are flame-retardant and may therefore have a specific use within construction for interiors. If the product becomes popular it could begin to reduce the burden on our forests to supply new timber.

In the USA, as with many countries around the world, 'disposable' nappies account for 3.5 million tonnes of waste going to landfill, or about 20 billion nappies. There are now roof tiles on the market that are made of salvaged nappies and other sanitary products, diverting them from landfill. A number of companies are developing products, such as roof tiles, that are made of material from salvaged nappies once they have had their numerous polymers separated in specialist recycling plants. It is early days for this product, and it is interesting that the company seems quite coy about the material source of their products despite big green credentials. Maybe it is a bit too challenging to expect people to specify this roof tile for the foreseeable future.

CLOCKWISE FROM TOP

FIG. 2.25 Waste material source for reconstituted bricks

FIG. 2.26 Mixing waste materials to create new bricks

FIG. 2.27 TOP LEFT: brick waste in clay binder
TOP RIGHT: brick waste in lime binder
BOTTOM LEFT: waste chalk in lime binder
BOTTOM RIGHT: waste thermalite block in lime mortar

FIG. 2.28 Selection of reconstituted bricks by Stone Cycling

FROM TOP

FIG. 2.29 Öko-Pavillon, 2011, ITKE Stuttgart, demonstrating a selection of recycled and biobase materials.

FIG. 2.30 Bio-flexi material: a combination of elastic binders and agricultural fibres.

FIG. 2.31 STRAWave panels made from recycled agricultural natural fibres (straw and coconut) combined with bio-resins

There is also an interesting cluster of organic materials being developed into products like bricks, insulation and packing materials. These materials are literally grown in factory conditions. For example, one of the leading companies developing 'biomaterials', Ecovative, has a portfolio of organic materials that are marketed as 'safe, healthy and certified sustainable'. Mycro Board is like a timber particle board, but instead of using glues to bind the fibres, mycelium (the vegetative part of a fungus) is used. The same company produces the revolutionary Myco Foam, which could replace much of our ubiquitous plastic packaging, as well as thermal and acoustic insulation. Mycelium is grown to order, then mixed with other waste organic matter such as corn husks, waste timber, etc. Bricks have also been grown by mixing corn husks (waste agricultural by-product) with silica (abundant) and mycelium. The resultant brick is solid, lightweight and durable to a point, though not as durable as a clay brick – yet.

As well as growing new organic materials, there is a lot of research into the reuse of agro-fibres – residue of plant fibres from the vast agricultural industries that are often burnt, allowed to biodegrade or, worse, sent to landfill. For over 20 years a number of institutions have been looking into the potential of this waste material to benefit the automotive, aircraft, textile and construction industries. One of the leading centres for research is the Institute of Building Structures and Structural Design at the University of Stuttgart.

RECYCLING WASTE **STEP 1**

Junior professor Dr Hanaa Dahy, who leads the BioMat Department there, specialises in biobased materials and material cycles in architecture. Dahy and her colleagues are identifying sources of agro-fibres and testing their application in architecture. Prototypes are in the form of green biocomposites and agroplastic, where the natural fibres are bonded with biopolymers – all non-toxic and biodegradable. One of these developments is the Bio-flexi product, where elastic binders compound agricultural fibres to be applicable in various free-form applications and furniture. The materials have the potential to replace toxic, non-degradable, off-gassing plastics and participate in preserving forests, as wood fibres are being replaced by agro-fibres. Current product experiments include prefabricated external cladding modules for buildings, including products like TRAshell, STRAWave and others: composed of green agro-fibre thermoset composites, free-orientated short natural fibres and plant-based thermoset bioresin. Agro-based particles are sourced from plant residue streams including coconut shells, cereal straw and black coal ash used as an agro-filler. It is all very interesting for the near future – perhaps this is truly organic architecture.

StoneCycling appears simply to 'do what it says on the tin'. The company was started at the Design Academy in Eindhoven, the Netherlands, with an ambition to create new building materials from waste building materials. The founder of the company, Tom van Soest, 'started to grind, blend and process' these waste materials 'in different ways'. Among the numerous products van Soest has produced is a series of attractive building bricks made from construction rubble (ie bricks and mortar). As with many of these companies, there is a secret ingredient or two.

[OPINION]

We have seen from these case studies that there are two strategies for emerging materials. The first locates a troublesome waste material – something that is quickly filling up landfill sites and is difficult to reuse, a material such as disposable nappies or building rubble. It then reprocesses this material into a useful, perhaps reusable, product. The second strategy is to grow organic materials that could potentially replace unintelligent materials such as plastics. The second strategy is the most exciting and forward thinking, while the first begins to deal with the environmental problems associated with materials that, while they have only been around in a big way for a hundred years or so, and while they have been very useful, have had a massive negative impact on the planet.

INTERVIEW WITH AN EXPERT

Cyrill Gutsch, designer and creative entrepreneur, founder of Parley for the Oceans

DBB: Is recycling 'just slowing down the inevitable'?

CG: For me recycling is not a solution. It's really the first conversation, because when you look at material – and specifically I'm talking about plastic – people use something and toss it away, then it loses all value. It's very obvious now with plastic, but it was not perceived as a problem until recently. Obviously there are specialists who are well aware of the problems of plastic waste, but in the mainstream you couldn't find an awareness of plastic being any sort of problem when we started with Parley for the Oceans, even in so-called highly developed countries with an awareness of environmental issues. The idea of recycling, with its nicely designed logos stating 'recyclable', [is] quite disempowering for people, who tend to think that any plastic product with this type of symbol on it is being reused, because it doesn't make sense that it wouldn't be. This is an illusion that we need to disrupt: the illusion that 'somebody takes care of my trash'.

That's why I feel it is important to visualise the process and the efforts that go into retrieving these materials, all that waste – retrieving it from the shoreline or getting it out of the water.

DBB: You come from a design, marketing, brand-developing background. Had you always been preoccupied with environmental issues?

CG: No not at all. My career has always been about solving problems, but I gave up on the environment at a very young age. As a German growing up in southern Germany, you try to do all the right things. Then you realise that the problems are so big and you wonder 'How can we solve them?' So for a long time I was very cynical about the environment.

I wasn't interested in environmental issues for a long time, not until I met with Paul Watson [the marine wildlife conservationist and an environmental activist, who founded the Sea Shepherd Conservation Society] in 2012. When I met him, I asked him: 'Listen, Paul, how can you be so positive about all this? When you are fighting this cause, it looks so lost.' And he replied, 'The only causes that are worth fighting are the lost ones.' I thought 'That's cool. You are right.'

DBB: So how did you meet Paul Watson?

CG: It was in Frankfurt at a small little law firm. We had a mutual friend who I met up with in Basel in 2012. She told me that Paul had just been arrested in Frankfurt on suspicion of intending to 'cause a shipwreck' 10 years earlier. I was shocked because he was a hero for me. There wasn't really another environmental activist that I knew the name of. She told me he had been arrested and she said 'You should campaign for him: you should get him out.' So I went to Frankfurt to meet with him.

During this meeting I began to understand one thing that I had completely missed before, and that is that the oceans are under serious threat, and it is not something that is going to happen 200 years from now; you are speaking about a disaster within 10 or 15 years from now. Paul then told me about his story – where he started out from at the age of 13 by liberating and freeing animals from traps. I thought, 'I was so busy creating stuff and being in love with my skills.' However, I also thought that I could use what I did for brands or personalities for the oceans.

DBB: So on that day, what did you agree to do?

CG: I just saw very clearly that day that every environmental issue to do with the oceans is caused by a faulty and very old-fashioned business model. I then thought, well, this is what I do anyway! I am redesigning business models and redesigning brands, creating added value where there is none. I am shifting things, effecting change. So we have to find ways to make it more lucrative to protect the oceans rather than destroy them. Which means we have to change the whole way our systems function. I also realised that people in creative industries have more power than people think. We create businesses, technologies, we design stuff, we make things famous and we create trends – and trends can change things overnight! Technology and fashion trends are perhaps the fastest change agents we have. While there is a place for talking about these problems in a logical and rational way, it can take forever. We don't have that much time.

So what I realised in the office in Frankfurt in 2012 is this. There is a big problem: the oceans are collapsing. The idea that we could be powerful enough to destroy the sea was something crazy for me.

Often it is the consumer who is blamed for environmental problems, but it is so difficult to be well informed, so difficult to do the right thing, especially if there aren't the products out there to support better environmental practice. What can a consumer do apart from pick from the options offered?

Brands are often blamed for environmental problems as well. However, the truth is that many brands do not know who or what comprises their supply chain. They don't even invent their products anymore. They may design and assemble them, but they are not in control of their supply chain and they often don't have the knowledge to question their supply chain. So they are just depending upon what other people tell them.

So it comes down to material. Yes of course people want to sell what they have in stock. Nobody wants to change anything. Change comes with pain. You pretty much have to make a massive buzz with the consumer to get the brands understanding that there is a trend happening and then to create a demand for alternatives that have not yet been invented, which makes it difficult and very frustrating. But still, once these brands understand that the market has certain new [environmentally sensitive] requirements, then they have the power to push it through – if they make bold decisions. Where there is demand, there is always an immediate answer to that.

So that's what Parley is trying to tackle from different angles. First we educate the consumer about plastic pollution in the oceans and then we go to the brands and say 'Listen, you don't have to stand there stunned. Learn about your supply chain. Go deep and then you will identify the problems. Be nagging and demanding towards your suppliers and stuff will happen.' You can't expect miracles overnight. It's not as simple as identifying one thing, like plastic, that we all depend upon and then turning it off overnight. It's not possible.

I believe that we need a transition phase. [We need] a long-term solution and a short-term solution.

DBB: **So what is the role of these recycling strategies in a circular economy?**

CG: The final long-term solution for plastic pollution is reinventing the material, because plastic is a design failure.

DBB: **Is that not the big problem you have with plastic: by raising awareness of the problem and turning plastic into products such as training shoes and jeans, are you not just perpetuating the production of the toxic plastic in the first place?**

CG: Good question. The truth is that the short-term objective that we have developed in our AIR (Avoid, Intercept, Redesign) strategy is to accept plastic as a design failure. We have to accept that we will only solve this problem long term by developing new materials. However, in between, to prepare the market and to prepare the supply chains and then make it possible to solve the problem long term we need our replacement drug. Right now we are addicted to plastic. Yes, if you can avoid plastic then do it. But if you can't avoid it and you need all these attributes that plastic gives us, then use recycled plastic. That is the one step everybody can do now.

DBB: **What were your first ideas for Parley for the Oceans?**

CG: We decided when we started Parley that our first mission was overfishing, but we had huge problems getting people involved with the cause. We then realised that we had to start with something to make it easier for everybody – a gateway project, if you like, to the oceans. Plastic was the obvious choice because plastic is so graphic and it is not controversial, in a way. Nobody is anxious to speak about it and it is not so complicated to understand. It's material lying around on a beach. It's very, very simple to communicate the problems. Therefore in the first place it was just important to make the problem known.

DBB: **You are working with Paul Watson on these projects. What are the networks you are employing here? You obviously have contacts with large corporates because of your background.**

CG: Parley is a collaboration network. At the core of the creative industries there is the artist, then there are brands because they are super-influential, and then there are environmentalists, and finally there are governments. At the beginning we started working with Paul Watson and his Sea Shepherd Conservation Society. Now we are working with over 100 organisations. If you consider a mosaic, we are the glue that holds it together. The truth is that everything we need to solve our problems is already here. The knowledge is here. The specialists are here. All the environmental groups are here. Everything is in place, we are just about assembling it and developing strategies that actually cater for the different needs of different people. I think at this point there is nobody out there who should not win from turning their organisation, their brand, their private life into an ocean-friendly, environmentally-friendly situation.

DBB: You must be promoting this idea as a positive business strategy as well?

CG: Yes, of course it is, for different reasons. Our partners explain how they normally go about their business, particularly looking at areas where they feel there is little scope for changing practice. We will bring people in that do not normally work for large corporations to look at the business. We question everything, which is an idea that is often scary for many companies, but we create this collaboration stage where everybody can put everything on the table and just look at it and question everything. We then go back and say, 'OK, here is our ideal scenario: that would be the perfect world. Where do we stand today?' We then develop a road map and say, 'These are the things that we can aim for. This is our vision.' Companies become their own best consultants. They know what they have to do themselves.

DBB: In many ways then, you are doing what you have always done, just in a different way?

CG: Exactly, and that is the point. The decision I had to make when I was in that little office with Paul in 2012 was, 'Do I become an activist, go on a ship and skin potatoes, or do I just take my skills and do exactly what I have always done – redesigning stuff, reinventing things – but do it for a different objective?'

DBB: What are the big challenges for Parley in the short to medium term?

CG: The biggest change happened in 2015, because before then people felt that the whole environmental cause was something they can just touch a bit and perhaps play around with it, but there was no urgency. Then in 2015 two things happened. Firstly, some of the most conservative scientists began to recognise that we are entering the sixth mass extinction event. Films like Louie Psihoyos' *Racing Extinction* helped in a specific demographic to promote that knowledge. The second thing was COP21 in Paris [the United Nations conference on climate change] in December 2015. Even if this agreement has no legal value, it did something. It made clear that something has to happen. What I also see is that people finally understand that no superhero or one person will solve these problems. It will only work in collaboration. I never saw so much desire for collaboration than during 2016.

We have developed this strategy called AIR which we can break down for a single household or build up to the level of a government. We have created a lot of buzz that questions our collective decision back

FIG. 2.32 The factory processing ocean plastic into yarns for Adidas x Parley running shoes

FIG. 2.33 The woven components of an Adidas x Parley running shoe

in the day to put plastic into everything. We have created awareness of the problem. Now we can't leave people alone, we can't put the fingers on them and say, 'You made the mess, solve it yourself.' So we have to empower people and break it down for people who don't have a long attention span or much time, or can't afford to focus 100% on these issues. So we say, 'These are the three items to use,' or 'These are the five decisions that you and your company can make.'

We are starting with island communities because they are the contrast of beauty and fragility, and this is never so obvious as when you are in paradise, places such as the Maldives, the Seychelles or Caribbean islands. The oceans are dying. You see the coral reefs showing us the 'white flag'. It's like the oceans have surrendered and you can see it. So we are going country to country and forming national alliances.

DBB: **What happens with the Adidas training shoes? If they start mass-producing them, what is the mechanism for getting enough fishing nets or ocean plastic?**

CG: We are focusing on three types of plastic right now. One is the nylon from fishing nets. The other is PET, which you will know as plastic for water bottles, and the third one is HTP, which is all the other plastic you will know from shampoo bottles, or whatever.

So this experiment we did with Adidas: we said 'We need a symbol'. So we made a training shoe only six days before we had a big presentation with Parley at the United Nations on 29 June 2015, which was a pre-conference to COP21. We achieved something together. The conversation changed overnight. It became very pragmatic, very real, very creative. It's not about the shoe really. It was the catalyst.

Now, a year later we have a full supply chain, from collecting the material to creating a high-performance yarn that you can use on the highest-performance products. Every step in the manufacturing process is a Parley Certified Step. We have now established Parley Ocean Plastic. By using this material, companies show that they are part of Parley, but they also have to commit to AIR. They also have to contribute towards the funding of our ocean plastic programme. This pretty much brings AIR to life.

INTERVIEW WITH AN EXPERT | STEP 1 | 53

DBB: Does Parley have a lab? I'm trying to understand exactly what Parley does.

CG: Parley has four 'pillars'. One is communication and education. You will know about our talks and conferences. We are doing Parley Ocean School where we put people on an island to figure out problems and a lot of communication where we are working with artists, creating art projects. The second angle is direct action: going out into the oceans and collecting stuff, in this case plastic. The next pillar is research and development. We are also working with our own labs that we pay for, developing solutions to problems where perhaps other people wouldn't look. There is so much need for technology. We are doing this in different segments. One part is upcycling trash, another is replacing plastic; then intercepting as well. There are different ways to intercept plastic. One is the biotech way by eating it: the whole enzyme thing. One is a mechanical way, and finally there is another idea to find ways of attracting plastic, like a magnet for plastic.

DBB: Is that last idea a reality or a fantasy?

CG: It's a fantasy that is close to reality. I didn't get to explain Parley's fourth 'pillar'. The fourth 'pillar' is product innovation. So we are actively developing product concepts or pushing and supporting other people to do so. For example, if you go after very plastic-centric products like water bottles or plastic bags or packaging, you have to reinvent the product, not only the material.

DBB: How do you finance this work?

CG: In the beginning we just financed it with our own money. We took a big risk, plus a big load from friends and family. The second level is with membership fees – there are different ways to become a member, whether it's individuals, private companies or governments. They just contribute at different levels. The third way is via donations and grants – that is the newest way of funding. We are just starting the Parley Foundation that is focusing on areas where there is definitely more commercial interest. Then there is merchandising, as I call it. People will use our brands. We are very selective. You have to earn our brand. We have a very high rejection rate as we have to be very careful whom we take on.

DBB: In terms of the next two years, what are the products you have to launch?

CG: From the product angle, we are launching a full range of materials with all the partners. We are creating yarns and other materials for the fashion industry. With our Parley Ocean Plastic there is a tonne of stuff coming with very good manufacturers. From the brand angle, from every category we have identified the one brand who we would like to work with. We will open it up later: we will not stay exclusive, but we start with one brand. We are going into furniture, automotive design and (don't laugh!) super-yachting.

DBB: Well, these super-rich people are the ones with the huge carbon footprints – a hundred times bigger than most people. Reducing this is a big deal.

CG: Exactly. Transform the sinner! It is easy to go and specialise on the little brands that are already doing the right thing, but that is not challenging as they already do everything right. You want to change where change seems most impossible. There it gets surprising and then you get the 'ear' of people.

STEP 2 Reusing Waste

[DEFINITION]

STEP 2 PROJECTS
This step involves reusing either synthetic or organic material that would normally be thrown away. These products require inventive designers that see potentials in stuff others discard. Crucially, the following reuse projects do not reprocess waste material and therefore do not have the large carbon footprints associated with 'Step 1' recycling projects. This is a big leap forward from recycling, as the value of the 'waste' resource can stay the same or on occasion it can increase.

STEP 2 CASE STUDY No.1

Elvis & Kresse

commodity brokers | eco-entrepreneurs | designers | eco-activists

[THE STORY]

Kresse Wesling has had a longstanding fascination with waste. From an early age she used to visit the dump with her father and she enjoyed school visits to sewage treatment plants and recycling centres. In 2005 she had a chance meeting with the London Fire Brigade, who showed her their waste fire hoses. Although they are made of very tough nitrile rubber, extruded around and through a nylon woven core, and some of them last up to 25 years, once damaged they are scrapped, which in practice means they are burnt or sent to landfill. Wesling was drawn to their texture and rich red colour: she thought they were beautiful. Though the material is tough to work with, she made the decision to treat the material like expensive

FIG 2.34 A typical fire hose reused by Elvis & Kresse

CLOCKWISE FROM TOP LEFT (OPPOSITE)

FIG 2.35 Cutting old fire hoses for reuse

FIG 2.36 Hoses drying after being cut and washed in preparation for making into bags, belts, etc.

FIG 2.37 Sewing old fire hoses to make new belts

FIG 2.38 The Weekender bag by Elvis & Kresse, made from 100% old fire hoses

leather and employ top-quality designers and makers to produce top-end fashion items such as belts, bags and IT accessories. Fast-forward ten years, and Elvis & Kresse, based in Kent, currently buys up the world's annual supply of damaged fire hoses and has prevented over 200 tonnes of waste going to landfill.

Formative experiences studying politics and Chinese, and working as a venture capitalist, have enabled Wesling to source resources others would discard and match them with potential customers. Currently the company deals with 12 different waste sources, proving, as Wesling says, that it is 'easy to be good'. Future Elvis & Kresse projects include matching biomass to boiler suppliers and waste leather with soft furnishing companies.

Wesling's first project with the London Fire Brigade is also a social enterprise – 50% of profits made on fire hose products goes towards The Fire Fighters Charity.

PART 2 CIRCULAR INSPIRATIONS

[**OPINION**]

Elvis & Kresse is interesting because it is an example of a traditional model – that of the venture capitalist finding and then exploiting an opportunity. However, I like the positivity and intelligence of this project, together with the strong moral position and social benefits. It also adds value to the waste product in question.

This project isn't just green for moral reasons. It's green because green is the best option for many sound reasons. Of course, as with all products in this section, recycling the waste material is only slowing up its inevitable journey to landfill, although turning waste fire hoses into more valuable and desirable fashion accessories will make the customer think twice about throwing it away. It also helps reduce the amount of raw materials used within the fashion industry and that reduces the burden on Planet Earth to supply these. There is a possible issue that today's desirable fashion object is tomorrow's cliché. However, Wesling is expanding the range of products she designs using this material, and the fire hose range has been going since 2009. That's over 28 fashion seasons of change!

REUSING WASTE STEP 2 57

STEP 2 CASE STUDY No.2

Rural Studio

social activists | design pioneers | educators | makers | new material flows

[THE STORY]

The Rural Studio programme of the School of Architecture, Planning and Landscape Architecture at Auburn University, Alabama, USA, has a worldwide reputation. It has more than 20 years' experience of inspiring undergraduates, and has made hundreds of beautiful buildings for the sort of money more affluent people would spend on a new kitchen. For many architects and designers, it is the epitome of the well-informed, well-meaning architecture practice, for it is a practice as well as a school of architecture, with a strong ethical position. It also pretty much single-handedly made 'live' projects the de rigueur pedagogic tool for modern schools of architecture.

Rural Studio came to the attention of many people in 1994, when it completed the first of its 'Client Houses' in Mason's Bend, a community of only 100 people. The Bryant (Hay Bale) House was quickly followed by a number of distinctive houses employing unusual material sources, such as car tyres, straw or carpet tiles. The idea was to expose students to 'the classroom of the community'. However, students were also exposed to the idea of inventing new construction techniques and finding alternative material resources as the budgets for these projects were so small: $15,000 per house. The early works were distinctive: they were visually striking and often beautiful, particularly the Glass Chapel in Mason's Bend from 2000, reusing 80 car windscreens scavenged from a nearby breaker's yards, and elegant Antioch Baptist Church from 2002.

Those early projects were inspiring, but they were creative 'one-offs', and some were less successful than others. In 2010, the Rural Studio Strategic Plan called for all the buildings to be renovated so they would consume less energy or even generate it. Rural Studio started to concentrate more on improving its own facilities: looking at ways of growing food by setting up its own farm on its own land, creating a 'solar greenhouse', a 'food forest' and a commercial kitchen. Water collection and irrigation is also integral to the Strategic Plan.

The second decade of Rural Studio's practice was marked by an increased emphasis on considering ways in which its architecture

....

CLOCKWISE FROM TOP LEFT (OPPOSITE)

FIG 2.39 Two of Rural Studio's most recent '20k Houses'

FIG 2.40 Construction of Newbern Town Hall

FIG 2.41 Newbern Town Hall corner detail

FIG 2.42 Opening of Newbern Town Hall in 2011, with Newbern Fire Station (2004) in the foreground

FIG 2.43 Opening of Newbern Fire Station, 2004

REUSING WASTE **STEP 2** 59

could fit into the local vernacular and local needs. Projects such as Newbern Fire Station (2004) and Town Hall (2011) were developed after local officials approached Rural Studio, not the other way around. Some of the early projects had satisfied an individual's needs while leaving many in the community feeling confused or even angry. As Andrew Freear, director of Rural Studio since 2002, reflected, 'In my initial years at Studio, the design/build process was pretty hit or miss, quite undisciplined. Students would just start building and assume it would be OK. Frequently their decisions were a response to earlier mistakes in the building process – artful camouflage.'

Learning from earlier mistakes (and successes) and being open and transparent about them is perhaps one of the most inspirational aspects of Rural Studio's approach It has now put its one-off 'Client House' programme on hold in favour of its '20K Home Product Line', which aims to provide well-designed, cheap housing for a wider audience. At first glance these homes look a lot less interesting (especially for architecture students) as they adopt the much-loved features of local vernacular homes. However, upon closer inspection they are just as inventive, but less visually flamboyant, and they work with local resources that can include waste or low-grade materials. The '20K House' programme also aims to provide dwellings that are easy and cheap to maintain and straightforward to raise a mortgage on.

After more than 20 years of teaching and practice, it is perhaps the larger-scale projects where Rural Studio's combination of design inventiveness, community collaboration and cost-effectiveness has been most successful.

For example, the large playground (or 'playscape' as they call it) in Lions Park from 2010 is a perfect mix of a carefully considered brief and typically inventive Rural Studio design focusing on demonstrating the adaptability of a valuable product destined for recycling – in this case an unlimited supply of 55 high-grade galvanised steel barrels. The project budget could not afford concrete, so when Damon Smith of mint-oil supplier IP Callison turned up at one of Rural Studio's Soup Roast Reviews offering to donate an unlimited supply of these barrels, Freear and his students began thinking of ways they could work with this valuable resource. They are manufactured in India and then sent over to the USA, where they are filled with mint oil used in the manufacture of chewing gum and toothpaste. By giving them to Rural Studio, IP Callison avoided the cost of crushing and recycling these barrels as dictated to them by industry standards. As usual, Freear is candid about the successes and challenges this project presented to the team. The design solution used free material resources in an efficient manner: 'One detail, a welder, a calibrating level and a crane', as Freear states. However, as is often the case with the realities of reusing materials, there is a lot of repetitive manual labour, often with boring tasks such as de-nailing second-hand timber. In this case it was what Freear describes as 'a monotonous, soul-destroying building process', although that actually sounds like many construction processes. However, it does point out that reusing materials destined to be thrown away does not save money, it saves natural resources. It is a conscious decision made by clients, designers and makers to be material efficient, but it often comes with a higher labour input.

[OPINION]

After making a big impact in the mid to late 1990s, Rural Studio has steadily evolved. Creating student accommodation finished with car number plates or a chapel using car windscreens as curtain walling was inspiring at the turn of the 21st century. To create buildings in collaboration with some of the most disenfranchised communities in the USA, and to make these buildings look so self-assured and beautiful, was awe-inspiring. However, these early buildings were perhaps too experimental, and the Rural Studio team were sometimes too quick to solve a problem with a new building. They successfully identified material resources previously overlooked, but as projects were always built on a meagre budget, as with all 'prototypes', sometimes bits of them failed. The problem with the 'Client House' projects is that people were living their everyday lives in these experiments. The larger-scale community and infrastructure projects – the bridges, birding towers, baseball grounds, chapels and playgrounds – were better places to be experimental.

Rural Studio has reflected upon this. It is now concentrating on reworking existing buildings, whether they are old buildings brought back to life or its own 'first generation' buildings requiring a 'green' retrofit, as well as building more modest-looking, but even better-considered housing projects. Since 2010, more time has been spent developing the facilities at Rural Studio's Morrisette House HQ, where the team are endeavouring to create most of their energy and food on site. In future the Rural Studio HQ will provide a more holistic teaching and learning resource, focusing on low-carbon solutions, not only for the students, but also for the surrounding communities on which they depend. They are an inspiration.

FIG. 2.44 Lions Park playground

REUSING WASTE STEP 2 61

STEP 2   CASE STUDY No.3

Superuse Studios

designers | inventors | systems + processes | new material flows | facilitating circular systems

[THE STORY]

Rotterdam-based Superuse's original name, 2012 Architects, came about because some of the founder members of the studio (including Jan Jongert) were living in a street where 18 houses were planned to be demolished. Jongert and his colleagues proposed an alternative vision that preserved all the houses, but rather audaciously asked the municipality to lend them the houses for 15 years, until 2012. The community renovated the houses and when 15 years had passed they were able to buy them from the municipality at affordable rates: a positive tale of social sustainability.

The current name, Superuse, comes from the idea of improving the value and usefulness of a product or material from its original intended use. Connecting different systems that are normally kept separate does this. So, for example, if a glass bottle is reused as a brick that forms part of a building, its life and usefulness are hugely extended from that originally intended. Jongert refers to this as 'the creative "click"; understanding that the function can change'. For him the difference between everyday reuse and 'superuse' is the ambition of the creative challenge involved. 'Superuse' requires people (often designers) to propose future scenarios for discarded material that extend its life and add value. This requires a new perception and understanding of the potentials of these materials to be substantially more useful than previously thought.

Similar in many ways to Rotor in Brussels (see page 82), Superuse is taking on the challenges of resource efficiency and closed-loop systems in a systematic manner. Its team produce academic papers on subjects pertaining to resource management and flows, they teach (Jongert is a professor at the Royal Academy of Art in The Hague), design buildings and advise their regional and national governments.

In 2005 Superuse completed what many people believe to be Europe's (if not the world's) first contemporary house made from a selection of waste material. Superuse procured this using its 'Harvest Mapping' methodology (see interview, page 75). The house famously reused steel profiles from a redundant textile machine for the main structure, as well as for one of the facades. Timber from massive cable reels was salvaged for other facades. Many other sources of waste material (including house 'for sale' signs for the linings of kitchen cupboards) were used to deliver this project.

OPPOSITE

FIG 2.45 The 'Harvest Map' digital platform

FIG 2.46 'Superuse.org' digital platform promoting and linking reuse projects around the world

PART 2 CIRCULAR INSPIRATIONS

REUSING WASTE **STEP 2** 63

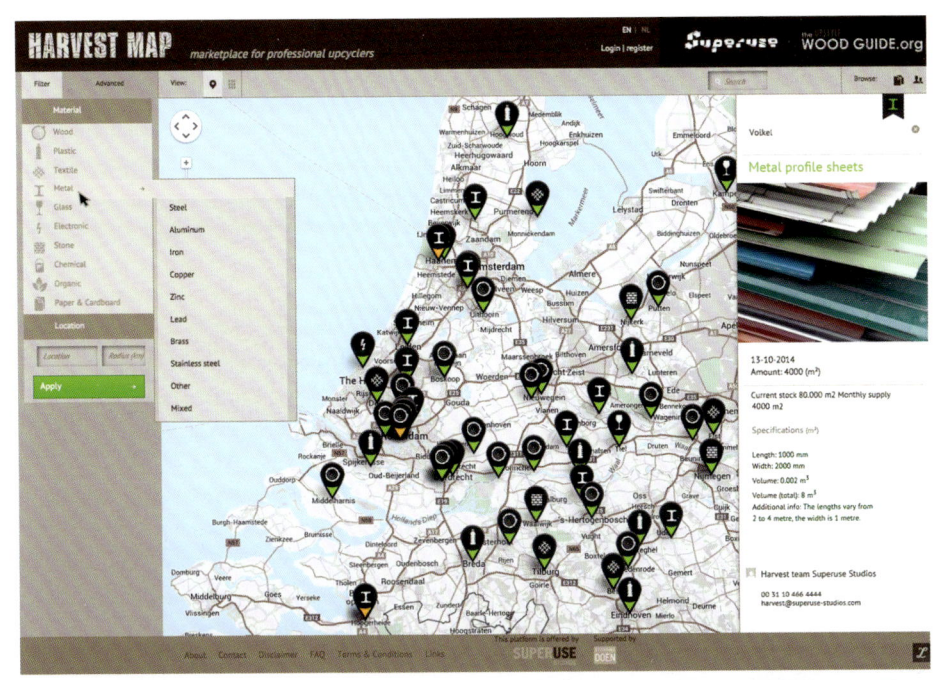

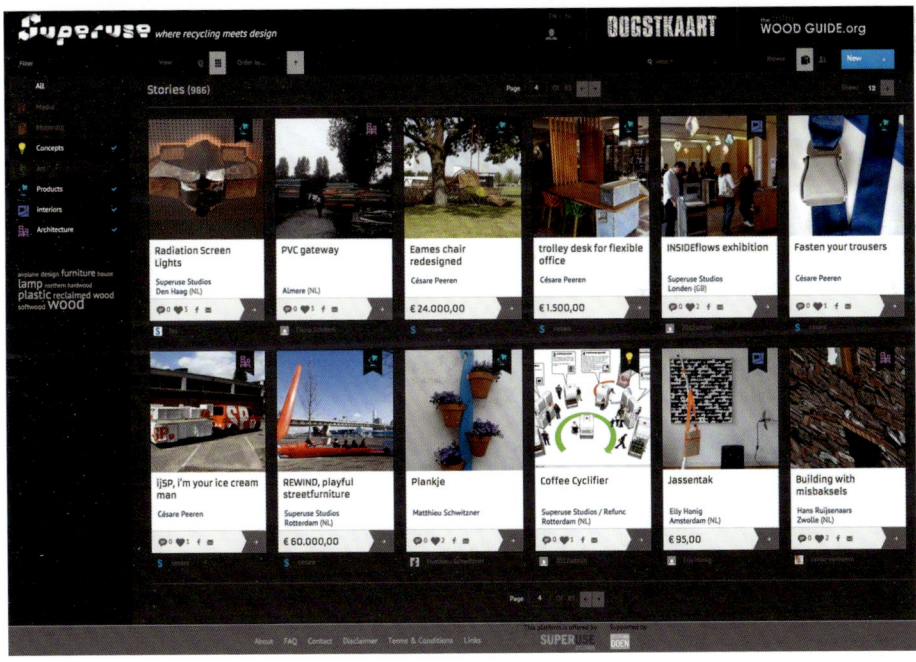

The project highlights very clearly some of the real challenges facing a client and their design team. For example, the design team cannot show their client exactly what the final building will look like until the material has been sourced. How does one design a building without understanding what all the finishing materials will actually be before starting on site? Designers working with so-called waste sources have to continue to be creative throughout the duration of a project, not just at its inception.

Superuse knew it could never be a normal design practice, and as a result of pursuing a 'material-experimental design approach', it has assembled a multidisciplinary team that includes chemists and environmental scientists, supporting designers and architects dedicated to 'turning cities into a living web of connected material processes and flows'. Obviously this is a slightly unconventional way of perceiving a city. In order to make this preoccupation relevant, and of course, financially viable, Superuse has developed a series of tools, such as the 'Relevance Indicator' and the 'Environmental Impact Calculator', that help ground its design strategies in rigorous scientific practice. Its Harvest Map uses geographic representations to help identify and prioritise waste materials near to a specific project site. As well as highlighting surplus and waste materials currently available via a 'live' interactive map, this platform also provides useful information to facilitate the repurposing of materials, elements and components that would otherwise be discarded. It also encourages people to become 'scouts' looking out for neglected material flows.

....

FIG 2.47 The 'Cyclifier' digital platform

FIG 2.48 'Inside Flows' digital platform, which identifies potentials for circular/closed-loop systems

64   PART 2   CIRCULAR INSPIRATIONS

[**OPINION**]

In many ways Superuse Studios looks like a conventional design studio, perhaps because its completed projects are extensively published in the design press. However, this practice is really a multidisciplinary group who are all focused on interrogating the challenges a circular economy presents. What sets the practice apart is the ability of its designers to identify these challenges and then, in partnership with the rest of the practice, create devices and working methodologies that enable a change from the current 'linear' system to something resembling a closed-loop system. Whether it is the 'Harvest Map' technique for identifying resource flows, the 'Cyclifier' platform introducing disconnected flows to each other, or 'Recyclicity', which connects individuals and organisations who are in the process of demolishing buildings in order to encourage reuse, Superuse is dedicated to providing inventive mechanisms that facilitate these processes. A combination of inquisitiveness, rigorous research, knowledge and creativity makes this practice highly significant within the world of reuse and closed-loop systems. Superuse is inventing some of the tools (as well as the words and phrases defining these) that we will all need to practise within a more circular economy.

FIG. 2.49 Interior space of Dordtyart Cultural Centre, fittted out with materials located using the Harvest Map method

REUSING WASTE **STEP 2**

STEP 2 CASE STUDY No.4

Traditional *Boro* clothing, Japan

historic | traditional | vernacular | reuse | austerity

[THE STORY]

The main focus of this book is to demonstrate ingenious contemporary design solutions answering questions presented in the 21st century, as we head for a world population of nine or ten billion people. I could have written two or three chapters dedicated to historical precedents of sophisticated, culturally integrated reuse behaviour from any continent you care to choose. (Before oil and international trade was ubiquitous, people had to make do with what they had. This resulted in countless examples of ingenious, robust and durable designs with fascinating strategies for reuse.) Instead of that, I have included this inspiring case study from Japan, which, in my opinion, epitomises human tenacity, creativity and invention.

The tradition of *Boro* (literally 'tattered rags') clothing dates back to the Edo period (1600s) when cotton was a very precious commodity in northern Japanese provinces: the climate was too cold to grow cotton plants. Until Japan started to import cotton from India and China, working-class people made clothes and household items from hemp and flax. If a working family got hold of cotton they treasured it, as it was far more comfortable to wear, and the cotton fabric would be repaired and handed down from mother to daughter and father to son. This tradition of *Boro* was born out of poverty and necessity. Worn-out indigo cotton clothes from the prosperous south were shipped up to the north-east of Japan, where working people developed techniques for patching, sewing, weaving and repairing. Sewing techniques such as *Sashiko*, a simple running stitch in repeating or interlocking patterns, layered small pieces of cotton and hemp into a patchwork material that was more durable, warmer and comfortable for Japanese farmers or fishermen than hemp garments. From this came other traditions of sewing techniques giving additional layers of meaning and cultural identity to these modest textiles. Out of *Boro* came the technique of *Zanshi*, which translates as 'vestige' or 'leftover'. Extra threads from fixed-pattern weavings and unravelled threads from spare, unwanted cotton fabric were rewoven into regionally and even family-distinctive styles. Another technique is *Sakiori*, which involves textiles being torn into strips, or pieces of *saki*, which are then woven together. The *Sakiori* were rolled into 13- to 16-inch lengths that were then loomed together to create casual kimono or working clothes.

FIG 2.50, 2.51 A Japanese farmer's *Boro* cotton vest from the 1800s, with numerous layers and patches

[OPINION]

Human beings can adapt and work within harsh situations. When cotton resources were scarce the Japanese working classes invented techniques to make their valuable clothes last for decades, if not centuries. Out of that adversity came an increased understanding of the potentials of a former waste material to become a valuable commodity. The technique of *Boro* also developed a sense of cultural identity reflected in the textiles themselves. At times *Boro* textiles were a social embarrassment, especially after World War II. Ironically, original 19th-century *Boro* textiles are now fetching thousands of pounds as there are many collectors wanting to own these often beautiful garments that hold onto decades of family history. To Western eyes, these garments have imbued meanings and authenticity that are often lacking in our day-to-day lives. We can, of course, learn from their beauty as well. If you design beautiful, functional things, they are less likely to be thrown away.

So what can we learn from this 'make do and mend' attitude? For a start, people do develop an emotional attachment to things, especially things passed down in families. This idea contrasts with the way we tend to acquire and dispose of stuff today. Adding 'emotional value' to products is a concept that is prized by today's manufacturers as they want you to be long term customers, but they don't want you to hold onto the object they sold you. They want your brand loyalty.[1] However, if things are designed to last longer they tend to get personalised and even cherished. Then they might get adapted rather than thrown away. It is interesting that there are hundreds of knitting circles in the UK and that some of them will only use wool from second-hand jumpers. They unravel the wool just as Japanese people did centuries before: a great example of the circular economy, and all very familiar.

REUSING WASTE | STEP 2

STEP 2 CASE STUDY No.5

Silo, zero-waste restaurant

pre-industrial food systems | closed-loop systems

[THE STORY]

Silo, in Brighton, was conceived in 2014 as a direct response to the huge amount of waste involved in the production and consumption of food around the world. Another aim was to widen the variety of food that we eat. Founder Douglas McMaster looks for alternative sources of nutritious foodstuffs from varied local and regional sources.

McMaster is an ambitious character. He not only wants to alter our narrow food-consuming habits, he also wants to inspire the whole food industry as well so that it 'demonstrates respect for the environment, respect for the way our food is generated and respect for the nourishment given to our bodies'. However, he is the first to point out the realities of trying to run what many people have called a 'zero-waste restaurant', admitting, 'I have ovens, toilet, fridges, appliances, etc that are not designed to Cradle to Cradle principles.'

McMaster had worked as a chef in some of the world's best restaurants, but the job that had the most influence on him was working for green entrepreneur Joost Bakker in Melbourne. Bakker came from a farming background so understands about supply chains for the catering business. It was while cooking in one of Bakker's restaurants that McMaster tested his ideas for a zero-waste supply chain to and from his kitchen. He explains, 'I was exposed to the idea of zero waste by people I truly admired. When you can see something for how it needs to be, it is hard to ignore it.'

Silo doesn't have any bins! That is quite incredible for any restaurant, but for one in a city centre it is even more challenging. This is achieved by installing an aerobic digester that can generate up to 60kg of compost in only 24 hours. The restaurant makes so much compost that it gives it away to neighbours. Silo doesn't accept plastic or non-biodegradable packaging from its suppliers, and reduces road, sea and air miles associated with the transporting of food by growing as much as it can on site. It has its own brewery, called 'Old Tree', which creates fermented drinks using foraged and intercepted plants, herbs, vegetables and fruits. A traditional flour mill that turns ancient varieties of wheat into flour for bread is also on site. The restaurant even churns its own butter and makes its own almond milk and cheese, as well as rolling oats. The website states, 'We support a nose-to-tail ideology, meaning that if an animal dies for food we will maximise the whole beast.' All this from a small but ambitious restaurant seating 50 guests.

McMaster has applied his zero-waste approach to the interior design of his kitchen and dining environments. His strategy is to

PART 2 CIRCULAR INSPIRATIONS

CLOCKWISE FROM TOP

FIG 2.52 Silo zero-waste restaurant

FIG 2.53 Bread baked on site with flour ground on site

FIG 2.54 A selection of locally sourced fruit juices

FIG 2.55 T-shirt advertising the unpasteurised milk

FIG 2.56 Roasted ox heart, raw and cooked patty pans and wild garlic oil

FIG 2.57 Silo mission statement

FIG 2.58 On-site flour mill

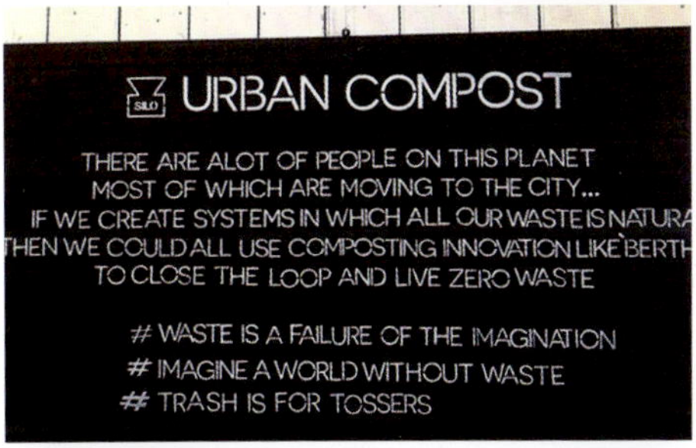

REUSING WASTE | **STEP 2**

upcycle and reuse material rather than use recycled material. Tables are made from galvanised steel 'tiles', formerly a raised floor in a commercial office space. Workbenches are formed from filing cabinet frames, and jam jars are used for glasses! There is a bit of reprocessing involved in the manufacture of Silo's plates: they are formed from old plastic bags and surprisingly (perhaps) look great and function perfectly.

Perhaps what is most interesting about Silo is what it produces – wonderful food. Described by McMaster as supporting 'a pre-industrial food system', Silo aspires to reacquaint us with sources of foodstuff that have been neglected for centuries or longer.

[OPINION]

The inspiration behind this project is very obviously linked with a moral stance towards living in harmony with the planet. McMaster is keen to point this out, saying, 'For me, reuse is more of a natural behaviour, both moral and ethical. When you understand natural systems, you will see circularity.'

McMaster acknowledges that most people who eat his food won't go home and stop using their bins. However, he is proving that a closed-loop system involving the growing, production, consumption and composting of food is possible to achieve with limited financial resources and limited space, in an urban environment. This start-up business is also making money: Silo's aerobic digester paid for itself within two years. The flour mill paid for itself within four months, and the electrolysed water filter should pay for itself by 2017: all crucial elements in eliminating the need for a bin!

FIG. 2.59 Interior of Silo restaurant, including furniture made from 'waste' material from the Brighton Waste House

70 PART 2 CIRCULAR INSPIRATIONS

STEP 2 CASE STUDY No.6

Hub 67, by LYN Atelier

London 2012 | building reuse | unconventional building | testing contract law

[**THE STORY**]

Andrew Lock founded LYN Atelier, a London-based architecture, interiors, exhibition and theatre design practice, in 2009 after winning a design competition. Fairly soon LYN was getting commissions for temporary buildings such as The Festival Village below the Queen Elizabeth Hall on London's South Bank. This project gave the practice the opportunity to explore collaborative design processes (in this case involving up to 200 artists).

In 2011, LYN Atelier was invited to bid for what became the 'Hub 67' project: a temporary community centre made from material collected in shipping containers after the Olympics closed in 2012. The Olympic Delivery Authority (ODA) had a huge site in the Lea Valley ('over ten football pitches in area', according to Lock), where structures such as temporary food kiosks and banks etc were being deconstructed, as well as running track, seating, concrete barriers and lots of other valuable material. The ODA was keen to prove that it could create something meaningful for one of the communities near to the Olympic site. Initially, Lock says, it was really difficult to assess the potential of the resources, as his team were only allowed an hour or so on site. Instead of providing a detailed design proposal for their winning bid, they produced more of what Lock called a 'statement of intent: a working methodology'.

Even when LYN got the commission, Lock says access to the site was limited: the contractors were busy doing other tasks for the ODA. Also, the ODA's bureaucracy was huge and cumbersome, set in place for multimillion-

FIG 2.60 Hub 67

REUSING WASTE **STEP 2**

CLOCKWISE FROM TOP LEFT

FIG 2.61 Members of the local community assembling cladding made from second-hand material

FIG 2.62 Second-hand building components from the 2012 London Olympics, waiting to be taken to site

FIG 2.63 Second-hand building components being assembled on their new site

FIG 2.64 The facade

FIG 2.65 Hub 67 interior, fitted out with second-hand material

pound stadium and infrastructure projects. Even though Hub 67 was only a £350,000 temporary community building, the ODA procurement route started off being the same as for these much larger projects. Whenever Lock and his colleagues needed to visit the material site, they had to complete a risk assessment, and then would have only about an hour on site. As a consequence, Lock developed a keen eye to spot potential building material. He soon noticed that there were a lot of steel frames with glazed and insulated composite metal panels, the remains of the banks and food vending machines. Lock secured nine of these to create the structure of Hub 67. Cladding came in the form of the external finishing for the Olympic Training Centre. Lock states that they only had to get one of the roof elements built from new, as there wasn't a correctly falling existing roof element to reuse.

The original suppliers of this material were supportive of Lock reusing their product, as they were keen to demonstrate how their product was indeed designed for 'remanufacture'. Nevertheless, the acquisition of this second-hand material was very time-consuming and stressful. The client (the ODA) had not had the time to think through the implications of constructing a building out of second-hand material. This was Lock's belief.

The contractual set-up was also not appropriate for a small construction project made of second-hand material. The main contractor for the project was a small building company not used to working with 500-page contracts such as the type the ODA normally issued. They successfully negotiated the contract size down to a mere 75 pages. However the contract was still a 'standard' NEC (New Engineering and Construction Contract), with its obligations for the building contractor to guarantee proper performance of the resultant construction. This immediately raised the question: 'How does one guarantee the performance of a building made from second-hand materials without the data that proves the quality or standards of these materials?' This issue reinforces the need for 'material passports' discussed later on in this book (see page 127). The contractor took an informed risk. They assumed that as the building would only be used for three years, they would probably not test this issue of building fabric performance ie, how the external fabric of this building performs from the point of view of insulation levels, airtightness (ability not to leak air through walls/roof etc) and therefore conserve energy and weatherproofing (all issues checked by Local Authority Building Control Departments).

The main challenge that Lock and his colleagues at LYN Atelier had to overcome was that the definition of a 'temporary building' as far as the Building Regulations is concerned is a building occupied for up to two years. The Hub 67 building needed to be occupied for over three years. The consequences of this were profound. The external fabric of Hub 67 had to meet the airtightness and insulation levels described in 'Part L2 2013', which was brand new legislation at that time. Thanks to the team pulling together (and somebody finding a gadget that could measure the U-value of the different materials as they were reassembled on site!) they were able to meet this additional challenge. The project was built on budget and on time (constructed in a little over 12 weeks), which considering the unusual constraints and challenges facing the design and construction team, and indeed the client, was a real achievement.

[OPINION]

LYN Atelier had to overcome an almost complete lack of information on the type of material they had to use, as well as limited information on the performance (thermal and other) of this material once it arrived on site. The construction contract made little, if any, allowance for the fact that this building was made out of second-hand materials. As a consequence the main contractors had to assume the normal responsibilities, as far as the structural integrity of the building. This included, in effect, stating that second-hand materials and construction systems were 'fit for purpose', when there were no written performance specifications, certificates, guarantees or evidence of any sort. It required the experience and expertise of the design and construction teams to overcome this challenge.

This project proves that if there is a clear objective and desire to deliver an innovative product, designers and makers can overcome huge obstacles to work things out. However, in this case it has been done at risk to the designer's professional indemnity insurance and the contractor's building insurance. This project was designed and delivered without any legislation or any systems or networks in place to assist in their vision to prove that a perfectly functioning new building could be constructed out of the second-hand remains of other buildings.

FIG. 2.66 Reused materials on the facade

74 PART 2 CIRCULAR INSPIRATIONS

INTERVIEW WITH AN EXPERT
Jan Jongert of Superuse Studios, Rotterdam

DBB: You founded Superuse in 1997 with Cesare Peeren. I notice that your studio is 'run by five engineers, all specialists in their own fields: interventions, design, architecture, urbanism and research'. Which one are you?

JJ: I'm an architect by education. In the meantime I have developed into the head of research at Superuse Studios. Now I am mainly involved with internal knowledge management, platform development and material flow analysis for building materials and urban districts.

DBB: I knew Superuse initially because of your Superuse.org website. How did that website resource come about?

JJ: In 2004 we launched our first platform called recyclicity.net, where we pretty much included everything we thought necessary to perform as resource-based architects and share that with our network. Unfortunately the technology was not yet far enough advanced. So we stopped the platform after two years and rebuilt it again in separate pieces. Superuse.org was the first piece, showcasing the creative reuse by our own network and open to everyone else to publish. That was until Pinterest took a big part of our market with reuse pinboards.

The first version of superuse.org was completely self-funded and ran for several years from 2007 onwards. In 2012 we were granted lottery funding that allowed us to reappropriate superuse.org to new standards (ie to make it easier to use and better connected to other web-focused platforms) and we connected the database to the new Harvest Map platform; later on we teamed up with Upstyle Industries to launch woodguide.org.

DBB: I really like the Upstyle Wood Guide. Are there plans for other such material-focused web platforms?

JJ: The site was connected to a grant for a study into wood processing. It was not our initiative, we were part of a larger team, but we decided to connect to Superuse.org and the Harvest Map platform in order to make it a real ecosystem in terms of knowledge. Of course if we could find research funding for steel, glass and other materials we could create other sustainable material user guides. Hopefully that will happen one day soon as we are discussing the idea with the Design Academy in Eindhoven.

DBB: Superuse Studios is obviously research-led. How is this afforded?

JJ: Most of our research is funded by our design projects and external sources such as the Dutch Creative Industry Fund and the Lottery Fund.

DBB: My book looks at four 'steps' towards the circular economy. Many of your projects look like Step 2 projects (reusing waste). Do you have any projects that are genuinely circular?

JJ: Our temporary projects all had different 'reappearances' in different cities. However, since our focus is on component and element reuse, we are playing on a little bit of a different field. We do not believe in promising a clean future, but want to do the best with what we have now. Of course we design for disassembly, so that even with low-tech means, adaptations to our projects can be made easily.

DBB: I am drawn to your description of 'reappearances' of your buildings. Could you be more specific?

JJ: A number of our projects have reappeared over the years. For example, we had a project made of washing machines that started off as a small unit with frames filled with washing machine fronts. It was modular so we could add a bit more and enlarged it so it could be an office. This mobile office was then moved to a festival and used there. Finally the Faculty of Architecture at TU Delft used it as a special bar. We also have a project reusing kitchen sinks that grew from small units into something quite big in Utrecht, changing shape and also collecting water. It then became a place for arts and now it's a mobile selling cart for a man growing mushrooms using old coffee granules.

DBB: In the UK we don't often have a lot of time between a project being demolished and the new building project commencing. How do you create the time to set up a Harvest Map project?

JJ: That's why circular building is indeed difficult. The potential, on the other hand, is huge. If we build up a good 'dataset' of existing building stock we can start finding the demand when the initial ideas for demolishing a build start to emerge.

DBB: Do you have such a 'dataset' of vacant buildings or buildings about to be demolished?

JJ: No. Developers will contact us and say that they have a building they want to demolish. They ask if we can quantify and sell materials for reuse. So we collect data from that specific building, but this is of little value once that building has been taken down.

DBB: Do you come across a lot of obstructions from the Dutch version of the Health and Safety Executive when proposing to harvest overlooked material for construction projects?

JJ: As long as we make sound and healthy decisions this is not a problem. We are not engaging in chemically polluted material flows. Additionally, we aim to make minimum alterations to a component when we salvage it, and that includes the minimal chemical alterations. When we have to, we comply with building regulations. We have expanded our activities to the food industry – providing bakers with spent beer grains or mushroom growers with spent coffee – and these issues, of course, are taken care of appropriately.

DBB: Are local building suppliers supportive of Harvest Mapping?

JJ: Building suppliers are not our typical suppliers, but their suppliers increasingly are. We often find our supplies from the car, train and airplane deconstruction industries.

DBB: Cars, trains and airplanes. This is big stuff. You must have a huge warehouse to store it all?

JJ: No, no. That is exactly why we have Harvest Map, to avoid the need for storage. In general, we collect data from the companies that demolish buildings or dismantle airplanes and order exactly the materials we or our customers require. We did try using our own storage facilities a few years ago, but then you become a warehouse manager, which is a different job.

DBB: What was the most surprising material that you were able to salvage for reuse?

JJ: Windmill (turbine) blades were the most successful components we reused. They were used to create children's playground furniture, climbing frames, even buildings – all depending on the cross-section size of the blade. We also very much like our 'white goods' experiments, with washing machines and sinks reused as cladding, and fridges reused as insulation.

DBB: One can imagine not only regional or national resource exchange networks, but worldwide networks using the Harvest Map model. Are you not treading on the toes of the large waste management companies?

JJ: On the contrary; we actually collaborate with Van Gansewinkel, the largest waste collector in the Netherlands, on the Harvest Map platform. It's like an extra service they provide. They also appreciate that they need to transfer their business model from incineration to procuring material and components for the construction and other industries.

DBB: What is the commercial model, the business plan, that informs the Harvest Map process?

JJ: Since we are a 'circular' company, Harvest Map is one of the five interlinked services we offer. Internally, Harvest Map provides us with an overview of available materials for the projects we design. Externally we are trying out several business models. Currently it drives two income flows as our office also trades materials for other companies. The first [income flow] is that Harvest Map serves as an advertisement for the material on sale. The second income flow is supplying dedicated platforms to other organisations and companies. The first licence of Harvest Map technology was sold to a start-up connecting empty buildings to groups of 'home-seekers'. We are preparing similar strategies with organisations in China, New Zealand, Italy, the USA and Austria.

DBB: I know you are in China setting up a Harvest Map network. How do you start up a Harvest Map in an unknown place?

JJ: We work with local entrepreneurs. It is impossible to process all the world's waste through Superuse Studios in Rotterdam. So we train and launch local scouts that are already starting to have their first successes. In China we connected a large furniture manufacturer to a prototyping company. Our local partner is increasingly involved in new connections.

DBB: **I can imagine the Harvest Map model getting very big and being rolled out around the world. Are you not attracting the attention of venture capitalists?**

JJ: No, not yet, and maybe that's good as I'm not sure we are ready for that. The Harvest Map model can be rolled out around the world. However in China they don't have access to Google, so we have to reformat the platform there. Also this circular approach is not easy to explain in one sentence and it's also hard to estimate what the profits would be. So maybe it's not established enough for venture capitalists. However, we have already had a company buy the Harvest Map model in order to set up its own platform, but the business model element of it we are still working on. Perhaps it will develop slowly instead, as it needs lots of different skills and information to work well.

DBB: **Many people are concerned with some of the perceived outcomes of a circular economy. For example, if a large lighting supplier leased lux levels (locking clients into 20-year contracts) rather than selling light fittings, then a circular economy could actually result in unfair monopolies as well as corporate resource responsibility. What is your thought on this issue?**

JJ: I have similar and more doubts. I think for short, cyclical products, leasing could be the best option. For long-lasting products like buildings, it is very awkward to think one can predict the best treatment and material price in 40 years. So on what value and business model should this circularity model be based? Moreover, by creating closed loops one could potentially prevent innovation by other companies that might have better processing solutions. Thirdly, natural robust systems (which production systems should be) need to be able to adapt to changing circumstances and be connected to more than one chain. I also fear that the user will have no sense of responsibility for the leased product, as the manufacturer will have that responsibility. In the end, sustainable development is something that has to be carried by all of us.

DBB: **Professor Dr Michael Braungart often cites reuse, and particularly recycling, as simply 'slowing down the inevitable route to senseless disposal'. What are your thoughts?**

JJ: Well, the material is there. We have to do something with it. For instance, when asked what to do with the current building stock, I do not believe the answer should be to eradicate everything we have and construct a new ideal future. It will probably generate its own errors and flaws. So I believe in building upon what is already there. Of course I applaud all activities to develop new materials according to this Cradle to Cradle philosophy.

DBB: **Is Superuse inventing and testing innovative business models?**

PART 2　CIRCULAR INSPIRATIONS

JJ: Yes that is what is happening. We are also continuing to develop to see where new opportunities are. We are working with many different parts of the chain. [To do well] you need to earn from these different parts. Margins are not very high for the individual parts – for example, it is hard to earn a living from just design. However, in the Netherlands you cannot practise as an architect and earn from the supply of materials on projects you have designed. This is a big problem for a circular designer. As it stands, the law encourages architects to only specify new materials off-site. I hope the law will change one day soon.

DBB: How do you get around this situation now?

JJ: We often oversee design-and-build projects. That makes it easier as we are designers, contractors and suppliers. The other way is when we act as consultants to clients and other architects by supplying reused materials and components.

DBB: How much of your own work could be described as architecture?

JJ: Not so much now, [I'm more involved] in the processes of running the studio. Two of my colleagues are more into the design of the projects.

DBB: Where do you see yourselves in five years' time?

JJ: At the moment we are like growing cells. The Chinese cell has already resulted in a project: in Beijing we have just opened a reuse market. We are also starting up research in the Shenzhen district. Obviously with the amounts of waste there, the potential for successful circular projects is high. We also have projects in the USA, specifically Detroit, where we have just won a commission to construct a playground. The environment for supplying construction waste is very good within established building material market. We are looking at ways our Harvest Map platform can complement the existing reuse networks.

FIG. 2.67 Retrofit of existing buildings, Palais de Tokyo, Paris

STEP 3 Reducing the Amount of Material Used

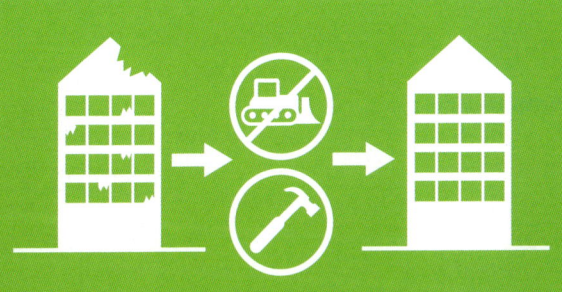

[DEFINITION]

STEP 3 PROJECTS
These are projects that demonstrate an ability to reduce the amount of material used during their whole life cycle. The products could still use materials that are not 'circular' and in effect merely stall the inevitable problem (unless someone solves the problem) of how to dispose of synthetic and toxic material. These projects require strategic thinkers from the outset of the design process, people who have a deep understanding of existing design and manufacture processes and, crucially, material flows. Once the existing systems are understood, these innovators unpack them and look at ingenious ways of providing the same 'stuff' but in a less resource-hungry way.

STEP 3 CASE STUDY No.1

Rotor & RotorDC

artists | designers | deconstructors | pathfinders | new material flows

[THE STORY]

I have interviewed more than 100 people for this book, all of them fully engaged with different aspects of designing systems and products that, to a greater or lesser degree, can be described as being on the way towards a circular economy. However, I have found that the team at the architectural practice Rotor, perhaps more than anybody else I have spoken to, are happy to try to unpack and critically evaluate the real challenges, intellectual and otherwise, facing 21st-century human settlements that endeavour to exist in harmony with the planet. However tedious the research or dismantling/making processes are, they will take the project on if they believe it will further their understanding of the potentials for a reuse economy.

I first came across Brussels-based Rotor when a colleague of mine, architect Anthony Roberts, reported back to me from the 2010 Venice Biennale. He had just stumbled across Rotor's 'Wear' exhibition for the Belgian Pavilion. It looked more like a 1960s installation by an minimalist artist and Anthony was struck by the precision of the curating, the beauty of the artefacts displayed, and the 'sheer amount of white space on the walls'. Entitled *'usus/usures'*, which literally means 'make/wear down', this exhibition considered the traces of use and wear on everyday building. Once you get past their beauty, these familiar objects reveal the effects of years of contact with human hands or feet. By being placed in the rarefied environment of a gallery, these objects were reappraised by visitors as abstract artefacts. Once their true 'self' became apparent again, one could re-evaluate them and consider the narratives behind, for example, a red carpet from a social housing apartment in Antwerp that clearly demonstrates the position of a pivot chair and a table. Although Rotor is keen to point out that this was not an exhibition about reuse, one can clearly see that it is linked to the company's focus on reappraising the value in discarded artefacts. According to Rotor, the exhibition and accompanying publication was 'the result of an intensive investigation carried out in Belgium, analysing "wear" as a material phenomenon and as an agent capable of influencing actions. Wear is approached not as a problem in itself, the result of an error of conception that must be avoided at all costs, but as an inevitable and potentially creative process.' On reading this statement, one can clearly see the link to Rotor's current focus on material reuse, or 'deconstruction' as they call it.

Rotor's 'Deconstruction' programme is the most pertinent part of its practice for this book. 'Rotor Deconstruction' is a hands-on

CLOCKWISE FROM TOP

FIG 2.68 Salvaged marble tiles waiting to be sold

FIG 2.69 Commercial office downlighting carefully removed for reuse

FIG 2.70 Carefully removing marble tiles for resale

FIG 2.71 Removing marble wall tiles for reuse

FIG 2.72 Carefully removing ceramic floor tiles for reuse

FIG 2.73 Removing a raised office floor for reuse

REDUCING THE AMOUNT OF MATERIAL USED **STEP 3** 83

FIG. 2.74 A selection of worn artefacts, Belgian Pavilion, Venice Biennale, 2010

FIG 2.75 Stair treads, Belgian Pavilion, Venice Biennale

84 | PART 2 CIRCULAR INSPIRATIONS

business that has resulted from almost a decade of research on the flows of materials in numerous industries, including construction. The programme is now a separate cooperative company that has the skills and knowledge to focus on the careful dismantling of parts or the whole of a building and then sell on the reusable materials. As the website (http://www.rotordc.com) states:

> Rotor Deconstruction facilitates reuse of building materials in large-scale projects. We help contractors and building owners to find markets for salvaged materials, we organise large-scale extraction operations, we advise design teams assessing the feasibility of on-site reuse strategies and help source locally available materials.

[OPINION]

Rotor has adapted its design practice so that it now provides a one-stop shop for deconstructing, redesigning and rebuilding projects, promising a complete circular process. Rotor is able to supply this service because of the different skills represented within the practice. This includes experienced architects, but also people such as Lionel Billiet (see interview on page 104) who have been prepared to work on in-depth research projects considering the real commercial potentials within the construction industry of reused materials and fittings. For example, when Rotor had the opportunity to work on a Belgian government report testing the legal frameworks required to support a national reuse industry, Billiet, together with other members of Rotor and legal experts, grabbed the opportunity. The resultant document, entitled *Vade Mecum For Off-Site Reuse*, is a manual with comprehensive guidelines for public works projects considering the reuse of building materials in the Brussels Capital Region. They are, of course, easy to adapt for other provinces in Belgium, elsewhere in Europe, and beyond. The *Vade Mecum* provides a step-by-step methodology helping clients to understand the processes of identification, reclamation and transfer of reusable materials, in order that it complies with public procurement legislation. This work has gained Rotor a national award, the 'Publica Award', which is given to the most innovative tendering strategy promoting sustainable design. Rotor's work makes it possible for people to salvage construction material for reuse that was previously designated as waste and in effect untouchable.

This rigorous approach to uncovering and solving the real challenges that present themselves to all designers trying to rework, adapt or rebuild projects sets Rotor's work ahead of most of its contemporaries. The fact that the team can turn their hands to writing interesting books, curating thought-provoking and beautiful exhibitions, writing legal handbooks and designing award-winning architectural projects, makes Rotor one of the true 'pathfinders' in the world of an emergent circular economy.

STEP 3 CASE STUDY No.2

Oslo Urban Mountain, by Schimdt Hammer Lassen Architects (SHL Architects)

testing material | supply chains | 'cradle to cradle' certification

[THE STORY]

In 2011 a group of architects working for the Danish practice Schmidt Hammer Lassen Architects enrolled on a week-long course arranged by 'Vugge til Vugge Denmark', the Danish representative for the EPEA (Environment Protection Encouragement Agency). EPEA was founded in 1987 by Professor Dr Michael Braungart. This institute undertakes scientific research exploring the potentials of circular systems. As it states on its website, EPFA combines 'chemistry, biology and environmental science with product optimisation and product development'. It also provides workshops and training for people who are interested in applying Cradle to Cradle principles to their own practice. The team at Schmidt Hammer Lassen Architects were committed to exploring 'C2C' principles further and applying them to their own architectural projects.

This investment quickly paid dividends. In 2012 'Nordic Built Innovation', a three-year programme launched by the Nordic Ministers for Trade and Industry (2012–2014) to develop innovative and sustainable building concepts for rehabilitating existing building stock, announced an open architectural design competition in five Nordic countries: 'The Nordic Built Challenge'. Schmidt Hammer Lassen Architects teamed up with engineers and specialists from the Cradle to Cradle network: LOOP Architects, COWI, Transsolar Energietechnik and Vugge til Vugge Denmark. They entered this competition armed with their mutual C2C knowledge. Their submission, known as 'Urban Mountain', won the Norwegian competition. The concept is based on rehabilitating an existing 50,000m^2 office tower situated next to the main railway station in central Oslo. The intention is to add two extra towers, increasing the building size to 79,000m^2, and to boost the building's performance efficiency.

A straightforward idea. However, the team also have C2C ambitions for this project. So as well as building Norway's first naturally ventilated high-rise building and aiming to achieve BREEAM certification 'Outstanding' due to its low carbon footprint and predicted energy consumption, this scheme has extremely ambitious resource-saving targets as well. For example, they intend to recycle as much as 90% of the material stripped out from the existing tower, and 80% of that material will be directly used in the newly refurbished building. Ingenuous ideas include reusing 50% of the glass from the existing facade as internal partitions. The other 50% of the glass facade will be recycled into Foamglas® insulation used in the new building skin. These are both interesting ideas, but for quite different reasons. Reusing glass from the facade for internal partitions is as

CLOCKWISE FROM TOP

FIG 2.76 Image of vertical atrium with living wall

FIG 2.77 Image of refurbished offices and vertical garden – Oslo Urban Mountain

FIG 2.78 Oslo Urban Mountain, Norway: proposed scheme to retrofit and extend the existing tower, while recycling 90% of the material stripped out

FIG 2.79 Detailed image of Oslo Urban Mountain, Norway

REDUCING THE AMOUNT OF MATERIAL USED **STEP 3**

radical as some of Rotor's 'Deconstruction' work, where they sell material stripped out of buildings back to the owner of the said building to reinstall (see page 105)! Assuming the glass is carefully dismantled and taken off site for cleaning, this process will save the client money and have a hugely reduced carbon footprint compared to the traditional approach of stripping out, throwing away, then installing new products.

To summarise the team's list of C2C strategies, some materials will be directly reused (such as the aforementioned facade glazing and aluminium panels in the existing facade), but most salvaged materials will be recycled and then returned to site as 'new products'. However basic recycling appears at first glance (reuse is always preferable if at all feasible), in this case it requires the team to have good relationships with construction industry suppliers. Some 50% of the facade glazing will be recycled and then used as 'Foamglas®' insulation on site; while 100% of the aluminium from the existing facade glazing will be recycled into mullions for the new facade. The team note that recycled aluminium has only 5% of the carbon footprint of new aluminium. Even the old asphalt from flat roofs will be recycled for the new roofs. New products for the project, such as precast steel and concrete composite structural systems, are selected because they are C2C Certified. Artificial light will be leased by the lux, and floor finishes will also be tendered as a 'take-back' agreement. This is a very thoughtful and innovative scheme.

There are other strategies worth mentioning. A number of glazed 'green lungs' will be planted with indigenous trees, shrubs and flowers. These will clean incoming air, raise levels of controlled natural light and create delightful communal areas for people working in the building. The team have also suggested using the vertical split between towers as glazed 'solar chimneys' harvesting useful surplus heat as energy that can be stored or distributed around the building.

[OPINION]

Unfortunately this scheme has not yet been built, but it will be. Planning approval has not yet been granted by city planning authorities in Oslo because of issues relating to the overall development of the urban area. That aside, what struck me about this project was how confident members of the design team were about delivering on the hugely ambitious reuse and recycling targets. Recycling or reusing 90% of material removed from the existing building is ambitious enough. Creating networks with suppliers and contractors to ensure that 80% of this product ends up back on the site it was taken from is even more ambitious. Upon further investigation and interrogation of their extremely detailed proposals, one can see exactly how this will be achieved. The team acquired the knowledge they needed by signing up to the EPEA C2C workshops. They assembled a design team that can deliver on these ambitious targets. All strategies proposed for this building are clear, appropriate and straightforward to comprehend. This is why I believe the Oslo Urban Mountain will be developed. The most remarkable thing about the scheme is the work that has gone into establishing the networks to deliver on the targets for material reuse. This proves to me that buildings of any vintage can be considered as 'material depots' for future generations to take advantage of, not send to landfill.

88 | PART 2 | CIRCULAR INSPIRATIONS

STEP 3 CASE STUDY No.3

Palais de Tokyo and La Tour Bois-le-Prêtre, by Lacaton & Vassal

lateral thinking | experts at using less | nurturing buildings + communities

[THE STORY]

For more than 25 years Anne Lacaton and Jean Philippe Vassal have been practising together from their studio in Paris. They have a very clear belief in the potential of design to benefit the day-to-day lives of individuals and communities. Their practice is characterised by a desire to work with the existing qualities of a site, seeing these as an opportunity and strength. They have a pragmatic approach towards issues of climate change and sustainability as a whole, never relying on expensive technological solutions, rather considering challenges in a genuinely holistic manner. When the partnership won a commission to overhaul and masterplan a town square in France, after exhaustive research they went back to their clients and confirmed that the current square was working perfectly well except for a couple of park benches that were valued by the community and needed repairing. This lost them a large commission, although it gained the practice huge credibility among its peers, and saved a huge amount of material resources as the client accepted their proposal.

They are, however, perhaps best known for having an acute awareness of how to make generous, beautiful spaces affordable: they make clients' money go further than most. One of their first projects that demonstrated this ability was the commission to retrofit the Palais de Tokyo in Paris. Originally opened in 1937, it had suffered from many decades of neglect. In the late 1990s Lacaton and Vassal received a rather unusual enquiry from the Palais de Tokyo team. Since the mid-1990s there had been plans to update the neoclassical buildings: they were in a poor state of repair and not suitable for curating late 20th-century contemporary art. However, by the time Lacaton and Vassal were contacted the Palais de Tokyo had just stopped renovation works on site: the construction and design team had spent three-quarters of the construction budget on one-quarter of the works! Lacaton and Vassal's challenge was to complete three-quarters of the works with one-quarter of the original budget. This they famously did.

Lacaton and Vassal's approach to this project was simple. They looked at the fabric of the building, which comprised an in situ cast concrete frame that the previous design team were spending substantial sums of money covering over, and pretty much left the interior spaces in a state of partial refurbishment. They spent money in an informed, frugal way (on materials/architectural features where people literally touched the building, but left the original building alone where it was less able

PART 2   CIRCULAR INSPIRATIONS

CLOCKWISE FROM TOP (OPPOSITE)

FIG. 2.80 An extremely 'light touch' retrofit of existing buildings, Palais de Tokyo, Paris

FIG. 2.81 The complete transformation of the tower, undertaken without demolition

FIG. 2.82 The interior of a typical flat before retrofitting works began

FIG. 2.83 A typical flat after the addition of a new 'winter garden' and balcony

FIG. 2.84 La Tour Bois-le-Prêtre after a previous refurbishment, in 1990

to be seen/comprehended), and delivered this successful project at build rates that were one-third of those originally anticipated.

This approach is not really frugal at all. Lacaton and Vassal have an extensive knowledge of construction materials and systems new and old, and they understand where to apply additional fabric and when to leave it alone. Their point of view is that by keeping everything 'raw' there is an honesty of materiality. As noted when we were commissioned in 2010 to expand the facilities of the Palais de Tokyo into under-utilised areas, 'we have distanced ourselves from the idea of seeking a form of aesthetic perfection and spectacular architecture'; we have 'reactivated' the original qualities of a building which had been unloved for a long time.

The second Lacaton and Vassal project I want to discuss is in many ways even more successful at demonstrating an informed, extremely cost-effective, resource-saving alternative solution to the norm. Lacaton and Vassal's approach to the challenge of creating a new 16-storey high-rise tower to replace the aging 1960s Tour Bois-le-Prêtre saved a whole lot of materials from going to landfill, reduced the energy consumption on site by over 50%, and, most importantly to the architects, provided hugely improved apartments for the tenants. The first smart move was not to demolish the building, but to partner with the original architect, Raymond Lopez, who obviously had an intimate knowledge of the building he designed. The team then proposed a radical solution to the idea of renovation. They decided to keep the interiors of the existing 96 'sheltered' apartments untouched but to remove the ugly precast concrete cladding system that had been applied in the 1970s and replace it with fully glazed 'winter gardens' that extended all the apartments by about 2m. The concrete panels were removed and each winter garden was applied while the tenants still occupied the apartments.

The new layer literally wraps the old building and in doing this provides greatly increased levels of natural light, increased natural ventilation, better quality of air and a reduced likelihood of overheating, which is a big problem with south-facing tower blocks. These unheated 'environmental buffer zones' keep the original apartments cooler in the summer and warmer in the winter. Crucially, all of these 'passive' low-tech 'devices' are controlled by the tenants occupying the apartments: different tenants can have different set-ups.

Since the completion of La Tour Bois-le-Prêtre in 2011, Lacaton and Vassal have applied the same strategies to a larger project known as 'Grand Parc' in Bordeaux. Again, this is a collaboration with the original architects who designed this collection of three large residential blocks, and again the tenants will not have to leave while this radical transformation of their homes takes place.

FIG. 2.85 A later project applying a similar strategy at Grand Parc in Bordeaux. Left, flats before retrofit, right, after retrofit.

When I spoke to Anne Lacaton, she was keen to stress that they are not 'green' or 'eco' architects. Their primary ambition 'is always to create amazing environments for all people. Intelligent design should always address all environments'.

[OPINION]

These two projects are inspiring, thought-provoking and, as with almost all good design, represent a simple, straightforward solution to a problem. Just think of how much waste material would have been created if the Tour Bois-le-Prêtre had been demolished and then simply replaced by another tower of a similar size, constructed in nearly identical materials. It is really only the facades and services of contemporary high-rise buildings that are radically different to those constructed from the middle of the 20th century.

Both projects identify the true value and potential of existing buildings, materials, systems and communities. By undertaking research at an almost forensic level, such as working with the original architect on the Tour Bois-le-Prêtre, Lacaton and Vassal unearth unrealised potentials. Both projects test the potential for our existing buildings to be 'material stores' for the future: even the so-called difficult ones made of monolithic 'plastic' materials such as concrete and cement.

As they stated in their 2012 publication *Druot, Lacaton & Vassal: Tour Bois-le-Prêtre*, 'Somebody who demolishes a building just to re-erect it on the same site but in a "contemporary look" has, in principle, gained absolutely nothing.'[1] They also said, 'For the money needed to tear down one apartment and to build a new one, you can renovate and expand three to four existing apartments.'

Lacaton and Vassal have been true innovators. They question 'normal practice' and use their skills as designers to create inspirational places for everybody, applying authentic, low-carbon solutions to everyday problems, such as 'How do we make cost-effective homes for people who are not rich?' And they do this with the minimum of fuss. They are truly inspirational.

STEP 3 CASE STUDY No.4

Rented House Life, by Sadaharu Komai

design | reuse | adapt | repeat

FIG. 2.86 A map of Kyoto, showing the sites used for the four 'rented houses'

[THE STORY]

Japanese architects have a well-deserved reputation for being resourceful, often developing ingenious buildings on the smallest of plots, and with the minimum of resources. This is exemplified by the work of Tokyo's Atelier Bow-wow. This case study is no less ingenious.

Sadaharu Komai is Associate Professor of Architecture at Nagoya University of Arts. While teaching architecture he has been building his own home in Kyoto for the past 25 years. Komai calls this project 'Rented House Life'. Komai has not been building the same property for 25 years, although many architects do find it difficult to complete their own projects! Over this time he has built and then rebuilt his home, on four separate occasions and on four separate sites. Komai finds a site and leases the land or, in the first three cases, a building. He moves home when needs dictate: normally when his family expands. What is unusual is that when he leaves his old home he dismantles it and takes it along to the new site. As each site to date has been bigger than the previous, he also brings new material in as well. So the home expands each time.

REDUCING THE AMOUNT OF MATERIAL USED **STEP 3** 93

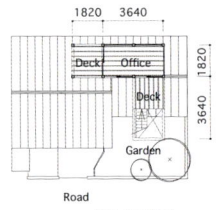

Rented house 1

Rented house 2

Rented house 3

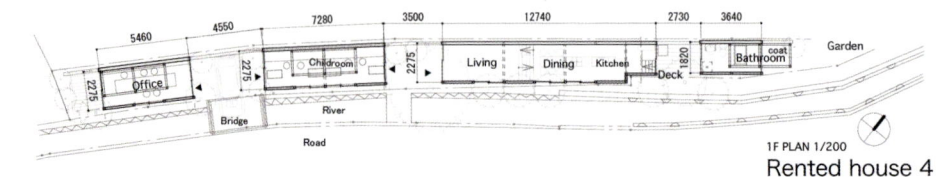

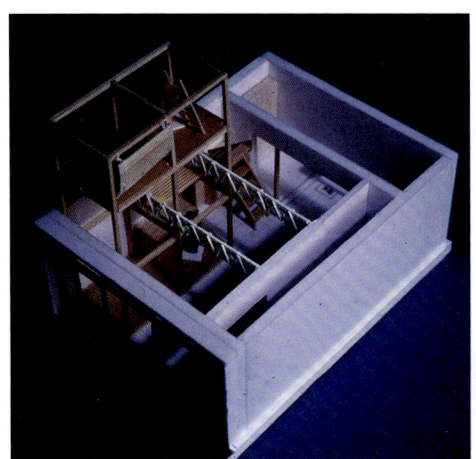

Rented house 4

CLOCKWISE FROM TOP

FIG. 2.87 Plans of the four iterations of Rented House 1-4

FIG. 2.88 Model of addition to 'Rented House 1'

FIG. 2.89 Room within a room in 'Rented House 3', being used by Professor Komai

FIG. 2.90 Model of 'Rented House 3' room within a room

94　PART 2　CIRCULAR INSPIRATIONS

FIG. 2.91 Timber from 'Rented House 1', creating washing and social space in 'Rented House 2'

FIG. 2.92 Room within a room created in 'Rented House 3' by material from 'Rented House 1 and 2'

Even the latest 'Rented House 4' is by no means a large dwelling, with its floor area of just over 90m^2 – and that includes 24m^2 of carport and office. However, the first iteration, 'Rented House 1', was actually a 20m^2 extension wrapping around and on top of an existing dwelling. Komai moved in when he was still a student. This minute building was his home and workplace until Komai got married and his wife was expecting their first child.

The timber structure from the first project was dismantled and then reassembled in the new property. Komai's attention to detail had ensured that the timber frame was originally assembled like flat-pack furniture. His building extensions were more akin to joinery.

In 1998 Komai, along with his wife and new baby, moved to 'Rented House 2'. Komai states that this site 'was blessed with a beautiful surrounding environment and the rented house was also good quality, although old'. However, it was not large enough for his family so Komai unpacked the two decks and the office structure from 'Rented House 1' and reassembled them at 'Rented House 2' to create a much-needed outdoor bathroom with adjacent living room/deck.

'Rented House 3' was a small warehouse previously used by a picture framer. The original timber frame from 'Rented House 1' was reassembled here inside the existing building, but turned on its head and added to, to create a three-storey intervention running through the vertical section of the building.

REDUCING THE AMOUNT OF MATERIAL USED **STEP 3**

It provided a home, office and gallery for this imaginative architect. The overall expansion of floor area created by this timber frame was only 8m², but the existing warehouse was substantially bigger than previous rented buildings, and it needed to be, as by this time Komai and his wife had four children.

The final iteration of this project presented quite a different challenge: there was no existing building, or conventional site for that matter. Komai's latest project, 'Rented House 4', sits on a former grass verge separated from a quiet residential road by a narrow river and backing onto a row of residential properties.

At just over 2m wide, this site is more door threshold than a site on which to build one's home. Again Komai dismantled the timber frame structures used in his previous homes and, working with the original 1820mm x 3640mm module, repeated this module by a factor of three to allow this new dwelling to materialise as a narrow (1.8m) two-storey modular structure running along for 40m. This is a modest yet beautiful home that also provides an office and gallery, accessed via a bridge over a small river lined with trees. It is an ingenious and delightful outcome from a talented architect working on a very challenging site.

CLOCKWISE FROM RIGHT

FIG. 2.93   Model of 'Rented House 4'

FIG. 2.94   The site for 'Rented House 4'

FIG. 2.95   'Rented House 4', completed

96   PART 2   CIRCULAR INSPIRATIONS

[OPINION]

One of the issues I had with this project was which 'step' I should put it in. The timber frame from 'Rented House 1' resides in 'Rented House 4', along with additional material from the other two dwellings. This method of building has resulted in a reduction of new material required for each new dwelling. 'Rented House 4' could be described as almost completely 'designed for remanufacture' – a 'material store' for a future house. As the project ran from its first to fourth iteration, it dealt with both the 'Reuse' and 'Reduce' steps, with 'Rented House 4' poised to demonstrate that it is a closed-loop system.

This project may appear modest and simple; however it completely depends on a designer to detail it for deconstruction in the first place. Komai stuck rigorously to the 1820mm x 3640mm module used in all four projects. From the first dwelling to the last, the same timber frame has been reused but with quite different outcomes. By adding to it with more of the same material, Komai has been able to expand this construction system into ever bigger spaces, but in quite different ways. This project demonstrates that with enough design ingenuity and foresight, closed-loop human-made systems are definitely achievable.

FIG. 2.96 3D sketches describing the reused elements from 'Rented House 2, 3 and 4'

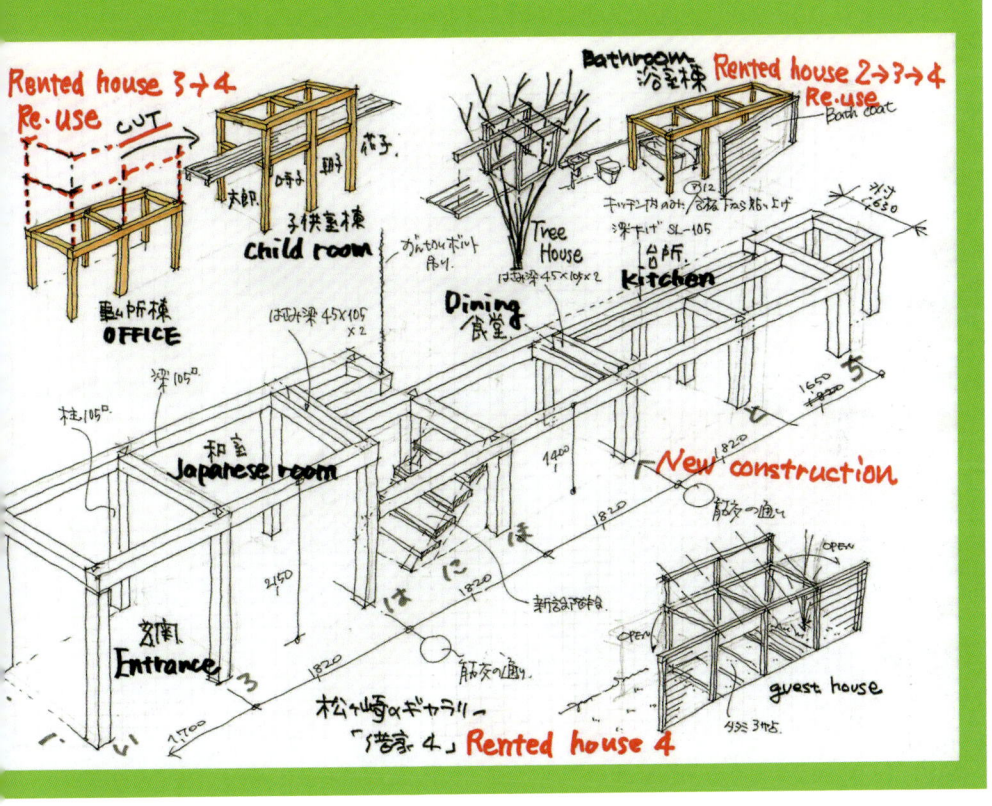

REDUCING THE AMOUNT OF MATERIAL USED **STEP 3**

STEP 3 CASE STUDY No.5

Retrofit: a 'reuse/reduce' opportunity

design | adapt | rework | buildings | communities

[THE STORY]

I had originally wanted to discuss one of my favourite retrofit projects, Jakob + MacFarlane's transformation of the Docks de Paris building from 1907 into the 'City of Fashion and Design'. The massive in situ cast concrete frame and floor plates from the original shipping depot were kept, with the architects designing what they call a 'plug-over', which is actually an external steel and glass skin complemented with timber and grassed decks. The new facade is pulled away from the old frame to allow for a new circulation zone. The roof is topped off with an array of solar photovoltaic panels.

The reason I like this building is simple: the architects have seen the value in this simple piece of concrete infrastructure from over a century ago. With the minimum of effort, Jakob + MacFarlane have transformed it into a centre for high culture, and they have done this in a visually expressive and exuberant manner that begs the viewer to ask questions of this clever retrofit project. They have also done this with the minimum of new material, as the lightweight steel and glass facade makes the most of the potentials of the old strong and thermally massive concrete frame to work hard for the new programme. But I'm not going to speak about this building as I think there is another linked topic that is more important to discuss in my *Re-Use Atlas*.

This topic is less glamorous, but I believe it is one of the biggest challenges we have as architects and designers. It is the task of adapting for climate resilience the buildings, neighbourhoods, towns and cities that are already built and inhabited. How can the retrofitting of our existing places be done in a creative, intelligent and sensitive way, so that it reduces humankind's carbon footprint, without displacing communities and perhaps obliterating centuries of cultural and social history?

The City of Fashion and Design is an ingenious solution to a design challenge. However, the large size of the site, and the single occupant, makes the project perhaps an easier nut to crack than what I believe to be the biggest retrofit challenge we have – how to convert multi-occupancy, unloved and poorly maintained housing estates. It is this challenge that I want to consider now, and I will do this by looking at the UK's housing retrofit challenge.

....

OPPOSITE

FIG. 2.97 The original Docks de Paris building, constructed in 1913

FIG. 2.98 Docks de Paris, transformed by Jakob + MacFarlane into the City of Fashion and Design

PART 2 CIRCULAR INSPIRATIONS

REDUCING THE AMOUNT OF MATERIAL USED **STEP 3** 99

The UK, which has more than 27 million homes, has some of the most energy inefficient dwellings in Europe. As a result they are also the most expensive in Europe to heat. Around 50% of these homes were built before 1960, with only 10% built since 1990. One of the consequences of this situation is that fuel poverty is also at a higher level in the UK than in any other comparable EU country. The definition of 'fuel poverty' is when a tenant is spending more than 10% of their net income on their fuel bills.[2] More than 10 million families live in 'fuel poverty' in properties with a leaking roof, damp walls and rotting windows. Despite this, UK CO_2 emissions have fallen by 35% when compared to 1990 levels.[3] However, the UK needs to reduce its CO_2 emissions by a total of 80% when compared to 1990 levels, and needs to do this by 2050. Recent CO_2 emission reductions have started to slow down. The UK, like all its European partners to a greater or lesser extent, has a huge challenge ahead to meet its CO_2 emission reduction targets by 2050. Another issue is that many experts estimate that 80% of the houses currently standing will be the structures trying to meet these ambitious targets. For numerous reasons, the UK doesn't build much housing, or demolish it.

The lack of demolition is a good thing for the environment. However, the high energy consumption associated with these leaky old structures is not. So with this in mind I wanted to dwell upon the big challenge of how to adapt existing UK housing, new and old, so that it is climate-change resilient. This challenge should not be underestimated. The temptation to demolish large housing estates from the 1950s to 1970s is great, but as the UK learnt with the wholesale destruction of its so-called slums to make way for these large estates, along with clearing the Victorian terraces, the bulldozers destroyed whole communities. As we have seen with a number of case studies in this chapter, a well-informed retrofit project has the potential to greatly enhance the performance of a place without destroying the community it supports.

Retrofit is complex though. The UK government's innovation agency, Innovate UK (formerly the Technology Strategy Board), has undertaken extensive research into this subject, supporting more than 80 retrofit case studies via its 'Retrofit the Future' initiative.[4] This programme gave architects and social landlords the challenge of retrofitting examples of UK social housing from the 1870s to the 1970s. All of the case studies were given a (large) budget of £150,000 to spend on often very modest buildings, with a goal of reducing CO_2 emissions to meet the UK government's 2050 targets. Only eight of the case studies met this target.

So it is early days for top-quality retrofit projects. There are not many designers, contractors or clients who understand the complexities and challenges that face them when trying to deliver a successful retrofit project. Many retrofit projects deal with only some of the problems that a building might have. For example, many buildings are being over-clad with external wall insulation that dramatically reduces heat loss through the building fabric. However, this fabric-focused approach often comes at a cost for the tenants, resulting in poor internal air quality due to a virtually airtight fabric and poor background ventilation. The knock-on effect, especially in winter, is mould on internal walls due to a build-up of moisture in the air. Another problem

CLOCKWISE FROM RIGHT

FIG. 2.99 Wilmcote House receiving a new insulating layer, wrapping the existing building

FIG. 2.100 Installing insulation between metal studwork at Wilmcote House. Note the new protruding window frames, anticipating another layer of insulation

FIG. 2.101 The final finish layer of render applied over rigid insulation at Wilmcote House

REDUCING THE AMOUNT OF MATERIAL USED **STEP 3** 101

many people are anticipating is a new type of 'fuel poverty' – the inability of some tenants to afford the bolt-on air-cooling devices needed to deal with overheating in the summer months. Retrofitting needs to be delivered in a holistic manner, where the design team and contractors have a deep understanding of building physics and a sensitivity towards the tenants they have to work around.

Having said all of the above, there are a number of architects and contractors who are doing an excellent job. One of these architecture practices is Gardener Stewart Architects (GSA), which is currently tackling some of the most challenging housing estates in the south-east of England. One of these is Wilmcote House, in Southsea in Portsmouth, which comprises 100 three-bed maisonettes plus seven one-bed flats. Constructed in 1968, this development utilises a precast concrete panel construction system, with a fully electric hot water and space heating system. Although cost-effective and swift to erect in the late 1960s, the apartments in this social housing scheme are cold and damp, and for many of the tenants, too expensive to heat, creating 'fuel poverty'. Maintenance costs are spiralling upwards, due in part to the coastal saline air and exposure to severe weather. The Le Corbusier inspired 'streets in the sky' external access decks create a security problem for tenants, and finally the projected economic and social costs of decanting and completely demolishing these buildings was not affordable.

GSA has attempted to solve all of these problems. The cold and leaky concrete skin is now wrapped with a new super-insulated and super-airtight wall that sits on its own foundations immediately in front of the old concrete walls, leaving them intact. New treble-glazed Passivhaus-standard windows have been installed, with access balconies given over either to extending apartments or the creation of private balconies/sunspaces. Mechanical Ventilation and Heat Recovery (MVHR) has been installed for a number of reasons. It will ensure hugely improved air quality (reduced moisture content in winter will reduce the likelihood of mildew) and reduced energy consumption. This 'fabric first' approach is also underpinned with the retrofit version of Passivhaus design principles, called EnerPhit. GSA predicts energy savings of 80 to 90% (down to less than 20kWh/m^2/yr). At £920/m^2 this project compares very favourably with 'normal' new-build costs. However, the running costs of this are negligible when compared to normal new-build housing projects, and, most impressively, the apartments have been increased in size, while the community has not been broken up and rehoused around the city; it has been kept intact. The hope is that the occupants of these homes will now not have to spend nearly so much of their wages on heating bills, and the aesthetics of the retrofitted buildings, together with the new communal and retail facilities, will help them live their lives in a more pleasant environment. Wilmcote House will hopefully meet, or even exceed, the UK government's CO_2 reduction commitments (80% by 2050) today rather than putting it off for tomorrow. Tenants will hopefully thrive in the new environments.

[OPINION]

The wholesale retrofitting of our cities and towns is one of society's biggest challenges. It will require an innovative and visionary approach that, above all, is well informed with the knowledge and skills to deliver better places for everybody to live, work and play in. External wall insulation and solar panels are only two of the tools at a designer's disposal: they will not create sustainable, circular cities on their own. However, there are exciting new construction systems emerging that will perhaps assist local authorities complete high-quality retrofit programmes across all our cities. Initiatives such as the Dutch government's Ministry of Interior and Kingdom Relations 'Energiesprong' (Energy Leap) programme are spreading across Europe.[5]

The hugely reduced carbon footprints required cannot be achieved without local, regional and central government's buy-in and support. For example in the UK, VAT laws actively encourage demolition of buildings by adding a 20% tax onto nearly all refurbishment (retrofit) works, while new-build projects are 'zero-rated'. Large utility companies responsible for the supply of gas, electricity and water have to step up to the challenge as well. Retrofitting our leaky homes and other buildings cannot achieve a low-carbon lifestyle in isolation. It requires joined-up thinking and education. To quote green designer Neil B Chambers: 'If your design team are telling you that the "green" version of their proposal is more expensive than the norm, tell them to try harder: if they can't, find a team that can.'[6]

It's all about knowledge and understanding and how to apply it.

INTERVIEW WITH AN EXPERT
Lionel Billiet of Rotor

DBB: How did you start working for Rotor? You aren't a designer or architect, are you?

LB: My first contact with Rotor was in 2007, as a helping hand on the construction of a temporary headquarters made out of reclaimed materials in the centre of Brussels. When I graduated as a biochemist in 2010, Rotor was looking for someone with a scientific profile to work on a research project related to building and demolition waste. I applied for the job and that's how I joined the team. Within Rotor, I was in the first years mainly involved as researcher and entrepreneur in the launching of Rotor Deconstruction.

DBB: What came first for Rotor: the live projects or the research projects?

LB: From what I know, the two aspects were both present since the beginning.

DBB: I would like to know more about Rotor's Vade Mecum, or Handbook for Off-site Reuse. How did this project come about?

LB: For a couple of years, there has been a political will to encourage reuse in the Brussels building sector. Public authorities were looking for the best ways to encourage such practices. Instead of trying to create a whole sector from scratch, we suggested it was maybe more relevant to learn [more about] the existing sector for reused materials, and to support its further development. This was the starting point of the Opalis project, a survey where we identified and documented more than 100 reclaimed materials dealers in Belgium and in the neighbouring regions (see www.opalis.be). With the Opalis website, local architects and builders were now able to find easily a supplier of reused materials for their projects. But these suppliers can also turn out to be purchasers when it comes to evacuating reusable components from a soon-to-be-demolished building. Our long-term vision is that before every large demolition or renovation, the option of organising a salvage phase should be at least considered. In the cases where it is feasible and relevant, the reusable components would be offered to a dedicated professional sector and the items that received interest would be extracted. The handbook allows public contracting authorities to be exemplary [in encouraging reuse], and to generate case studies that could support, one day, a change in regulation on that matter.

DBB: **Have any local authorities used this handbook?**

LB: The handbook was published in September 2015 and there are already two cases where it has been used in Brussels: for the sale of interior fittings and finishes from a 1930s social housing complex constructed by a municipality, and also for the donation of surplus roof tiles by another public contracting authority. Other operators are considering launching similar procedures.

DBB: **Do you have an English version of the handbook?**

LB: No, not yet. If you think of a funding opportunity for the translation work, you are welcome!

DBB: **I'd like to dwell upon Rotor's 'Deconstruction' project now. Could you explain how this initiative was launched?**

LB: Our first experimental project started back in 2013 when the sustainability manager of a large real estate company in Brussels contacted us as they were about to renovate a large office building: actually the HQ of Levi's [Levi Strauss]. The project was to strip out and renovate over 8,000m² of empty office. All partitions, ceilings, fittings and interior finishes were being removed. They had heard that Rotor was working on 'reuse' projects and asked if we could deal with the material being stripped out of the building. Until that point we thought we would work on reuse just as researchers, architects and – let's say – consultants. Because of this enquiry we made the step to become material salvagers for real.

Initially we worked with another building contractor who had the appropriate insurances as we couldn't get this completed in time for this first project. We still had to invent a process and a way to collaborate with this real estate company and actively look for people who were prepared to pay for these dismantled materials, as this project had to be financially sustainable.

DBB: **What motivated the client?**

LB: Our clients had done many projects improving energy and water-use efficiency on buildings. So they had made lots of effort in the past, but reached a kind of 'level'. They now felt that the issue of the huge loss of materials on every renovation needed to be addressed.

DBB: **So did they first hear about you because of your research: had this inspired them?**

LB: Yes they first heard about us through research projects that we had done.

DBB: **How did you find people who wanted the material?**

LB: Initially we just used our own direct networks – architects around us – but also because of our previous research we had good contacts with reclaimed material dealers, who were interested.

DBB: **You had no storage space, so did you sell materials straight from site?**

LB: We offered people the possibility to reserve or take an option on the materials before they were stripped out.

DBB: **And was that ultimately successful?**

LB: This operation broke even the first time. So we didn't lose money, but we decided to go further next time. The beginning was slow, but for nearly two years now it has become a regular activity. We now have a department that is focused on doing just these sorts of interventions in buildings, in terms of the reuse of components. We have about one intervention per month. Last year we kept more than 400 tonnes of material 'in the circuit'.

DBB: **So how are you doing that now? Have you got somewhere to store this material or are you doing it like you did the first commission?**

LB: So now we are equipped for it. We now have a warehouse of 1,000m² and another 1,000m² outside. We have four people who are working for us just on deconstruction projects: people with a technical background who can coordinate such projects. We have someone responsible for the material storage yard. Now the deconstruction projects (and spin-off activities) are taking more than half the working hours of Rotor.

DBB: **Do you have people approaching Rotor with deconstruction projects or are you actively looking for buildings?**

LB: It's both. We try to be proactive and identify potential sites. We try to have collaborations with real estate companies who are renovating on a regular basis. We also try to have access to exceptional buildings when they are going to be demolished or renovated. Perhaps what the difference is between what we do and other reclamation companies in Belgium is that we are mostly interested in buildings [such as] offices or schools, larger-scale buildings, and mostly from the 'modern movement' or what followed, including completely contemporary things or buildings from the 1960s or 1970s.

DBB: **What has drawn you to that era? Is it perhaps because other architectural salvage companies are less interested in it?**

LB: Yes that's one way to explain it. Maybe three years ago, we realised that there was a market for reused materials, but that this sector was mostly focused on pre-modern materials or a kind of 'ageless' material such as cobblestones or bricks or wood. We identified a gap in the market.

DBB: **Who is buying these materials?**

LB: Sometimes it is the building owner. We have been asked on several occasions to dismantle components within a building and then reassemble them in the same building once renovation was complete. In a lot of situations, building components that are still perfectly functional, attractive or interesting are doomed to being thrown away simply because it is 'normal' practice with demolition companies. For example, if an internal floor and wall finish need replacing, often the ceiling will be stripped out as well even if it is perfectly OK. It is seen as impractical to try and protect and preserve it. However, Rotor provides a service whereby we draft a full inventory of the components we have salvaged from a building, together with a handbook describing how to reassemble them. We can store these components until the building is renovated and ready to receive them again; this might be two years later. By providing these services we make some types of reuse that are not normally considered practically or economically viable, possible.

DBB: **How have you turned previously unwanted material into a desirable product?**

LB: We have to take good photographs of the materials installed on site. We do a historic investigation on the provenance of the materials and the building itself. By documenting a component you can quickly reveal its value. For example, we dismantled a ceramic floor from a modernist university building from the early 1930s. If we had tried to sell these tiles in their various colours (I think there were five) they would not have appeared that special or specific. Although the building was quite geometric and 'no-nonsense', the architects had had some fun with the patterns made by the floor tiles. So we photographed these complex patterns. We then encouraged our clients not to buy just the tiles, but to buy a certain area of a certain pattern. A few clients did this. So now, for example, there is a grocery in Ghent where there are different ceramic floor tile patterns in each room, and these patterns come from the old university building from the 1930s.

DBB: In addition to salvaging materials for reuse in the buildings they originated from, how do you find other customers for your projects?

LB: There is a link on our Rotor website (http://rotordb.org) under 'Deconstruction' to the Rotor Shop, where you can see everything we have in stock right now. However, a big part of the materials we actually deal with go straight from their deconstruction sites to their new use. Therefore a large number of the components we actually work with never appear on the website as we have a client for them already. The Rotor Shop is mainly used by architects or interior designers and their clients, whereas the people taking material directly from deconstruction sites are normally professional salvage companies or building contractors and developers.

DBB: To create the market for deconstruction in the first place, did it rely on your first project getting a lot of publicity? What creates that market?

LB: This is still an ongoing job. What we tried to do was make use of the existing networks we had and we try to fit things together that are likely to complement each other. So, for example, one of our partners is a company that sells second-hand furniture. They now also sell small construction components that look like furniture. As they already had a wide client base looking for second-hand material, they have been successful at taking these components from us. Some elements, such as second-hand flooring, have established markets that we work with. However, for some types of elements there are no established markets so we have to promote those in our shop.

DBB: How are you ascertaining the value of these second-hand materials?

LB: That is an interesting question. When it comes to contemporary anonymous materials you can still find on the market, most of the time people don't want to pay more than 50% of the new price. So that is our upper limit. Our lower limit relates to the money we actually invest in finding the material in the first place. We try to set a price between these two limits.

DBB: Is it you, personally, who goes into these buildings to carry out the resource inventory?

LB: I have done this often. For the moment, as we are still a small team, everybody is doing a bit of everything. However, a large part of my work is to work with the building owners to develop the brief, deal with the bureaucracy relating to deconstruction and to make the report of the reclamation operation. On some projects I have also followed the daily aspects of deconstructing a building, but that is something we can delegate to colleagues who are focused on this. Sometimes I work on the scientific aspects of these projects. For example, the first time we tried to reclaim a wooden floor we could see that it was fixed with a kind of black glue like asphalt. At first we were suspicious that this was toxic and would stop us reusing the wood. We came to the conclusion that if a wooden floor is from the 1950s or later then the black glue is asphalt not tar and therefore safe to reuse. If it is earlier, then it will be tar and therefore a dangerous product. We now send samples of suspicious materials to a laboratory for analysis before we decide to reuse.

DBB: **You have a scientific background. Did you know a lot about construction before you worked at Rotor?**

LB: Not much. I had a bit of experience with DIY. I was trained as a bio-engineer: a biochemist actually. I was interested in issues relating to materials, but without experiencing the building sector.

DBB: **I guess the work you are doing informs Rotor's architecture work as well?**

LB: A tiny part of what we dismantle ends up in Rotor projects. It's very nice to have the opportunity to take the materials directly from source and reuse them in our own design projects.

DBB: **How do you see the future for Rotor?**

LB: We are at a stage now where we can prove the 'floatability' of the business venture. In 2015 we salvaged over 400 tonnes of components from buildings, which when you consider that most of the materials are lightweight (it's not brick and concrete blocks), you see it is a substantial figure, but still this is just a drop when you compare this figure to other flows of materials. So yes, we want to increase this amount and also to stabilise the way we function. We have a few regular streams: stable flows. We are of course open for new things.

DBB: **You must have a lot of people from the construction and waste industries interested in your ideas and business models? You are adding value to stuff they normally burn or send to landfill.**

LB: Yes, but for the moment the discussion with people from the waste industry is mainly centred around their curiosity. We often quickly realise that we are dealing with completely different problems. From a financial and logistic point of view, it is completely different to dealing with stuff that can be thrown in a container. For example if you consider wood waste, you can sell a tonne of wood waste for a few euros. However, if you take wooden flooring made from similar wood the value might be €1,000 to €2,000 per tonne.

DBB: **What is your view on the publication by the European Commission of the Circular Economy Package in December 2015?**

LB: We have heard a lot about it from local authorities that now feel they need a circular economy strategy or plan, or at least a vision. So it has given us extra arguments to advocate for things we stand for.

STEP 4 — The Circular Economy

BIO-SPHERE

TECH-SPHERE

[DEFINITION]

STEP 4 PROJECTS
These are projects that create zero waste during their life – from design, through to manufacture, use and reuse. They are designed for perpetual reuse without undermining their initial sophistication; in fact they never generate any waste at all and function as part of a healthy circular economy. These are the type of designs that the Cradle to Cradle Products Innovation Institute[1] will certify.

STEP 4 CASE STUDY No.1

Circular economy pedagogic methods, by Professor Dirk Hebel

innovative pedagogies | live projects | buildings as material banks

[THE STORY]

Professor Dirk Hebel, Assistant Professor of Architecture and Construction at ETH Zurich, has been pushing the boundaries of architectural teaching for over 15 years. His work considers ways to 'activate' unusual building materials, which over the years have included air, water (BLUR Building with Diller Scofidio + Renfro), bamboo, and, most recently, locating sources of waste material. Hebel has worked in many contrasting environments around the world, including the National Research Foundation in Singapore and The Ethiopian Institute of Architecture, Building Construction and City Development in Addis Ababa, where he was Director. This has allowed him to experience the development of architecture in hugely contrasting environments from the perspective of resource consumption. Hebel states on his website that his current research 'concentrates on a metabolic understanding of resources and investigates alternative building materials and construction techniques and their applications in developed as well as developing territories.'[2]

This case study is unusual because it partners the pedagogic practice of Hebel, who currently teaches architecture at ETH Zurich, with a large residential construction development in the heart of District 4 in Zurich. The project, in partnership with housing cooperative GMBZ, involves the design and construction of 140 apartments plus a kindergarten, common areas for residents and a shared laundry. All elements will follow the principles of 'building for disassembly'. The development aims to test the idea that buildings can be developed so they are a 'material store' for the future: all materials used in this development will be genuinely reusable. However, there are not many examples of contemporary buildings delivering upon these ideals, let alone large residential developments designed, as this is, by students.

This project highlights that many natural resources are becoming increasingly scarce, even aggregates such as sand and gravel for concrete production. It also focuses on the potentials of other material sources or 'flows' that have piled up over centuries – the materials that constitute our towns and cities that can now be conceived as our future 'mines'. Cities that of late have been purely consuming entities can now become providers of valuable material resources to repair and rebuild new and existing cities. This takes the pressure off the natural world to provide this material, which in turn could allow it to begin to flourish again.

FIG. 2.102 (OPPOSITE) Front cover of the brief issued to Dirk Hebel's students, who are creating apartments 'designed for disassembly'

PART 2 CIRCULAR INSPIRATIONS

ILEK Werner Sobek

Architectural Design V–IX
Start: 23.02.2016, 10 Uhr, HIQ C 11

DIRK E. HEBEL · ETH · ARCHITECTURE AND CONSTRUCTION · ASSISTANT PROFESSORSHIP

Ressource Stadt
Building for Disassembly

Von planen gemeinsam mit der Gemeinnützigen Bau- und Mietergenossenschaft Zürich (GBMZ) der neue wird in dem Kreis 4 in Zürich. Wir verfolgen unsere Gebäude nach dem Prinzip des Building for Disassembly zu nicht nur den Aufbau sondern auch den kompletten Rückbau und somit die sortenreine Wiederverwendbarkeit aller Materialien zu ermöglichen.

Natürliche Ressourcen zur Herstellung von Bauten werden immer knapper – dies gilt selbst für vermeintlich im Überfluss vorhandene Materialien wie Sand und Kies zur Herstellung von Beton. Gleichzeitig haben sich viele potentielle Ressourcen über Jahrhunderte in unseren Städten in Form von Bauwerken aufgetürmt. Während unsere traditionellen Rohstoffquellen langsam zur Neige gehen werden unsere Städte die neuen Minen der Zukunft. Städte werden gleichzeitig Verbraucher und Lieferanten von Ressourcen in einem – sie benutzen sich selbst zur eigenen Reproduktion.

Gebäude werden heute kaum als temporäre Ressourcenspeicher der Stadt gesehen. Der Rückbau und Einsatz von recyclinggerechten Materialien sind nur in den aller seltensten Fällen integraler Bestandteil der Planung. Und selbst da, wo der Rückbau gezielt geplant wird, scheitert eine ressourcengerechte Realisierung allzu oft an nicht recyclinggerechten Produkten und ungeeigneten Verbindungstechniken.

Wir werden in enger Kooperation mit Werner Sobek und dem Institut für Leichtbau Entwerfen und Konstruieren (ILEK) an der Technischen Universität Stuttgart eine architektonische und konstruktive Planung von städtebaulichen Fragen bis hin zur Ausarbeitung innovativer Fügungstechniken im Massstab 1:1 entwickeln. Der architektonische Entwurf soll ein relevanter Beitrag zu einer zukunftsorientierten Baukultur in Europa sein, welcher die gesellschaftliche und ressourcenrelevante Situation unserer Generation aufnimmt.

Die Semesteraufgabe wird eine reale Bauaufgabe darstellen, die GBMZ in den kommenden Jahren umsetzen wird und die durch Baugenossenschaft wahrend des Semesters begleitet wird.

Die von uns organisierte Seminarwoche unter dem Thema Zukunft des Bauens wird interessierten Studierenden dringend empfohlen.

Die erstellten Entwürfe beinhalten materialspezifische, architektonische sowie konstruktive Untersuchungen, Zeichnungen und Modelle.

Die Professur bietet den Entwurf mit der integrierten Disziplin Konstruktion an. Ebenfalls versuchen wir in Zusammenarbeit mit der EMPA eine integrierte Disziplin zum Thema Life Cycle Assessment zu ermöglichen.

Asst. Prof. Dirk E. Hebel
Patrick Chladek, Amélie Fibicher,
Felix Heisel, Philippe Jorisch,
Hans-Christian Rufer,
Marta H. Wisniewska

**ARCHITECTURE AND CONSTRUCTION
ASSISTANT PROFESSOR DIRK E. HEBEL**

ETHzürich   **D**ARCH   (FCL) FUTURE CITIES LABORATORY

THE CIRCULAR ECONOMY STEP 4 111

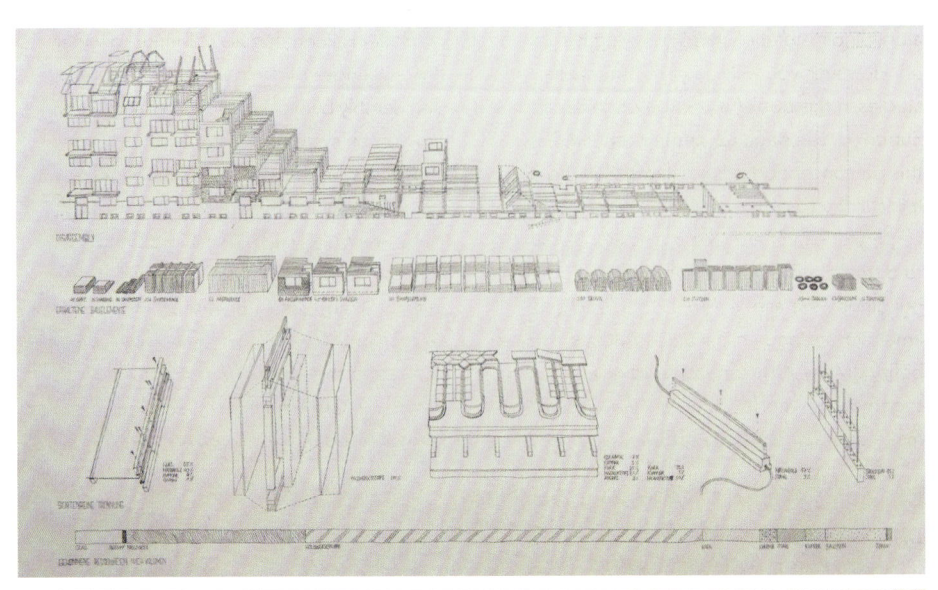

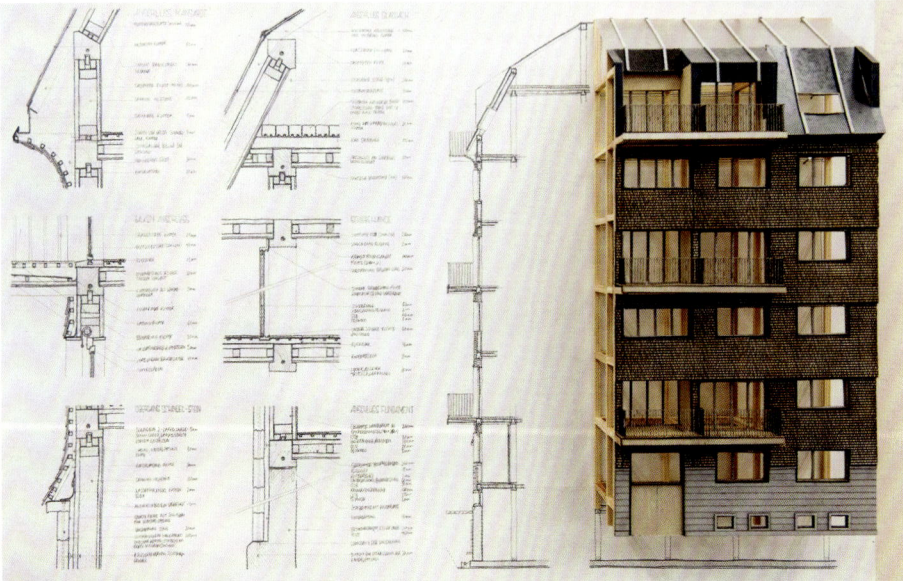

FIG. 2.103 Student drawing describing the construction and disassembly processes

FIG. 2.104 Student drawing and model of the Zurich apartments 'designed for disassembly'

The technique of reusing material that constitutes our cities is called 'urban mining'. In practice, it can be time-consuming (and therefore expensive) to dismantle or unpack

112   PART 2   CIRCULAR INSPIRATIONS

a building instead of simply blowing it up. However, you will see from other case studies in this book (Rotor, see page 82, and Superuse, see page 62, among others) that this preconception is now being challenged. It is still the case that buildings from the 19th century or earlier are far more straightforward to dismantle. This is mainly because of the way buildings were assembled: bricks used soft lime mortars, and timber and steel frames were bolted. Many 20th-century buildings are stuck together with mortar, glues and welds that make disassembly impractical.

Hebel is keen that his students consider the challenges of designing architecture for disassembly by looking at a wide range of issues, from urban systems through to the design of jointing techniques at full scale. It is hoped that by designing in this holistic manner, a genuine circularity can be achieved and this new development of 140 apartments will address 'the social and resource-related situation of our generation'.[3] Once the students have developed and tested the design brief with their tutors and client (GBMZ), the resultant design will be implemented over the coming years.

[OPINION]

Buildings are rarely considered a material or product resource for the future. However, 'urban mining' clearly demonstrates how waste can be reused at the end of its conventional lifespan, and used and reused on numerous occasions thereafter. It also brings to the forefront the need for designers to facilitate this by considering the 'waste state' of a product at the beginning of its life. This point is made very clearly by Sophie Thomas, former director of circular economy at the RSA, who points out that '80% of decisions made at the beginning of the design process either lock or unlock the potential for a product or building to be reused'.[4] So to enable more straightforward disassembling of buildings designers must to a certain extent relearn how to design.

In their text *Mine the City*,[5] Ilka and Andreas Ruby describe how contemporary culture is beginning to become aware of the fact that many everyday raw materials that are becoming rather scarce in the 'natural realm' are actually more common within the 'cultural domain' of our buildings. They state, 'The material resources of construction are becoming increasingly exhausted at the place of their natural origins, while inversely accumulating within buildings. For example, today there is more copper to be found in buildings than in earth. As mines become increasingly empty, our buildings become mines in themselves.' In other words, our cities are containers of buildings and these can be considered as mines supplying resources for future development.

This concept is pursued further by Thomas E Graedel from the Yale School of Forestry and Environmental Science.[6] Graedel considers the question of how much energy is saved by the reusing or even recycling of material normally destined for landfill or incineration. Aluminium, for example, is a material commonly used in contemporary buildings. As a number of our *Re-Use Atlas* case studies can demonstrate, aluminium is relatively straightforward to recycle. This process consumes energy. However, it requires only 5% of the energy originally used in its production to recycle it into a 'new' product such as a window frame. Graedel therefore argues that 'it is not inaccurate to regard this aluminium as "urban ore" and cities as "urban mines"'.

THE CIRCULAR ECONOMY **STEP 4**

STEP 4 CASE STUDY No.2

School buildings and others in Burkina Faso, by Francis Kéré

architect | pathfinder | vernacular materials | contemporary design

[THE STORY]

It is almost impossible to write about the work of Kéré Architecture without reference to the story of how its founder, Francis Kéré, became an architect. He was born in the village of Gando in Burkino Faso and was lucky enough to be the first child from his village to be sent to school. This education led to Kéré becoming a carpenter, which in turn led to him gaining a scholarship from the Carl Duisberg Society in Germany to complete an apprenticeship in development aid. Afterwards, he went on to study architecture at the Technical University of Berlin, where today Kéré bases his practice. However, while studying, Kéré never forgot where he came from: his final diploma project was a design for a school in his home village of Gando, which had more than 3,000 inhabitants but no school. Kéré was determined to give something back to the family and friends who had helped him achieve academic success. In 1998 he set up Schulbausteine für Gando, or Building Blocks for Gando, to fund the construction of a primary school, which was completed as his diploma project in 2004.

This was a hugely ambitious project involving most members of the village, as there was little money. Children from the village collected stones for over a year to form the foundations of the building. Women prepared the beautiful compacted earth floors, while men made bricks. Perhaps the biggest challenge Kéré faced was convincing his fellow villagers that large buildings, such as the new primary school for 700 pupils, could be made of mud and timber, as these materials were considered sub-standard and only for poor people who couldn't afford 'proper' materials. Villagers were also concerned that adobe walls would be washed away after a storm or two. Kéré overcame this issue by designing a gently curving roof that over-sailed the walls to protect them. He also remembered how hot the tin roofs made the classroom he learnt to write in. So he lifted the roof up to allow

....

CLOCKWISE FROM TOP LEFT (OPPOSITE)

FIG. 2.105 Villagers constructing part of the Opera Village, with sun-baked, hand-thrown clay bricks, Laongo, Burkina Faso

FIG. 2.106 Villagers utilise old clay pots to create rooflights for the Gando School Library

FIG. 2.107 Interior image of the stunning natural light in the Gando School Library

FIG. 2.108 Women making a rammed earth floor for the Gando School extension

FIG. 2.109 Young women carry rocks for the foundations of the Gando School extension

THE CIRCULAR ECONOMY STEP 4 115

FIG. 2.110 School pupils stand outside the completed Gando School extension

the natural cross-ventilation of air, while still providing rain protection. More than 12 years later the school is still standing: now it is one of a cluster of buildings, including a library, teachers' houses, an extension to the original school and a new secondary school, which is still under construction. All these buildings were constructed by the villagers themselves.

The resultant ensemble of large buildings has not only empowered the citizens of Gando, but many other people throughout Burkino Faso. Kéré deliberately developed a contemporary architectural language for his new buildings in Gando to overcome local prejudices against local materials. At the same time, by developing designs for these buildings with the villagers themselves, Kéré has empowered people to believe again that they can be responsible for the significant infrastructure projects more often outsourced to European or Chinese mega-companies.

PART 2 CIRCULAR INSPIRATIONS

[OPINION]

So why are these projects interesting to us as far as the circular economy is concerned? In short, the Kéré-designed buildings are constructed primarily out of organic material (stone, earth and timber) that one day will compost or return to the ground beneath the villagers' feet. The steel roof structures and roof finishes are easy to disassemble in the future for reuse. These two separate outcomes are the two 'circular systems' that describe the circular economy, which is fed by either organic or inorganic 'nutrients'. Remember, waste is 'food' for the circular economy.

Kéré has identified the potential of his people to relearn skills that were lost or undervalued due to more than 100 years of colonialism and the forced dependency upon outside funding and resources that resulted. Kéré has also allowed his fellow countrymen and women to reacquaint themselves with material resources that their forefathers knew well. This has given this community a sense of confidence to investigate new and emerging design techniques to create genuinely comfortable and beautiful buildings. They also feel confident enough in their newly acquired skills to experiment with the materials they formerly viewed as second-rate. Gando is now the site of many architectural and construction experiments that involve the whole community in their development. One of the by-products of this fascinating situation is that the carbon footprint of these substantial new buildings is almost non-existent and the material sources are completely 'circular'.

Kéré Architecture has plans for even bigger buildings, such as a new people's parliament building in Burkina Faso. Let's wait and see how its European, Chinese and North American commissions compare as circular systems. Kéré's work in Burkina Faso deals with the circular system in such a complete way, addressing material sources, design and construction techniques, as well as education and cultural empowerment.

FIG. 2.111 School pupils enjoy the shade under the roof of the Gando School extension

THE CIRCULAR ECONOMY **STEP 4**

STEP 4 CASE STUDY No.3

Hy-Fi organic compostable tower, by The Living

innovative design process | new material flows | bio-waste

[THE STORY]

To achieve a true state of circularity many people have identified a need to divide resources into 'technical' and 'organic' nutrients, or flows. The organic cycles or ecosystems already exist in nature of course, and the technical ones will hopefully exist when things large and small are designed for disassembly, incorporating new intelligent synthetic materials. The idea of constructing products and buildings with materials that are organic and capable of composting is not a new one. Historically many buildings and artefacts have been made in this way. However, contemporary designers have tended to avoid organic materials, although there are a number of interesting practices and scientists who are considering ways of literally growing their buildings. One of these is Brooklyn-based design practice The Living, comprising architects, artists and researchers and formed in 2006 with a mission of 'creating the architecture of the future' through the exploration of 'how new technologies come to life in the built environment'. Its projects blur the boundaries of avant-garde art, design and horticulture. In 2012 its 'Mussel Choir' formed part of the US Pavilion at the Venice Biennale. Mussels were used as 'biosensors', which were able to vocalise changes in water quality by combining natural and artificial intelligences.

The Living is perhaps best known for its Hy-Fi installation for the contemporary art institution MoMA PS1, based at Long Island City, New York. These temporary towers were constructed using more than 10,000 bricks that, incredibly, were grown rather than manufactured, using a combination of agricultural by-products (chopped-up corn stalks) and mushroom mycelium, which acts as a natural glue. The project was carried out in partnership with Ecovative, a company which specialises in developing organic grown materials and whose own mission is to 'rid the world of toxic, unsustainable materials'.

....

FIG. 2.112 How to grow a brick

PART 2 CIRCULAR INSPIRATIONS

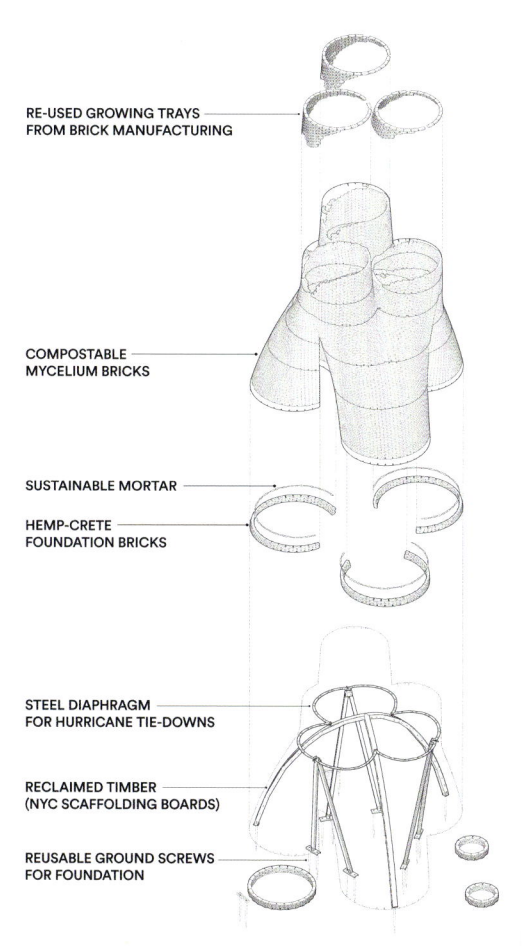

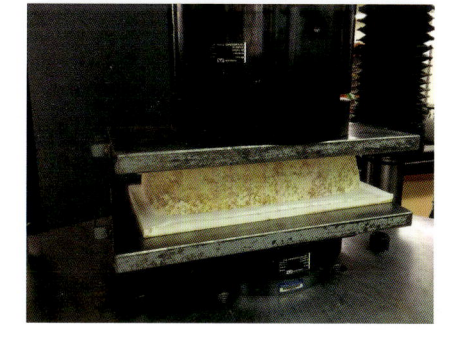

Labels on exploded axonometric:
- RE-USED GROWING TRAYS FROM BRICK MANUFACTURING
- COMPOSTABLE MYCELIUM BRICKS
- SUSTAINABLE MORTAR
- HEMP-CRETE FOUNDATION BRICKS
- STEEL DIAPHRAGM FOR HURRICANE TIE-DOWNS
- RECLAIMED TIMBER (NYC SCAFFOLDING BOARDS)
- REUSABLE GROUND SCREWS FOR FOUNDATION

CLOCKWISE FROM TOP LEFT

FIG. 2.113 Exploded axonometric drawing describing the elements that created the Hy-Fi tower

FIG. 2.114 Mycelium bricks, incubating for three days

FIG. 2.115 Mycelium bricks in their moulds

FIG. 2.116 Sample mycelium bricks broken in two to reveal corn husk aggregate

FIG. 2.117 Testing the compressive strength of mycelium bricks

THE CIRCULAR ECONOMY STEP 4

The Living created brick-shaped moulds that Ecovative used to grow their mycelium-based material in. Through a process of iterative design, growing and physical testing, The Living and its collaborators (including Ecovative, Arup for structural engineering, and a materials testing lab at Columbia University) developed bricks that were strong, load-bearing and tolerant of bad weather – they were designed to last outdoors for three months without any change in mechanical properties. So it is now possible to build with bricks that one day, if they cannot be reused, can be composted. It should also be noted that growing these bricks does not have to consume fossil fuels: the chemical process does not require heat. This is one of the big issues associated with conventional clay bricks, which have a huge carbon footprint. Ironically for a project with the ability to compost organically, Hy-Fi was eventually acquired for MoMA's permanent collection.

FIG. 2.118 Constructing the Hy-Fi tower

FIG. 2.119 The Hy-Fi tower installed

[**OPINION**]

The Living could be classified as a practice of avant-garde architects. This may be so. However, their ideas are rooted in very tangible goals to observe and learn from nature. In the case of Hy-Fi, they turned a linear process into a circular one. Designing contemporary structures that introduce these systems into the everyday is to be commended and many people believe that in future many new buildings will be grown. The Living's 'Amphibious Envelope' project is perhaps more a thought-provoker than a strategy to be rolled out again and again. It wraps part of an existing building with timber-framed glass tanks housing snails and frogs! However, the 'Bionic Partition' (in partnership with Autodesk) for Airbus tries a different tack. It creates a new type of partition wall separating the plane's galley from the passenger seating area. In an industry trying to reduce energy consumption by making aircraft lighter, The Living designed its 'Bionic Partition' with a 40% saving in weight. This was possible by utilising 3D printing, using new algorithms based on the concepts behind slime mould and bone growth. So on this occasion they learned from natural systems rather than emulating them. With a saving in weight over the current partition of 40%, they more than met the client's brief to reduce the weight by 30%.

Despite appearing to be on the fringes of the design world, The Living's projects are increasingly influential, attracting numerous awards from around the world. Fast Company recently ranked the practice third in its list of the World's Most Innovative Companies in Architecture.

The Living is definitely onto something.

FIG. 2.120 Looking up from inside the Hy-Fi tower

STEP 4 CASE STUDY No.4

The Enterprise Centre, UEA, by Architype

pathfinders | eco-architects | new material flows | bio-base | grown buildings

[THE STORY]

The University of East Anglia (UEA) was established in 1963. It has a longstanding tradition of commissioning innovative buildings from leading UK architects, starting with its famous Ziggurats, designed by Sir Denys Lasdun, the Sainsbury Centre for Visual Arts, designed by Sir Norman Foster, and 'Europe's largest low-energy building project' in 1992, student accommodation by Rick Mather Architects. In 2012, together with Morgan Sindall and the Adapt Low Carbon Group, UEA continued this worthy tradition by appointing Architype to design a new building dedicated to nurturing the growth of small and start-up businesses, as well as providing educational and conference facilities. Architype has a long-established record of delivering buildings with authentic 'green' credentials and is perhaps the UK's most successful exponent of sustainable design solutions.

The team behind the project took advantage of this unusual commission to test the viability of constructing a large (3,425m²) university office building using locally sourced materials, whether that meant organic and grown, second-hand or material from local waste streams. Not specifically 'designed for remanufacture', the focus here is to reduce the 'carbon footprint' of the project, from the inception of the design, through the construction process and of course while occupied. Architype predicts that the complete CO_2 'footprint' for this building will be 500kgCO_2/m² over a 100-year life cycle. This might not mean too much to many people, until you put the figure into the context of a similar university building built to 'best practice' standards, which can expect to have emitted 800–900kgCO_2/m² by the first day of occupation.

This has been achieved by specifying locally sourced materials to reduce road, air and sea miles to the minimum, and by using as much 'grown' material as possible because it 'locks' CO_2 until it is burnt or composted. The team also specified the reuse of local second-hand materials discarded by others, and complemented this with a policy of using local tradespeople and suppliers whenever possible. These strategies have created a series of closed-loop systems, as well as at least 27 new permanent jobs for local people.

....

CLOCKWISE FROM TOP LEFT (OPPOSITE)

FIG. 2.121 Thatch panels in construction near the site

FIG. 2.122 Thatch panels in construction

FIG. 2.123 Trimming thatch panels once installed

FIG. 2.124 Thatchers installing roof finish

FIG. 2.125 Detail of thatch panels and timber cladding

PART 2 CIRCULAR INSPIRATIONS

THE CIRCULAR ECONOMY **STEP 4** 123

124 | PART 2 CIRCULAR INSPIRATIONS

These are permanent jobs formed in the supply chain serving the construction industry, not on-site construction jobs. Over two years the team, endeavoured to collect local timber, which is normally overlooked as substandard, to provide the timber frame for the building. The external timber columns are formed of glue-laminated larch sourced from Thetford Forest, within 30 miles of the site.

However, this project has achieved its fame because of the unusual material it is wrapped in. The Enterprise Centre has a vast and spectacular thatch roof and, unique to this building, similar thatch cladding. This material combines the robust carbon-locking rain screen with organic cellulose insulation made from either waste paper or waste wood fibre. Architype provided me with the following statistics:

- 47% of external walls (by mass) are locally grown thatch.
- 11% of roofs by mass are locally grown reed.
- 70% of studwork forming walls is local Thetford Corsican pine, with the balance comprising Irish Sitka spruce.
- 40% by volume of all material is sourced within 100 miles of the site. This includes the thatch, studwork timber, glulam columns to the canopy, aggregates and oak cladding.
- 50% by volume of all material used can be composted one day.

Soon after receiving the commission to design the building, members of the design team contacted local farmers and bought up future crops of wheat to provide material for the thatch wall cladding and reed from the Norfolk Broads for the roofs. They thought of specifying heather thatch for the roof, but abandoned the idea as it would have had to be sourced from Northumberland. The resultant thatch cladding was developed by the team. It comprises prefabricated timber cassettes in-filled with 'Yeoman' wheat straw that has a slightly shorter stem than that used for roofs. This innovation could only happen because the suppliers and installers, specifically the Thatching Straw Growers Association, worked closely with the design team to create a closed-loop cladding system for a high-specification university building. Stephen Letch was the thatcher who facilitated much of the procurement and implementation for this unique and epic project. Letch saw the potential benefits for the project, as well as for the construction industry as a whole. He also identified smaller closed-loop systems that could result from the thatching process: the wheat's off-cuts were turned into flour and wheat beer.

Architype located other local material sources for the project. Flints from Holt were used in the lecture theatre, SUDs pool and around the building perimeter, as well as on the roof of the lecture theatre. Above the main entrance are panels of planed African Iroko (a rare and protected hardwood normally off-limits to eco-friendly projects) that was salvaged from old lab desks recovered from the university's chemistry building, designed by Denys Lasdun. The timber species was confirmed by the building's original project architect, Gordon Forbes. The remainder of the cladding is 20-year-old seasoned oak from a local timber yard, which originated from a local estate. Even the new reception desk is actually an old reception desk designed by Norman Foster for the nearby Sainsbury Centre.

OPPOSITE

FIG. 2.126 Main elevation

FIG. 2.127 Facade and columns utilising African Iroko from salvaged chemistry worktops

THE CIRCULAR ECONOMY STEP 4

[OPINION]

When completed, The Enterprise Centre was recognised as the greenest building in the UK for many sound reasons. Architype has ensured that the building is certified to Passivhaus standards, is 'carbon neutral' regarding energy consumed by the building in use, is extremely airtight and achieves BREEAM 'Outstanding' – all the 'normal' sustainable best-practice benchmarks. If that had been it, the project wouldn't be in our *Re-Use Atlas*. What is significant about this project is Architype's rigour and tenacity when considering genuinely low-carbon, closed-loop material sources and construction systems. About 40% of this high-spec building comes from the surrounding landscape, where it was grown. Around 50% of the building is compostable. Its very existence has created at least 27 new permanent jobs (as jobs formed in the supply chain serving the construction industry, not on site construction jobs) and acts as an advertisement for the potential of wealth-creating, closed-loop systems.

The cost of constructing this building, at about £2,800+VAT/m^2, is competitive when compared to a normal build rate for a building of this type and quality. The Enterprise Centre at UEA will, over its 100-year life, treat the planet with more kindness than most buildings occupied in the UK and beyond. In many ways there are parallels here with the work of Francis Kéré (see page 114). Just like Kéré, Architype has highlighted the true value of local organic materials that have been neglected, forgotten even, by the construction industry. By rediscovering the potentials of these materials to do a 'proper' job, perhaps The Enterprise Centre can provide a clear way forward for humankind to develop in a circular way. Nearly half of this building was supplied by the local landscape. One day it may return the favour and feed the landscape that has recently nourished it, or perhaps it will be dismantled and reused for future buildings, just like timber frame and thatch buildings from previous centuries.

FIG. 2.128 Most of the material in this image locks CO^2 and will compost one day

PART 2   CIRCULAR INSPIRATIONS

STEP 4 CASE STUDY No.5

Brummen Town Hall and a new HQ for Alliander, by RAU Architects and Turntoo

Eco-architects | c2c visionaries | supply chain innovators

[THE STORY]

RAU Architects was formed in the early 1990s with a remit to deliver buildings creating the smallest possible ecological footprint. Issues of energy consumption and material sources have particularly interested the practice. By the early 21st century the founder, Thomas Rau, had a high profile as both a successful architect and future thinker, keen to consider forms of development that were less dependent on raw material and so less damaging to the environment.

Not content to stick with designing buildings, in 2010 Rau, together with Sabine Oberhuber, formed Turntoo, a company dedicated to working on new 'circular' business models. The company now develops closed-loop systems, products and services for private and public organisations, which it hopes will 'facilitate the continuity of life on Earth'. The ambition is to develop an open network of companies that act as closed-loop suppliers for architectural projects. Once constructed, the buildings can be considered as 'material depots' for future projects. Turntoo has also created the concept of 'material passports' for second-hand material flows and components. By researching a particular waste source, Turntoo adds value to it, believing that 'information turns waste into valuable material'. A 'material passport' will document all the materials used in a building, noting their exact specification, including level of toxicity, location in the building (structure, skin, etc), function, as well as their ability to be dismantled for reuse or recycling. The project is still in development.

CIRCULAR LIGHTING

Perhaps the most famous partnership Turntoo has developed is its 'circular lighting' concept with Philips Lighting. The idea is simple, but quite possibly brilliant. Instead of buying light fittings, customers lease light – or, to be more precise, they lease the appropriate lux level for the function required. Leasing lux for 10 or 15 years instead of buying light fittings puts the responsibility for the maintenance, performance and disposal of said fittings firmly with the manufacturer. The idea is that this will encourage far greater levels of corporate responsibility. So, for example, as manufacturers will have to deal with the light fittings at the end of their functioning life, perhaps they will be more inclined to design their fittings for remanufacture: perhaps they will consider their products as a material resource to reuse in the future.

> **LEASE-A-JEANS**
>
> Inspired by the 'circular lighting' concept, the founder of MUD Jeans set up a lease-a-jeans company, in partnership with Turntoo. MUD Jeans states that 'on average 30% of all garments in our cupboards have not been worn for almost a year'. A year or so after you have leased your MUD Jeans, the company will accept the worn-out garment and recycle it into 'new' garments to lease. This is a particularly big deal when one considers that cotton currently has the nickname of a 'dirty crop' because although only 2.4% of the world's cultivated land is dedicated to growing cotton, it accounts for about 24% of the world's toxic insecticide market, making cotton the most toxic crop on the planet!

Two recent RAU Architects building projects that are worth considering are both situated in the Netherlands. They are the new HQ for Alliander in Duiven, which involves the reworking and extension of existing buildings, and an extension to Brummen Town Hall. Both projects are extensions to existing buildings, although Brummen Town Hall has the added challenge of conservation of a designated monument.

The original town hall in Brummen was designed as a stand-alone villa, dating from 1890. As with many municipal buildings, the original fabric had been altered and extended to such an extent as to almost obliterate the original valuable architectural heritage. RAU Architects' approach was to restore the original fabric of the villa using materials that matched the original 19th-century specifications. Materials from earlier alterations were mostly 'remanufactured' (for example, stone was crushed and the blockwork was used for the facade of the basement).

The new extension was designed to use as little material as possible, incorporating a prefabricated and modular supporting structure, with timber used for the floors and facade. This approach helped reduce the initial ecological footprint of the development and allowed for simple dismantling at the end of the building's life. It also reduced the construction time significantly. However what is more unusual, and more ambitious, is the actual design of the timber columns and beams. Rather than being designed for the specific situation on site, they have been cut in sections and lengths that are commonly used in building construction, to ensure the broadest options for reuse at the end of their time at Brummen Town Hall. Many other components and materials used on site are Cradle to Cradle Certified, which means that during their whole life cycle they have a minimum environmental impact. The lighting and flooring are on the Turntoo-type lease agreements previously mentioned.

The new Brummen Town Hall was constructed by BAM Utiliteitsbouw. The biggest challenge for these contractors was the guidelines RAU put into the construction contract – in other words, the particular way the building was to be assembled to allow 'dry' processes to replace normal 'wet trades' such as in situ cast concrete, plaster and mortar joints, as well as bolting steel elements together instead of welding.

CLOCKWISE FROM TOP (OPPOSITE)

FIG. 2.129 Work in progress on the site

FIG. 2.130 Aggregates from buildings demolished on site, being reused for new buildings on site

FIG. 2.131 Low-grade timber salvaged from pallets and used to overclad existing and new buildings

FIG. 2.132 Detail of existing building, overclad with insulation and reclaimed timber

THE CIRCULAR ECONOMY STEP 4

CLOCKWISE FROM TOP

FIG. 2.133 Photovoltaic solar panels were installed at the beginning of the construction process to power construction equipment, as well as the building in-use.

FIG. 2.134 Interior environment, highlighting reuse of reclaimed timber

FIG. 2.135 Completed building

PART 2 CIRCULAR INSPIRATIONS

The second RAU Architects project to discuss is the headquarters building for energy company Alliander, in Duiven, the Netherlands. At first glance this looks like a brand new building. However it is actually a retrofit and extension of an existing structure – an overcrowded 30-year-old office building. It was originally designed to accommodate 600 people, but the new brief asked for facilities to be expanded to allow for 1,500 people.

In RAU's design for the new headquarters, the original buildings are not immediately apparent as their original facades, including the windows, have had an additional 'skin' of second-hand, low-grade timber overlay. This provides additional insulation, which in turn reduces both heat loss and heat gain. The timber has been heated up in a controlled environment, which adds to the material's ability to be weatherproof. The insulation used with this new layer of cladding was made from shredded clothing.

A new roof over-sails both the original and new enclosed accommodation, allowing for well-lit communal social spaces and environmental 'buffer zones'. Large windows open onto the new central atrium, which helps create better levels of natural ventilation, air quality, and increased levels of natural light, and therefore greater levels of wellbeing.

Despite what appears to be a wholesale rebuild, RAU states that:

- 90% of building material remained on site, either in its original state or as material recycled on site to provide material for the new buildings created on site.
- 50% of all materials used were reused from the old buildings
- 84% of the remaining 50% of 'new' materials were tagged 'recyclable' by the NIBE (Dutch Institute for Building Ecology).

Second-hand salvaged timber was specified for the new-build elements as well as the retrofit elements. Concrete stripped out of some of the existing buildings was reused on site, as was steelwork. Asphalt from existing roofs was reused on site, as well as existing toilets and ceiling plates. Even existing doors were turned into furniture. The steel structure for the new mega-roof was designed with the help of a roller-coaster manufacturer with experience in designing with the minimum amount of material. The resultant structure was 30% lighter than normal, using 35% less material, and allows for disassembly at the end of the building's life. 'Raw material passports' were applied to all materials supplied to this development. RAU is confident this will ensure that the potential for this building to be a material depot for future developments will be met.

This building is 'carbon neutral' as far as in-use energy consumption is concerned: the building generates a surplus of energy which is distributed via a local energy grid. However, it was also the first 'energy positive' construction site in the Netherlands, if not Europe. That was achieved by using renewable energy generated by photovoltaic panels installed on the roof of the parking deck. These same cells now produce energy for the completed building. The construction site was also the cleanest construction site in the Netherlands. All surplus materials were sorted and prepared for reuse and recycling.

By creating the infrastructure, systems and knowledge to support a circular system, RAU Architects appears to have ensured that this building will in time become a valuable material resource for future generations who may not have access to the raw materials we take for granted today.

[OPINION]

Turntoo critically unpacks conventional procurement methods, material specifications, contracts with suppliers and maintenance agreements. RAU Architects has established a reputation as an imaginative practice testing ideas of sustainable development. However, it is with Turntoo that it has the potential to create the mechanisms (the specifications and contractual agreements) and crucially the new concepts (leasing products, 'material passports', buildings as material stores) that the design and manufacturing industries need if we are to start changing well-established unintelligent linear processes into genuine circular closed-loop systems.

FIG. 2.136 The ultra-lightweight steel roof, designed by a roller-coaster manufacturer, is bolted together for easy reuse

132   PART 2   CIRCULAR INSPIRATIONS

STEP 4 CASE STUDY No.6

New City Hall, Venlo, the Netherlands, by C2C ExpoLAB with Kraaijvanger Architects

C2C-branded city | C2C-certified supply chain

[THE STORY]

When Bas van de Westerlo of C2C ExpoLAB completed his building engineering Masters thesis in 2008, by his own admission he had no interest in sustainable design, which he dismissed as just 'being less bad'. However this all changed when he saw the documentary 'Waste = Food'.[7] So moved was he by the concept of Cradle to Cradle that within a year van de Westerlo had attended a C2C training course in Hamburg at what is nicknamed 'the Cradle of Cradle to Cradle' – the Environment Protection Encouragement Agency (EPEA), formed by Michael Braungart. Van de Westerlo is now a certified Cradle to Cradle Consultant in the built environment and governmental processes at the C2C ExpoLAB.

When van de Westerlo joined C2C ExpoLAB in 2010, the company was employed as project manager and C2C advisor for the new city hall in Venlo, the Netherlands. Since 2008 the city of Venlo had committed to the principles of Cradle to Cradle by investing in a C2C Master Plan, overseen by Cradle to Cradle authors Michael Braungart and William McDonough.[8] It was hoped that the principles of Cradle to Cradle could potentially give Venlo a new visionary identity and increase sustainable economic growth.

In 2008 when Venlo embraced its C2C Master Plan many within the municipal council didn't actually know what this meant: it was a leap of faith. However, this approach gave the team at C2C ExpoLAB an extraordinary opportunity to apply their recently gained skills as C2C consultants. All they needed was a design team and building contractors who could deliver on the city's visionary ideals.

With the support of the city, ExpoLAB drafted a brief for an open architectural design competition that had, as van de Westerlo states, 'a red line focused on Cradle to Cradle principles running through the entire process'. The competition attracted 54 submissions from across Europe and five teams were shortlisted. They were given a one-day 'C2C inspiration workshop' with McDonough+Partners and Braungart, then had a further two weeks to produce their vision of what a C2C city hall would look like – and, crucially, *how* it would be delivered. Kraaijvanger Architects from Rotterdam won.

The design process was interesting as the team needed to flush out in very little time what was achievable as far as C2C principles were concerned. The design team employed a technique van de Westerlo calls 'pressure cooker sessions'. Over five long days in one week the whole design team sat in one studio. They invited many suppliers and experts in and

PART 2 CIRCULAR INSPIRATIONS

asked them questions about the viability of C2C products, systems, design techniques, etc. By the end of that week they had a detailed sketch scheme for the building. This technique was employed every month after that for the whole of the design development process.

The financial context for this project was testing, with Venlo facing economic difficulties. Capital projects needed to be cut back by €20 million in one year alone. C2C was seen by the controlling city council as an economic principle as much as anything else – C2C-inspired buildings should not attract costs in excess of 'normal' construction rates. At over €46 million, the city hall was by far the largest project and ripe for cost cuts. So van de Westerlo and his colleagues were asked to 'value engineer' out the vast green wall designed to purify air for the building's interiors, as well as acting as a 'lung' emitting clean air to its immediate surroundings. The large array of photovoltaic panels creating clean energy for future occupants was also to be omitted. Over €3.4 million of savings were identified: so far so normal. However, C2C ExpoLAB and the design team then did something quite unusual – they calculated the amount of cost savings these omitted items would bring to the city if they were installed during the 40-year lifespan of the building. This resulted in an estimated €16.9

....

CLOCKWISE FROM TOP LEFT (OPPOSITE)

FIG. 2.137 Exposed concrete frame at Venlo City Hall, one of the 'less bad' decisions the design team had to make to meet the construction budget

FIG. 2.138 View of Venlo City Hall

FIG. 2.139 View of Venlo City Hall's green 'breathing' wall

FIG. 2.140 Central garden court at Venlo City Hall

FIG. 2.141 Detail of green 'breathing' wall

million benefit to the city if the green wall and photovoltaic panels were kept in the project. Both elements were retained. The design team sees this as one of the most positive outcomes of the project.

The next success for this project was the number of new C2C Certified products created because of this development. At the beginning of the design process there were only five products with a C2C Certificate, so the design team did extensive market research throughout the design process. They invited many suppliers to their studios and convinced them to change their manufacturing processes, supply chains, and the way they provided their products to clients. They convinced more than 30 suppliers to change their linear processes into circular ones, including the green wall suppliers.

The value of the interior fitting for this building is over €2 million. C2C ExpoLAB wrote a short clause in the tender documents that asked for the suppliers of these fittings to estimate the amount of money that they would be prepared to pay the clients to receive back these fittings in ten years' time, at the so-called 'end of their useful life'. The successful company stated that it would guarantee paying the clients 18% of the value of these fittings, which amounts to around €360,000. This money will benefit the city hall, but also shows that the suppliers are seeing their products as a material store for the future.

The design team did have to omit one big idea from their plans. The concrete frame for the building is cast in situ so it cannot be disassembled at the end of the building's life. Concrete also has a very large carbon footprint. The design team had wanted a timber frame for this 11-storey building. It was not cost-effective and C2C buildings must be that to be credible.

THE CIRCULAR ECONOMY **STEP 4** 135

Subsequently, they had tried to reuse the concrete frame from the old city hall but that was found to contain toxins and so was not safe for recycling. The old frame was then crushed up and 'down-cycled' to provide hard core for a new road. So the team interviewed concrete manufacturers and tried to find solutions to this difficult challenge, to take the first steps towards a circular construction. They found a supplier that was prepared to change the make-up of its product so that it was not as carbon-hungry as normal by specifying up to '100% granulate in some instances'. Van de Westerlo points out that when the building is in use the frame is a 'carbon sink' that reduces CO_2 omissions due to heating and cooling. This is an argument that people in the world of sustainable design have used for decades to justify the use of concrete, although C2C advocates would dismiss this as 'being less bad'.

[OPINION]

It is difficult to judge what the real successes of this project will be – when I interviewed van de Westerlo the building had been occupied for only one week. It will take time to assess its real impact, not just on its occupants and the city of Venlo, but also on those people who are putting their faith in Cradle to Cradle's ambitious view of what a circular economy might look like. I am assured that the building is being rigorously monitored post-occupation. As well as the normal points of interest – such as energy consumption ($kgCO_2/m^2/$annum), levels of rainwater harvesting and black water filtration – air quality (from the green 'lung' that is the growing wall system) and the quantity of materials coming in and leaving the building are also to be recorded for evaluation. So one day soon we will see if this investment in C2C philosophies is paying dividends.

At the point of going to press it was not even possible to ascertain what percentage of this building was constructed to C2C principles and therefore how successful it is from that point of view. How much of this building, for example, can be considered a 'material store for the future'? It is interesting that when defending a decision for specifying a concrete frame over the more costly timber one, the designers had to resort to 'being less bad', which goes against the ethos of Cradle to Cradle principles. However, these are very early days in the world of procuring truly C2C buildings. What we can say is that the new City Hall in Venlo is one of the best examples of a building completely inspired by the C2C ethos, and it's hard to knock a design team actively trying to do good 'for people, the environment and the economy'.

I am particularly impressed by the fact that at the beginning of the design process there were only five Cradle to Cradle Certified products specified for this project. However, due to the rigorous interrogation of their supply chain (no mean feat), the design team was able to convince many of their suppliers to alter the supply, manufacture and life-cycle processes of another 30–40 products so that they could achieve C2C Certification.

PART 2 CIRCULAR INSPIRATIONS

INTERVIEW WITH AN EXPERT

Nigel Stansfield, Vice President and Chief Supply Chain Officer at Interface

Interface is a large multinational company that has been producing carpet tiles for the interior design industry since 1973. Since 1994 the company has been considering how to make the process of producing carpet tiles less harmful to the natural environment. Here I interview Nigel Stansfield, who has recently taken up the post of Vice President and Chief Supply Chain Officer, which among other tasks makes him responsible for delivering on the company's 'Mission Zero' declaration by 2020, as well as nurturing the hugely interesting Net-Works initiative.

DBB: How long have you worked at Interface?

NS: I've been in the industry all my working life. The carpet and weaving company I worked for was acquired by Interface in 1997, and I have been here ever since.

DBB: Tell me about Interface's commitment to reducing its negative impact on Planet Earth.

NS: The founder of our business announced our intent in 1994, but with nothing to refer to we had to build our 'road map' from scratch. We looked at our emissions, energy use and how much of that was from renewables. We also looked at how much material we used, including waste, and how much went into product that provided value to clients, and a variety of different metrics which we called 'Eco-metrics'.

We have used the same set of metrics since 1996 and every year we release the latest data and compare it to the previous year's.

DBB: Who devised your plan in the first place?

NS: We started by forming an 'Eco Dream Team' which had a number of independent green thinkers, such as Amory B Lovins from the Rocky Mountain Institute, Paul Hawken, who wrote The Ecology of Commerce, Janine Benyus, who wrote Biomimicry: Innovation inspired by nature [9] and the scientist Karl-Henrik Robèrt, who wrote The Natural Step: a framework for achieving sustainability in our organisations.[10] We also had Bill McDonough (Cradle to Cradle) and environmentalist and writer Jonathon Porritt. We used the system conditions outlined within The Natural Step as the 'founding father', if you like, of our

INTERVIEW WITH AN EXPERT   STEP 4

sustainability agenda, which allowed us to plot the path to what we called 'Mission Zero'. The whole business went through seven measurement metrics, called 'the Seven Fronts to Sustainability', which also inform our eco-metrics. This methodology is still used today even though we are much more mature in our sustainable development thinking. We are far more 'systems thinking' orientated now, but the objectives and goals agreed over 20 years ago are still important.

DBB: **So do you have an independent agency auditing this?**

NS: Any claims we make around renewable energy or recycled content have to come with third-party verification, and we ask the same of our suppliers. They get third-party verification of the product from organisations such as Bureau Veritas or Lloyds of London, depending upon the product. However, we always look for independent corroboration.

DBB: **Interface has famously pledged, via its Mission Statement, to be the first company to show the entire industrial world what sustainability is, in all its forms, by 2020. How is this progressing?**

NS: We [have] mapped the last four or five years just to see what needs to be done. Obviously as we get closer to achieving 'Mission Zero' the goals get more difficult to achieve, and more expensive. Before I took up my current post I was running the Global Sustainability Leadership Team for Interface. We plotted the road map to delivering 'Mission Zero' by 2020, looking at what we needed to do to make it work financially and technically. We also re-formed part of the 'Green Team' to look at what we needed to do beyond 2020.

[Since this interview, Interface has announced its new 'Climate Take Back' mission statement, which replaces 'Mission Zero'. The new mission statement includes four key commitments:

- We will bring carbon home and reverse climate change.
- We will create supply chains that benefit all life.
- We will make factories that are like forests.
- We will transform dispersed materials into products and goodness.]

DBB: **These are exciting times then. You are on the last push to reach your 'Mission Zero Targets' after more than 20 years.**

NS: Yes, but 'Mission Zero' has always been about doing 'less harm', about minimising the impact towards this mystical point of zero. Frankly, doing less harm is just not good enough anymore.

DBB: **From the point of view of Interface's production of goods that have a genuine zero impact, the manufacturing and distribution processes will need to be carbon neutral (at least) as well. How are you tackling these challenges?**

NS: We have six manufacturing plants around the world: one in North America, two in Europe, one in Australia, one in China and one in Thailand, which all run on 100% renewable electricity. In Holland we were able to move over to biogas from an anaerobic digestion plant nearby. Last year we were able to convert our factory in the USA, which is our biggest plant, to bio-directed gas as well. So our overall gas and electricity renewal footprint over our entire manufacturing process is now at about 85%.

DBB: So with the reduction in conventional energy needs and your ever-increasing reliance on waste materials to create your products, is Interface seeing increased profits as a direct result of the 'Mission Zero' initiatives?

NS: Renewable energy is generally quite a bit more expensive compared to the 'brown' sources. You make the company more energy efficient so that when you move to renewable energy the cost is not burdensome. Since the mid-1990s, when we created our 'baseline', we have reduced the amount of energy required to make a square metre of product by about 45%. We are now at a point where we can financially justify switching to renewables, but it's more about a whole holistic philosophy around how you tackle each of these issues. It's a similar point with waste to landfill. We have virtually no waste to landfill from our manufacturing plants. In theory, anybody could claim this statistic if they collected their waste and incinerated it, but that is not the right philosophy. First of all we reduced the amount of material we need to make a square metre of product by 'de-materialising' them without compromising their performance or aesthetics. As you de-materialise your products and bring in alternate product streams such as bio-base fibres etc, you become more process-efficient through your manufacturing and you get less by-product. We measure everything during the manufacturing process, including activity-based waste, process waste and product waste, with the idea of eliminating all waste as a by-product of manufacturing our products. This gives you a completely different philosophy about waste: it is no longer waste, it is 'food' for another process.

DBB: Could we now dwell on Interface's hugely inspiring 'Net-Works' programme? How did it come about?

NS: We started what became 'Net-Works' by exploring the idea of a socially inclusive supply chain in 2005. Our products were beginning to 'speak' about environmental issues relating to what they were made of and how they were made, but they hadn't considered social sustainability. We now wanted to see how we could introduce a social dimension into our products so that they would communicate environmental and social sustainability as well. We started to look for business models that were socially inclusive. The World Business Council for Sustainable Development (WBCSD) had been working on 'The Sustainable Livelihoods Business Model', which broadly supported what we now refer to as 'inclusive business'. The principle suggested that there is a way of connecting some of the poorest people in the world to your supply chain in a transparent and fair way so that you and your supply chain all benefit in the long term. It is about developing fair and inclusive business models that have longevity and are not dependent on the big organisations being charitable.

DBB: So how did you start this programme?

NS: We started in India, as it famously has a very long heritage of weaving using natural fibres such as river grass, bamboo, coconut fibres, etc. We found some partners, including the National Institute of Design in Ahmedabad and an NGO, and started to develop an idea for products made completely from material and skills indigenous to this particular area of India. We eventually produced a handmade carpet tile that we could sell into our European markets as a representative of social sustainability. Although we learned an awful lot, unfortunately commercially it was unsuccessful. The product was so far removed from everything else we did that it became a really niche product. After that we realised that if we were to continue with a socially inclusive business model we needed to make sure that the product we made was representative of our standard products.

At the same time as we deduced this, we had been working with one of our suppliers, a company in northern Italy called Aquafil (www.aquafil.com), pioneering the development of recycled nylon under the 'Econyl' brand and the Econyl regeneration system. Aquafil had been a partner of Interface since the mid-1990s so they had been with us all the way on the 'Mission Zero' journey. They developed a 'depolymerisation' technology that takes waste nylon and breaks it back down to its raw material constituents so that it could be rebuilt back up to 'new' nylon again. They invested about €60 million in building a material recycling plant, which now receives lots of different nylon waste streams. While doing research on potential material opportunities for this facility, the owner found that there was a big opportunity in reprocessing commercial fishing nets. For years he has been collecting these massive commercial fishing nets, mainly from large fishing farms in Scotland and Norway, and recycling them using the process. We looked into the viability of finding waste fishing nets from other sources that complemented this process. In the meantime we would be connecting some of the poorest communities in the world into our supply chain by setting up systems and a process of collecting their fishing nets from their island communities.

During the development of the project that became 'Net-Works' we held a workshop in London in about 2010. One of the participants was Dr Nick Hill of The Zoological Society of London (ZSL), who had completed his PhD in the Philippines. He said that there were a lot of discarded fishing nets on beaches and in the coral reefs surrounding the Philippines. So we sponsored him to go back and study the situation in depth while appraising the potential for an inclusive business opportunity. We then decided to set up just such a partnership with these fishing communities, who traditionally throw away their crab fishing nets every couple of months as they are not repairable. The problem associated with these discarded nets is massive. They have ruined beaches, trapping and killing turtles, fish, sharks and birds, and they are killing off the coral reefs. However by setting up these fishing communities as independent businesses, they were empowered and we now had another supply chain. As a material source, the nets collected in the Philippines are indistinguishable from those collected in Scotland or Norway. In each of the sites where we set up Net-Works we have either piggy-backed onto an existing micro-financing scheme or we have set up our own, so that funds can be controlled and a successful business model can be used. Now each of these communities has access to finance and the appropriate banking infrastructure. They run Net-Works through that but they also run other businesses through it and they all now stand on their own feet as independent businesses.

DBB: This is such a great good news story.

NS: It is so gratifying to be involved in these projects. I've been out to the Philippines to these villages and watched the community banking meetings take place. Without doubt Net-Works is one of the proudest things people in our company talk about.

We originally piloted Net-Works in two areas of the Philippines and they have been running for a couple of years. It takes about 18 months to two years to set them up. It is quite a complicated process. So we are now building a Net-Works toolkit which will be available to other people who want to do this sort of thing.

DBB: You now have a successful working model. There are a lot of waste fishing nets out there. Could Interface not become a material supplier to other companies?

NS: Absolutely. We are speaking to some of Aquafil's customers. We are now setting up other Net-Work initiatives. We have three sites now in the Philippines and are looking to expand. A year ago we set up in Cameroon and they are only just starting to collect discarded nets. We will also have other sites coming on stream in the near future. We are currently preparing a proposal for our main board that considers a plan to expand the Net-Works idea exponentially.

DBB: So your company will be partially responsible for cleaning up our oceans and shorelines. That's quite an accomplishment.

NS: It demonstrates what inclusive business is all about. It's good for us as an organisation, it's good for the individuals and it's good for the environment. We can see a time when Marine Protection Areas (MPAs) will be expanded and Net-Works will be one of the ingredients that has facilitated that.

DBB: Could I now change the subject a little bit. My book tries to answer some of the challenges laid down in Cradle to Cradle. Am I correct in thinking that Interface hasn't tried to get any of its products Cradle to Cradle Certified?

NS: That is correct. We don't adopt the Cradle to Cradle (C2C) labelling system, but some of the philosophy of C2C we obviously adopt. We were applying a lot of these principles before the term 'circular economy' was widely understood.

DBB: So perhaps as Interface has been pursuing C2C principles for a long time, and also because you have an independent auditing system, Interface doesn't need the C2C Certification process to prove that its products address the aspirations of a circular economy?

NS: To be perfectly honest we were very sceptical of the C2C Certification process in the beginning. This was mainly because initially both authors were also responsible for the certification process. It wasn't a transparent self-certification system when it was first launched. The methodology wasn't clear, and you had to buy into the process to understand what it was. In effect, the people selling you the methodology were the same people validating the methodology. So we stuck with our original strategy of having our 'Mission Zero' annually audited by independent third-party assessors. The Cradle to Cradle Certification process is now independently audited by a third party outside of their organisation. However, the people sitting on that auditing committee all appear to be practitioners of Cradle to Cradle.

DBB: **Could you comment on a Cradle to Cradle/circular economy concept that is gaining popularity, that of selling a 'service' rather than selling a 'product'. Is it something Interface is considering?**

NS: There were two strategies we launched in the mid-1990s. The first was our 'Re-entry Programme' from 1995, an initiative to take back old carpet material. We also launched 'Evergreen Lease', our product leasing programme. They were both linked to each other because if you have a product leasing programme you need a system in place to deal with said material at the end of its life, ie the 'Re-entry Programme'. The 'Re-entry Programme' has taken back nearly 136,000 tonnes of material and then recycled it into Interface carpet tiles. At the beginning we were only collecting our own product. Now we collect other companies' product for recycling into our product. We have also developed social reuse programmes as well, and sometimes the returned product can be resold instead of recycled. What we have learned from how nature works (biomimicry) is that invariably nature does not recycle its own waste within its own 'kingdom'. This showed us that we had to find partners to support us with this recycling, so we supply other industries with our waste for recycling and other industries supply us with material. This leads us towards one of our key activities beyond 2020: to stop thinking of materials as waste and start thinking about them as raw materials, and start 'harvesting' these materials from other industries. We have been doing that for the last ten years, with fishing nets being an obvious example. We also use waste from the construction industry. So the 'Re-entry Programme' has developed and grown from its inception in 1995. We are now actively looking to harvest waste material and bring it into our supply chain.

The leasing concept still exists for us. However it has not been popular and remains a challenge for us. Invariably carpets installed in new-build projects are fixed under 'capital' not under 'revenue'. That capital budget sits with one person and the revenue budget, where lease agreements normally sit, is elsewhere. So we have found it very difficult to find a successful continuous path to deliver lease agreements for carpets, although we continue to offer it as an option. However I don't believe that by not having a leasing option for our products we preclude the 'circular economy' in the way we function.

PART 3

The Waste House Story

[A STEP 2 PROJECT]

Duncan Baker-Brown

THE STORY

IN JUNE 2014 THE AUTHOR completed the construction of the Brighton Waste House, Europe's first permanent building made of approximately 90% materials others threw away or discarded.[1] It is also a low-energy building with an EPC rating of A, as well as being classified as a 'carbon negative' building, because it creates 25% more energy than it consumes. It was originally commissioned by the University of Brighton as a vehicle for the author to test the idea that collaborative 'live' construction projects were excellent pedagogic tools for young designers and makers (and older ones) to learn about the challenges of delivering on the ideals of sustainable design. The Waste House also aimed to prove that under-valued so-called waste material has potential to become a valuable resource and therefore prove 'that there is no such thing as waste, just stuff in the wrong place'. It also aims to prove that a contemporary, innovative, low-energy building can be constructed almost entirely by young people studying construction trades, architecture and design. To this end, over 360 students from the University of Brighton and City College, supported by apprentices and an experienced site agent from The Mears Group, worked together on the project, which was initially fabricated in the workshops of City College, and then assembled and completed on site by students and apprentices between May 2013 and April 2014.

More of a provocation than a future way to construct buildings, the Waste House is a 'live' research project that gets people thinking about where materials come from and where they end up. Materials that have gone into the house include old vinyl banners that you might see tied to street lamps during festivals. These tend to be date-sensitive and are therefore only used once, but in the Waste House they are being reused as internal vapour control layers. Construction waste such as bricks, ply sheets, timber off-cuts and plasterboard are supplemented with everyday domestic 'rubbish' including thousands of toothbrushes, 2 tonnes of denim, 4,000 DVDs and 4,000 video cassettes, which were slotted into wall cavities creating low-grade insulation for the house. These unusual walls are currently being monitored by a PhD student from the Faculty of Science and Engineering, to see how efficient their insulation qualities are. Old floppy discs are also being used in the wall cavities, while 10 tonnes of chalk, destined for landfill, creates a rammed chalk wall, with help from a compressor and pneumatic rammer. Heavy material such as rammed earth can contribute to the overall energy efficiency of buildings by storing heat until it is needed.

Introduction

Themes influencing the project

1 The UK generated 200 million tonnes of waste in 2012; 50% of this was generated by construction. Commercial and industrial activities generated 24%, with households responsible for a further 14%.[2]

2 Approximately 20% of all material arriving on building sites ends up incinerated or going to landfill: 30% of this is new material never used. Finding ways to reduce or eliminate waste from the construction process could help reduce environmental destruction from mining etc, as well as add value to material resource currently defined as waste.[3]

3 Many large corporations are very concerned about resource security and high levels of taxation associated with corporate responsibility (including dealing with waste/end of life products). They are taking issues of reuse and by association principles laid out in *Cradle to Cradle*[4] very seriously. The circular economy has the potential to galvanise industries that are looking to make money providing services and goods while working in harmony with the planet.

4 Proving that material currently discarded as waste can make a contemporary public building that performs to very high standards will draw attention to waste's potential as a valuable resource. This could lead to a reduction in the amount of waste created in the future, a change in construction techniques to promote low-waste alternatives such as off-site fabrication, and designing for demolition/remanufacture, while creating new jobs within this sector.

5 Learning about designing and constructing buildings is often undertaken in academic and vocational 'silos'. The need to share research data, whether academic or from a 'live' construction site, is particularly important in the UK as many so-called 'low-energy' projects do not perform as well as expected when occupied.[5] Designing and constructing in a 'circular' or sustainable manner is hugely challenging and currently very difficult to achieve. Getting the whole design team (designers, makers, suppliers and constructors) to work together, so they can learn together and from each other, and to document the outcomes, is perhaps the main objective of this ongoing project.

Methodology

'The House that Kevin Built', 2008

The Brighton Waste House was originally conceived as the rebuild of 'The House that Kevin Built' from 2008.

'The House that Kevin Built' or 'THTKB'[6] was designed utilising two construction systems that promoted the use of timber and other organic, plant-based materials. Both systems were designed by architects passionate about creating genuinely sustainable developments, with a consideration of the amount of CO_2 emissions and energy consumption associated with the manufacturing process. Both systems specified locally sourced, sustainably managed material.

The first system is ModCell®. These are prefabricated panels constructed of highly engineered 400mm-deep (front to back) timber box frames in-filled with either Limecrete® or straw bales. We used the straw bale system because these heavyweight panels, which exhibit both high levels of insulation and thermal mass, were constructed near to the building site in a barn that ModCell® refers to as a 'flying factory'. ModCell® assembles its engineered frames in the barn and then uses straw to infill the panels, before finishing them off on both sides with lime render. ModCell® can then legitimately claim to be specifying local organic materials. ModCell® panels (approx 3m wide and 2.7m high) weigh about 1.5 tonnes each, so we used them on the ground floor of THTKB.

The design team then specified a lightweight ply box construction system using 12mm ply sheet. This system, known as Facit®, was fabricated using a computer-controlled CNC laser cutter. The first floor walls and roof were designed with 3D CAD software. Every Facit® box was individually numbered and cut out with the CNC laser cutter. There was virtually no wastage as the computer ensured that as many panels as possible were cut out of each sheet. The computer guaranteed an amazing degree of accuracy, resulting in no errors on site and therefore no waste material. We used the same CAD system and laser cutter system to create the louvred rain screen cladding to finish off the upper floor external walls. These two systems (ModCell® and Facit®) were assembled on site in less than three days and created the external fabric of the house. The Facit® boxes were filled with cellulose insulation made from waste paper blown into pre-drilled holes in the boxes.

The roof was finished in an array of solar tiles, creating electricity and hot water for the underfloor heating system. These solar panels were some of the first to be fully integrated into a roof and form the actual waterproof layer.

THTKB: the rebuild

THTKB took just six days to construct. It was presented by Kevin McCloud, filmed and aired each evening on Channel 4 to over 5 million viewers as 'Grand Designs Live'. Although a success in as much as this innovative construction project was completed and built on time, I was frustrated that there seemed little understanding of why this project was in fact innovative. THTKB was dismantled two days after completion and put into temporary storage. Though there had been plans to rebuild THTKB at the Building Research Establishment (BRE) in its Innovation Park in Gaston, Watford, this did not come to fruition, which provided an opportunity to try and get the building reconstructed in Brighton.

The idea emerged of reconstructing this unusual building on the campus of the University of Brighton, which would allow the process to involve architecture, design and construction students, and enable it to become an innovative and effective pedagogic tool. However, it was not possible to rebuild the original building, so the original material and components were returned to their suppliers. The ground floor walls supplied by ModCell® now form part of a demonstration research project at the University of Bath.

It wasn't looking good for the rebuild project, but the idea of a 'live' research construction project had struck a chord with the Dean of the Faculty of Arts and Humanities at the University of Brighton, who instigated a fundraising campaign in October 2010 to rebuild THTKB reusing new material to the exact specification of the original.

In 2011, the University of Brighton gifted a piece of land that would place the project within the campus of the Faculty of Arts and Humanities, in central Brighton. This positioning was crucial to facilitating another ambition for the project, that of public accessibility. It was envisioned that THTKB would be a community 'hub', a place shared by academics and students from the university, as well as local community groups, businesses and schools.

Developing the design thesis and design team

The UK construction industry is wasteful, often discarding around 20% of all material that arrives on a construction site. I became convinced that we could create a new construction project tackling broader issues than those embraced by THTKB, and deliver the UK's first permanent building made from material discarded by the construction industry.

To prove that it was possible to construct a building using waste material, it was crucial that this project would not be another temporary shed or bus shelter. We had to create a permanent building, with very high levels of energy efficiency that attained full planning and Building Regulations approval. This would ensure that all students and other partners involved would learn how to construct an authentic low-energy building, something that was lacking within the design and construction industry, and that this process would be properly recorded for others to learn from.

In April 2012 I called a mini 'waste summit', where I met Cat Fletcher, who helped form Freegle UK, 'an exchange for unwanted stuff', with over 2.2 million subscribers. Together we met with Dr Ryan Woodard, a Research Fellow at the University of Brighton, who has been working in waste management research for more than 15 years, along with product designer and academic Nick Gant and Diana Lock from the environmental management consultancy Remade South East. We contrived a plan for redesigning the build so that it was constructed of waste and surplus material from the construction industry. Following Fletcher's suggestion, we also considered collecting items of waste material currently flooding domestic waste sites – material such as VHS videotapes and CDs. The idea developed from a project that focused only on waste from the construction industry to one that would raise awareness of how wasteful we all are in our everyday domestic lives. This would open up the project to a bigger audience, as well as changing it from an exemplar construction project that could directly inform the construction of many other buildings to something more akin to a polemic, a thought provoker. As the judges of the 2015 RIBA Stephen Lawrence Prize noted: 'The Brighton Waste House has sufficient scientific integrity to be taken seriously by the construction industry and just enough political clout to influence recycling policy. It is clear this interesting project will continue to question important issues of recycling that affect everyone.'[7]

The design team for the Waste House comprised architects (BBM Sustainable Design), structural engineers (BBP Consulting Engineers) and environmental engineers (Robinson Associates). My role was brief definer, coordinator and academic. This team had previously worked very successfully on THTKB four years earlier.

Developing the detail design

It was agreed that the building should be designed to be as energy efficient as possible. Due to the unusual constraint of being built with waste, the design team didn't try to deliver a project that met Code for Sustainable Homes or BREEAM requirements. It was decided to run an IES (Integrated Environmental Solutions) digital model to set energy-efficiency benchmarks relating to the site, the programme, the form and orientation, levels of U-values required through the external fabric, as well as ideas for the cost-effective primary energy source (conventional and renewable). It was decided that the building would be electric as far as heat and power were concerned due to services constraints on site. Also, the mechanical, electrical and power installations would be designed to be as efficient as possible: the building would not show an array of 'green technologies' as many demonstration eco-houses do, as these buildings are often overly complicated and too expensive. The team wanted to prove that this low-energy building made of waste would be cost effective, fuel efficient, and that it could be built on time and on budget.

The first challenge was to decide on the design of the load-bearing walls or frame for the building. The team had previously been successful at sourcing second-hand timber from skips and ply sheeting from large top tier construction contractors for temporary pavilions exhibiting student work. It was decided to take advantage of this by designing a timber and ply frame comprising 400x400mm section beams and 400x400mm section columns at approximately 2.5m centres. In between the columns we designed 400mm-deep, 900mm-wide and 2400mm-high ply boxes (like cupboards). We called these boxes 'cassettes', which would later prove a bit confusing. However, it was these cassettes that provided the opportunity for collecting, and in effect storing, waste material from sources other than the construction industry.

The vaulted roof structure over the top-floor studio was initially designed as a glue-laminated timber truss. (Enquiries into sourcing a glue-lamination press led to me finding one of the best partners for the project, discussed later on in this chapter.)

A 4kW array of photovoltaic solar panels sits on the largest south-facing facet of the roof. It provides approximately 25% more electricity than the building requires over a year.

Current Building Regulations U-value levels for the roof, external walls and ground floor were achieved by applying 'returned' and/or damaged polyurethane insulation (normally used in the construction of buildings), secured to the outer face of the 400x400mm timber box frame and 'cassettes'. This 400mm external 'wall zone' was used for 'storing' waste material, either heavyweight material providing internal air temperature stabilising 'thermal mass' or lightweight material providing, to various degrees of success, additional insulation. All walls were to be monitored for condensation, temperature and off-gassing.

It was decided that external windows and doors would be supplied as new high-performance units. Second-hand units are not easy to source and their thermal effectiveness could not be relied upon. The team felt that waiting for second-hand high-performance units would delay the project for a year or so, as the whole design revolved around the size of external openings.

The design of the foundations and 'over-site' was agreed as low-carbon concrete – concrete with a 40%-reduced cement content (replaced with pulverised fuel ash), plus aggregates from demolished concrete buildings. It was not possible on this project to avoid the specification of cement. The ground conditions were quite unstable as they were made-up ground with (rather ironically) a high degree of spoil (including composting rubbish) from a former car park.

In addition to the specification of below-ground drainage and generic 'performance specifications' for other key elements, this was the extent of the design that initially went to Building Control for a Conditional Building Regulations Approval. Building Control was hugely supportive of this project, allowing us to develop the rest of the design during the construction of the building. The Building Control Officer even attended design development meetings on site.

The construction team

The Mears Group, a national contractor charged with servicing and maintaining a large percentage of the UK's social housing stock, including Brighton and Hove's, was keen to help build the project as it had a healthy apprenticeship scheme in Brighton and wanted an opportunity for its apprentices. In the spring of 2011 the Mears Team stabilised the ground on site, constructed the foundations, installed the drainage and cast the ground floor slab for the Waste House. Mears also agreed to provide an experienced site agent to run the construction site, together with its apprentices. We planned to start works on site in the autumn of 2012.

It was during this period that I had a fortuitous meeting with tutors delivering construction courses at City College Brighton and Hove, as I wanted to see if they could construct a glue-laminated timber beam for the roof of the building. City College couldn't make a glue-lam beam, but they did want to build the Waste House: every year they build the equivalent of a new house in their three-storey workshops. In addition to this, the team employed Cat Fletcher of Freegle UK to source waste material for the project. The team was finalised.

Results

The construction and learning process

Mears took control of the construction site and was responsible for security, coordination and all aspects of health and safety. In addition, Mears supplied up to four apprentices every day. However, the Mears team was on standby to do 'normal' Mears work on nearby housing estates, so they would often have to leave site. Mears was the 'main contractor'. In addition to this, the project had City College student carpenters, electricians, plumbers, bricklayers, decorators and so on, supervised by qualified tutors. They were the subcontractors. City College students would be on site two or three times a week; however, the site agent wouldn't know if he had two students to work with or 30. Managing a construction site with an unknown number of relatively untrained subcontractors was one of the biggest challenges for this project. Despite this, the building frame was constructed within three months by students in City College workshops and then assembled and completed by 360 students, apprentices and volunteers on site in only 12 months. In addition, we had specialist suppliers who would often install their products or systems in partnership with our young constructors and their tutors.

During the on-site construction period there was a Volunteer Summer School Camp in 2013. More than 50 students completed the most challenging part of the construction process during this period – the vaulted roof structure. Some 25 of the volunteers were City College students, and another 25 were architecture students, with many of those from the Interior Architecture School (part of the University of Brighton's School of Architecture and Design). This was perhaps the most profitable time for skills and learning exchange among students, apprentices and the professional tradespeople we had on site. It was the one period of time where design students could spend three, four, maybe six weeks in a row working on site. Some of these committed design students became so adept at their new trade that they ran small teams of volunteer carpenters on site – teams that included City College carpentry students. It was during this time that Mears promoted five City College students to apprentices because of their work on our project. A number of our students received Achievement Awards from Mears.

We also worked with deaf students, as well as a number of students with learning and behavioural difficulties. Construction sites have always been a social and intellectual leveller, and so it proved with the Waste House. We recorded 25 short films during the construction period that included interviews with students from all institutions taking part. We also welcomed more than 750 pupils from local primary and secondary schools, as well as other technical colleges from around the south-east. This unusual learning environment was completely facilitated by our immensely patient site agent David Pendegrass, who had to do a health and safety induction for every person who arrived on site, whether they wanted to work or simply visit; and remember, he also had to get the Waste House built on budget and on time. This he did.

Locating appropriate waste material

I would meet the construction team on site every week to check progress and identify materials and products that needed to be sourced. Often the conversation would involve the site agent and Cat Fletcher. There were two strategies in place to find material. The first strategy was the conventional one: Mears, BBM and City College Brighton and Hove employed their contacts and networks within the construction industry to source second-hand, surplus and waste construction material.

The second strategy was less conventional. Cat Fletcher used her Freegle UK social media networks to locate waste material. Individuals, local authorities, building contractors and suppliers, schools and businesses from all over the UK supplied the project with materials such as 25,000 toothbrushes from Gatwick Airport, 2 tonnes of waste denim, 4,000 VHS video cassettes and 4,000 DVDs.

In addition, I sourced waste material from demolition sites that my practice, BBM, were working on. UK VAT rules dictate that retrofit and extension works to residential properties attract VAT at 20%, but new-build residential projects are 'zero-rated' and attract no VAT. BBM was working on a project where, to avoid VAT in excess of £360,000, the client instructed that his home be completely demolished. BBM collected timber from the demolition and reused it to form the vaulted roof structure of the Waste House. As an aside, I am currently campaigning with the Green Party to alter VAT to favour retrofit projects over new-builds.

Utilising waste from the Waste House

It is estimated that over 40 tonnes of waste was diverted from landfill or incineration by constructing the Waste House. However, the process of constructing the Waste House itself created waste material. Architecture students created designs and built them after locating and using waste from the Waste House. In addition, a local zero-waste restaurant called Silo (see page 68) constructed tables and shelving from surplus material from the Waste House. A local community group used waste material to create chairs, and an allotment shed nearby used surplus carpet tiles, vinyl banners and timber from the Waste House.

Specifying new material and products

Some types of products and systems that contemporary buildings require cannot be second-hand. Electrical circuits comprising wire stripped out of buildings will require too many joints or junction boxes to be reliable. Second-hand above- and below-ground drainage and waste pipes are technically a health hazard and not appropriate to reinstall without a professional cleaning operation. We sourced second-hand light fittings: five of them from a scrapped 60-year-old container ship. However, light bulbs have to be new.

In short, it is difficult to reinstall what the construction industry calls 'first fix' services: piping work and wiring. However, the 'fittings', such as sinks, wc pans, IT equipment, Mechanical Ventilation and Heat Recovery systems, and even flat screens for presentations, were second-hand and straight forward to source.

Achieving Building Regulations approval

Brighton and Hove City Building Control were very supportive of the Waste House and were an integral part of the design team, attending design and progress meetings. Installing DVDs, videos and denim into external wall cavities does not in fact test Building Regulations as they are separated from the internal environment by the internal wall linings. The Waste House is constructed primarily of timber and ply sheets with various second-hand plastics acting as low-grade insulation. Most homes built in the UK in the 21st century are timber framed with plastic insulation infilling wall cavities and plastic vapour control membranes sitting behind internal plaster or timber wall linings: pretty similar to the Waste House, in fact.

The most challenging aspects for the Building Control Officer were proving the fire and flame resistance of the 2,000 second-hand carpet tiles used for external wall cladding, and the ply wall linings used in the main first-floor studio. To satisfy these queries we set up a test rig of 15 carpet tiles fixed on a brick wall, as they would be installed on the Waste House. In the presence of the Building Control Officer, our site agent directed a hand-held blowtorch onto the tiles for 5 seconds and then for 10 seconds. On both occasions the tiles started to smoke quite heavily. However, as soon as the blowtorch was taken away, the tiles immediately extinguished.

The first-floor wall linings were more straightforward. They were constructed of third-hand ply sheet that had previously been used by the team to create a 9m-high 'waste totem' at EcoBuild 2013. Material for the totem had to be flame-proofed before it was decorated with second-hand paint and installed in the exhibition hall. This flame retardant ensured that we could reuse this material as the internal wall finish of the first-floor studio space without any fear of Building Control not approving it fit for purpose.

The academic legacy

The Waste House is an ongoing research project, involving new generations of students being set projects testing, improving and updating the house, whose performance is being constantly monitored by the University of Brighton's School of Science and Engineering. Since the inception of the Waste House in 2010, the University of Brighton has hosted a website focusing on its development, from an idea through to completion. It is regularly updated and serves as an archive and learning resource.

The themes and challenges embraced by the Waste House have influenced the core curriculum of the undergraduate architecture and interior architecture courses at the university, as well as at partner institution City College Brighton and Hove. I coordinate architecture 'technology' and 'practices' modules, which use the process of designing and then constructing the Waste House as an inspiration, awareness raiser, and vehicle to deliver RIBA-approved learning outcomes.

Architecture students have considered design projects tackling issues associated with valuing waste as a resource, as well as broader issues relating to the circular economy. One undergraduate architecture student designed a timber construction system that inspired the 'cassettes' used in the Waste House. Construction students from City College completed learning modules of their carpentry, electrics, plumbing, bricklaying, plastering, decorating and maintenance by working initially in the workshop, but then crucially on the 'live' construction site. Cat Fletcher and I delivered lectures to City College construction students, as well as architecture students, as part of their core curriculum. We also gave presentations about waste and designing for a circular economy to children. As part of the University of Brighton's ongoing Widening Participation Programme, over 750 young people were shown around the construction site during the construction period.

The Waste House has served as an inspiration for many visiting students from regional tertiary colleges, as well as students from the university's School of Science and Engineering. Indeed, while on site a Jordanian PhD student approached the university asking if he could be involved in the digital monitoring of the external wall fabric. He moved to the UK to do just this. The Waste House also hosts regular school visits on Wednesdays, where open design workshops are held.

In March 2013 Nick Gant and I curated a three-day seminar entitled 'The WasteZone' as part of EcoBuild 2013. Twelve guest speakers discussed the idea of waste as a valuable resource from many different perspectives. The Waste House team also designed and erected the 9m-tall 'waste totem', drawing the attention of the 65,000 visitors towards issues of reuse. Since this event, a new reuse-themed zone, called 'Resource', has been launched at EcoBuild. We feel we may have played a small role in enabling that to happen.

The Waste House also hosts the University of Brighton's Sustainable Design MA, with students working in the first-floor studio two days a week. Professor Jonathan Chapman and Nick Gant

have their office on the ground floor. Community groups, local schools and other educational establishments, as well as local and international businesses and local authority groups, use the Waste House. The building hosts meetings, lectures and symposia with large construction contractors as well as commercial enterprises such as The Body Shop and Marks & Spencer.

Perhaps the biggest legacy the Waste House project leaves is that of raising awareness of the negative issues associated with society's linear, throwaway, consumer-led lifestyle. The building has many stories associated with the materials collected and residing within it. For example, an airline cabin-service company at Gatwick Airport collected 25,000 plastic toothbrushes for the project in only four days. These statistics stop you in your tracks, as it were, and get you thinking about where 'stuff' comes from and where it currently ends up. Perhaps it will also encourage more people to realise the potentials for reuse and, more particularly, the potential for designers to play a huge part in our future circular economy, and, of course, to understand that 'there is no such thing as waste, just stuff in the wrong place'.[8]

CLOCKWISE FROM TOP RIGHT (OPPOSITE)

FIG. 3.1 Launching the construction of the Waste House

FIG. 3.2 Installing the timber frame, made from surplus ply and timber from skips

FIG. 3.3 Schoolchildren, visiting the site, drop off their old toothbrushes

FIG. 3.4 Some 2 tonnes of denim, formerly the legs of jeans cut off to make shorts, was used as insulation

FIG. 3.5 Some of the 50 summer camp volunteers who built the vaulted roof

FIG. 3.6 Some of the 4,000 vhs video cassettes used as low grade insulation

THE WASTE HOUSE STORY PART 3 155

CLOCKWISE FROM TOP RIGHT

FIG. 3.7 Part of the open studio, lined with third-hand decorated ply that had previously been the 9m-high 'waste totem'

FIG. 3.8 Street elevation of the Waste House

FIG. 3.9 Some of the team, celebrating the opening of the Brighton Waste House

FIG. 3.10 Detail of gorgeous rammed chalk wall

156 PART 3   THE WASTE HOUSE STORY

Lessons learnt

Lesson 1

Designing structural beams and columns using second-hand, waste and surplus material raises unusual challenges for a structural engineer. If you don't know where the timber materials originate from you won't know the stress grade and therefore the actual strength of the product. Our structural engineer had to assume it was the weakest material on the market. This initially manifested itself in a draft design from the engineer that suggested larger structural beams and columns than normal and thus far more material than normal. It was only when the design was refined over a number of weeks, so that it became more specific to the actual loads on each structural member, that it became more material efficient. During the manufacture of these elements the structural engineer had to oversee and approve every structural element in the workshop: they were constructed by young people with as little as two months' experience on a carpentry course.

Lesson 2

The team designed a timber-framed building assuming we could source over 400 sheets of waste ply and approximately 2km of timber studwork: we had, after all, done this before when constructing temporary graduation pavilions. However, in 2012 we were not able to do this because of the wet weather: we were receiving water-saturated and delaminated ply that was not appropriate to use. It took the team two months to find ply suitable to use and delayed the project.

We learnt to find material first and then think about whether it might be useful or not, instead of assuming materials would be available: a completely different design process to normal.

Lesson 3

Materials would often be offered weeks or even months before they were needed. It was crucial to the success of this project that we could store material, keeping it safe and dry. Brighton and Hove City Council let us borrow a building nearby to use as a temporary resource store.

Lesson 4

If properly briefed and supported, young people with limited skills and experience within the construction industry can construct a building using unusual materials that performs at very high levels of energy efficiency.

Lesson 5

A 'live' construction site can run effectively while shutting down for an hour a week to allow visiting tours from more than 750 schoolchildren interested in the project.

Lesson 6

Young people from different backgrounds, and with different skill sets, can learn successfully from each other and work together to deliver a complex construction project.

Conclusion

The Brighton Waste House started out as a design-and-build project, as well as an inclusive learning process to prove that construction waste and surplus material was worth salvaging and not throwing away. Via further research and a policy of inclusive design, the project evolved into more of a polemic rather than an exemplar for the UK housing industry to copy. The Waste House is a vessel containing hundreds of stories associated with the salvaged materials it contains. These stories and narratives resonate through the building and ensure that students, consultants, academics, and whoever asks questions when they use the building, will know more about where stuff comes from and where it normally ends up. Then, perhaps, they might ponder how things might be done differently: how our unintelligent 'linear economy', which finds material, then processes it into things that we then throw away, could be changed into a 'circular economy' where materials and goods are in a state of perpetual reuse.

The Waste House acquired more than 40 partners during its development. Many of these partners are able to use the building. Schools visit the Waste House and take part in sustainable design workshops with designers, poets, writers, artists and constructors. The University of Brighton's MA in Sustainable Design is based in the building, and many community groups use it as well.

The unusual external fabric of the building is being monitored to see how it performs compared with more straightforward materials. This information will be published in due course.

Over 450 articles have been published around the world via newspapers, web-based magazines, TV and radio. This project has got people speaking about waste as a valuable resource. To date it has won ten awards and is currently nominated for five more. It appears to have struck a chord.

The Waste House still inspires students on campus as new generations are encouraged to add their design ideas to the building. It is an ongoing, 'live' research project. The team, comprising different academic and vocational establishments, the local authority and local contractors, are currently bidding for European grants for future collaborative, innovative construction projects, and the idea of a 'Live Projects Office' is a reality for the Faculty of Arts and Humanities.

PART 4

Looking Forward

161   CHAPTER 1
Product Moments, Material Eternities
Professor Jonathan Chapman

166   CHAPTER 2
Educating the Circular Economy (or Learning in Circles)
Professor Anne Boddington

173   CHAPTER 3
How are Closed-Loop Systems Relevant?
Duncan Baker-Brown

CHAPTER 1

Product Moments, Material Eternities

Professor Jonathan Chapman,
Professor of Sustainable Design at the University of Brighton

AT ITS BEST, DESIGN IS A powerful tool for cracking problems and leveraging opportunities for new products, services and systems that drive a more resource-efficient economy and create value for policymakers, businesses and consumers. However, despite being an incredibly dynamic and vibrant cultural phenomenon, design is an extremely wasteful and destructive one too. This is largely due to its ephemeral nature, fuelled by the ceaseless consumer hunt for change, novelty and innovation. This chapter shows how sustainable design recalibrates the parameters of good design in an unsustainable age. It advances and broadens the agenda of the design system – with its established emphasis on economic sustainability and development, at all costs – so that it's fit for purpose in unravelling the Gordian knots of sustainability, through the design of more sustainable goods and services.

Better, not more

Simply having more stuff stopped making people in Britain, the USA and other wealthy countries happier decades ago; we need an economy of *better*, not *more*; one in which things last longer, age gracefully and can be repaired many times before being recycled. The UK government is one of several proposing an economy where resources are used sustainably through design for longer life, upgrading, reuse or repair. Product life extension strategies – like *emotionally durable design*[1] – have a vital role to play here: combatting rising levels of e-waste and obsolescence; tackling the challenge of weaning people off their desire for the new; helping shape new sustainable business models; supporting users in keeping products, components and materials at their highest utility and value throughout their lifetime. Indeed, the success of a resource-efficient, and circular, economy depends on new business models that are able to truly capitalise on longer product lifespans over time.[2] Simply put, it helps us design products that are built to last longer, and provide a longer-term experience. The term 'emotional' is used here because wasteful patterns of consumption and waste are driven, in large part, by emotional and experiential factors – we tire of things, novelty wears off all too quickly and we fall out of love with them, so to speak.

By questioning the very primacy of design production itself, of acts of *designing* in favour of acts of *use*, it is then a careful attentiveness to modes, experiences and patterns of consumption that needs to be fostered. Why are people drawn to certain objects, only to then rapidly discard them while they are still able to perform their practical tasks perfectly? Deluges of manufactured objects flow through our lives, providing mere glimpses of meaning along the way. From paperclips, cutlery and footwear, to armchairs, kettles and cars, we engage with this stuff in the hope that it will fulfil some kind of need, or lack, yet it seldom does. Sociologist Robert Bocock tells us that 'consumption is founded on a lack – a desire always for something not there. Modern/postmodern consumers, therefore, will never be satisfied. The more they consume, the more they will desire to consume'.[3] Bocock claims that consumer motivation, or the awakening of human need, is catalysed by a sense of imbalance or lack that steadily cultivates a restless state of being. Compulsory material over-consumption is therefore motivated when discrepancies are continuously experienced between *actual* and *desired* conditions.

From linear to circular

Conventionally, industrial activity involves a linear production–consumption system with inbuilt environmental destruction at either end; sustainable product design activity over the past 45 years has made these wasteful and inefficient ends of the scale marginally less wasteful and inefficient. The Earth is finite, balanced, synergistic and reactive, and yet we design the world as though it were separable, mechanical and lasting, leading to what Bateson refers to as a fundamental epistemological error[4] that shapes practically all that we do, and one that can be found at the very root of unsustainability. Indeed, human destruction of the natural world is a crisis of behaviour, and not one simply of energy and material alone, as is often assumed in design;

the decisions we make as an industry, the values we share as a society and the dreams we pursue as individuals collectively drive all that we accomplish, while shaping the ecological impact of our development as a species.

We need to move away from linearity in our design thinking, to reconnect with design on a more circular and systemic level, if we are to achieve the degrees of transformation our current situation demands. These new approaches require designers and manufacturers to take greater control over material flows; closing the loop through clear and systematised processes of product design, production, delivery and take-back. A circular economy is one in which resources are kept in use for as long as possible. The maximum value is extracted from them, while materials and energy are recovered or recycled as much as possible at the end of any product's life. In the circular economy, materials and resources *flow through* products and into new ones, as opposed to being designed into products, then locked into landfill.

Global businesses, supported by governments, are also beginning to look at product life extension as a viable route to waste reduction, and value creation. Electronic waste (e-waste) in particular is growing at three times the speed of any other form of waste in the EU. Today, practically everything is disposable – it is culturally permissible to throw away anything from a barely used smartphone, television or vacuum cleaner, to an entire three-piece suite or fitted bathroom.[5] Given the huge quantities of precious resources (including gold and other rare metals) that find their way into our gadgets, it would surely be worth us taking more care of them, repairing them when broken, and keeping them for longer.

In fact, the opposite is happening: product lifespans are shortening as material culture becomes increasingly disposable.[6] Hence, we live in a world drowning in objects:[7] households with a television in each room; kitchen cupboards stuffed with waffle makers, blenders and cappuccino whisks; drawers filled to bursting with pocket-sized devices powered by batteries – batteries which themselves take a thousand times more energy to make than they will ever provide. A child's remote-control tank, for example, contains a thumbnail-sized microchip, containing over 65% of the elements in the periodic table. There is more gold in a tonne of phones than a tonne of rock from a gold mine. Due to their design and manufacture, the rock-bound gold is more economically viable to extract than its phone-bound counterpart.

In the circular economy materials flow purposefully through products, adopting diverse forms throughout their lifetime, in continuous flux. Change is part of the basic nature of some, if not all, things. Whether we are talking about major changes in state – such as the demolition of a 40-storey block (one minute it is there, the next it is not) – or something more discreet – such as the barely noticeable growth of our fingernails – change is all around us. Of course, our experience of the everyday tends to happen through a series of fleeting glimpses, which provide a fragmented, artificial portrayal of reality. These passing snapshots capture isolated moments in a far longer and more complex timeline of an object, material or building, for example. Only through sustained and attentive engagement with a given thing – be it a house, armchair, car or pen – can we begin to understand it in the lengthier context of *flow* and change over time.

As if to disprove this, we fabricate the made world as though it can be fixed, set in place and frozen. Through this, we form expectations of permanence, of things that last for centuries, unchanged. This is, of course, folly.

This idea of *flow* draws from the famed Greek remark *panta rhei,* in English literally 'everything flows', originally attributed to pre-Socratic philosopher Heraclitus and later reported in the writings of Plato and Simplicius in particular. The Heraclitean concept of *panta rhei* uses the image of the river to evoke the eternal flow of time and change – a continually moving, shifting thing in constant flux. This remark serves to remind us that, in our pursuit of permanence, we are fundamentally at odds with the most essential underlying principle of the natural world – change. Indeed, Heraclitus' river itself could be described as a different river from moment to moment, since what composes it – the water flowing – is different from moment to moment. This concept is essentially meant to stress the uniqueness of each discrete experience of the world. On an atomic level, this principle is true of all physical things, no matter how solid and stationary they may seem. For example, a child constantly changes, and we are predisposed to accept, and expect this. Importantly – unlike the changing Heraclitean river – the child doesn't become a different child with each change. Rather, the child has changed and adapted in some way, hence becoming a slightly 'evolved' version of what it was before. As users we are in a permanent state of becoming, whereas the objects we attempt to engage with have already become. In this scenario, obsolescence is a somewhat inevitable outcome – the story, effectively, has nowhere to go as it has already been fully told.

Reflecting on this unfolding process,

Cameron Tonkinwise asks the compelling question of 'whether designers are capable of designing things that are not finished'.[8] Whether directly, or by proximity, a concern with the finished, complete nature of products has been a steady presence in design practice and theory, particularly post turn of the century. Several conceptualisations of this issue have attempted to grapple with its implications for both acts of designing and acts of using. 'Continuous design and redesign',[9] 'tactical formlessness',[10] 'design after design'[11] or 'metadesign'[12]: these are some of the better-known labels adopted to discuss the topic. What these perspectives seem to share is their intentions to question designers' absolute authorial claims, to instead promote user agency precisely by blurring the threshold between acts of design and acts of use. Amplifying the 'voice' and agency of users through the object's open-endedness is certainly a step in the right direction in that it widens the user's sphere of action. This holds true at least until objects will be provided with the ability to *respond* in their own terms, rather than being programmed to do so or forced to oblige in any possible way. To be clear, such a brief is by no means meant to encourage a dystopian 'nightmare in which tyrannical things command our daily lives'.[13] Rather, it speaks of things emerging in their eventfulness and asserting their own voices throughout person–thing encounters. That is, it speaks of the capacity for objects to *really* have an inherent process of their own, as Tonkinwise puts it.

The imperative significance of *change* has been a central concern across a number of fields. In evolutionary biology, for instance, 'it is not the most intellectual of the species that survives; it is not the strongest that survives; but the species that survives is the one that is able to best adapt and adjust to the changing environments in which it finds itself'.[14] Similarly, in 'resilience thinking', the capacity to absorb disturbance, and accept change – rather than defensively resist and block it – is considered key to success. Adaptive resilience, says Mark Robinson, Director of Thinking Practice, is 'the capacity to remain productive and true to core purpose and identity whilst absorbing disturbance and adapting with integrity in response to changing circumstances'.[15]

There is a growing sense that the consumer electronics industry must transition from a linear to a circular economy; one in which resources are kept in use for as long as possible. The maximum value is extracted from them, while materials and energy are recovered or recycled as much as possible at the end of any product's life. This is a seismic shift in thinking, affecting everything from the design and delivery of short-life throwaway products, to that of longer-lasting material experiences. Of course, the notion of a 'throwaway society' is nothing new. American economist Bernard London first introduced the term 'planned obsolescence' in 1932 as a means to stimulate spending among the few consumers who had disposable income during the Great Depression. The concept was popularised by Vance Packard in his seminal book *The Waste Makers* (1964).[16] Though informed by the work of both Bernard London (1932)[17] and Earnest Elmo Calkins (1932)[18] on consumer engineering, Packard's dualistic theories of *functional obsolescence* and *psychological obsolescence* assert that the deliberate shortening of product lifespans was unethical, both in its profit-focused manipulating of consumer spending, and its devastating ecological impact through the nurturing of wasteful purchasing behaviours. In fact, the concept of disposability was a necessary condition for America's cultural rejection of tradition and acceptance of change.[19]

Over the past decade, issues of sustainability have become well established within design – strategies like design for recycling, disassembly, service and energy efficiency, for example, have become commonplace in today's process. Designing for *emotionally durable* products and user experiences helps reduce the consumption and waste of resources by building lasting relationships between users and the products they buy. A deeper understanding of acts of use can be helpful in extending both the physical and emotional durability of products, enabling designers to encourage longer-lasting interactions with products and services, consequently minimising the consumption of resources.

Can sustainable design drive change?

Promoting sustainability by production can be intended as a response to the ecological impact of relentlessly wasteful manufacturing practices. The constant flood of products, interventions, experimental and conceptual work adopting strategies such as recycling or upcycling is clear testament to a predominant focus on production-related concerns within design discourses. It could be argued that the dominance of such methodologies, which don't risk 'offending' existing commercial and capitalist conventions is, on some level, a compliant approach to sustainable transition.[20] This conservative modus operandi, as it were, then liberates consumers' consciences and, in doing so, generates even more waste. By refusing to understand and engage with the problem of sustainability at a level of foundational causality, designers thus fail again and again to grasp the deeper roots of what Tony Fry defined as 'structural unsustainability'.[21] Until these roots are firmly grasped, sustainable design will always teeter around the edges of impact, but never drive the transformational changes it so passionately advocates. In this way, a truly sustainable design discipline has to undergo a radical cultural shift that would hinge upon a concern for *immaterial* issues, prior to and as a precondition for *material* ones.

In design terms, we can support greater levels of emotional longevity when we specify materials that age gracefully, and that develop quality over time. We can design products that are easier to repair, upgrade and maintain throughout their lifespan. These are effective product life extension strategies, and while they can come at an increased cost at point of purchase, they generate revenue downstream, through the introduction of service and upgrade packages. Extending the life of a product has significant ecological benefits. For example, take a toaster that lasts about 12 months. Even if the toaster's life is extended to just 18 months through more durable design, the extra longevity would lead to a 50% reduction in the waste consumption associated with manufacturing and distributing it. Scale this up to a national or international population of toaster-buyers, and it's clear how significant an impact this could be. Designing products that can be kept for longer also nurtures a deeper relationship with both the product and the brand, which increases the likelihood of brand loyalty maturing. Therefore, such emotionally durable design doesn't just make sense from an environmental and resources perspective, but can be seen as a commercially viable business strategy in an increasingly competitive globalised world.

CHAPTER 2

Educating the Circular Economy (or Learning in Circles)

Professor Anne Boddington,
Dean of the College of Arts and Humanities, University of Brighton

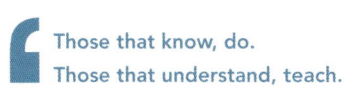

> Those that know, do.
> Those that understand, teach.
> Aristotle (attrib.)

> While we teach, we learn.
> Seneca (attrib.)

To teach is to know, understand and share and, importantly, to be aware of what one doesn't yet know or understand. Thinking and working within a circular economy challenges the profligate use of our resources, material and energies. It forces us to question whether, through our collective and creative ingenuity, we can rethink, re-engineer and rebalance our cultural and social behaviours such that we become more mindful of the value and finite nature of the world's resources, however these may be constituted and defined. Dirt is 'matter out of place' as the anthropologist Mary Douglas noted in suggesting that dirt is part of the natural and received order of things.[1] What constitutes 'dirt', or the unclean, varies between different cultural and social contexts, which may enhance worth or render 'matter' as 'unpalatable'. Or in the context of the circular economy and to cite Alex Steffen, 'There is no such thing as waste, just "stuff" in the wrong place'.[2]

Thinking, seeing and working within the circular economy, in contradistinction with the more dominant linear economy, re-evaluates our conceptions as to what in Douglas's terms we might consider 'palatable', what we consider as 'waste' or valuable, or what does, or does not, have worth in our contemporary intellectual, aesthetic and emotional schema. Its premise is a more finely balanced ecology, situated between what might be appropriately and justifiably linear and what might be more closely aligned to the social constructs of an exchange or 'gift economy'.[3]

Founded in 2010, the Ellen MacArthur Foundation has been at the forefront of promoting the principles of, and transition to, a more circular economy, in part by creating a framework of key sets of questions as the basis for a curriculum for higher education.[4] While the matrix provides a comparative list of the defining features of both the linear and circular economies and promotes the use of 'rich feedback' mechanisms in its delivery, perhaps what notably remains unchallenged are the pedagogic methods and the cultural, social and economic structures that underpin and drive higher education, both in the UK and internationally.

Higher education institutions (HEIs) are complex and ostensibly intelligent institutions. What I wish to examine here is whether, through adaptations to their infrastructure and societal positioning, they could enhance their performance and develop more contemporary and innovative educational experiences by embedding the principles of the circular economy within their academic structures, processes and practices. I suggest that to do so could open up new and different opportunities for future generations of students and academics alike and reposition the societal role higher education might play in a future and finite world challenged by scarcity, security, economic and political frailties and human conflict.

Manuel Castells in his 2001 essay 'Universities as dynamic systems of contradictory functions' identified a number of key factors that underpin the role of universities worldwide, including addressing the challenges that face the world at any given time; the socialisation and development of a society's elite or leaders (because higher education remains a selective sector); the development of new knowledge; and the development of the workforce for an unknown future labour market.[5]

While it would be naive to suggest the transformation of higher education in its entirety, potentially discarding the valuable opportunities it currently provides for many students, the tactical overlay of the principles of the circular economy on the infrastructural complexities of their existing academic strategies could usefully accelerate and potentially strengthen their responsiveness and societal impact. This could, to a degree, arrest the diminishing value proposition of higher education in a world that is changing far more rapidly than its systems generally permit.

This begs the question of what might change: what might academic practices applying the principles of the circular economy look like and how might they differentiate themselves from the current transactional models that underpin the majority of the world's higher education?[6]

Potentially this would require some conceptual adaptations and a willingness to think beyond the basis of higher education conceived principally as the transfer of content in our curricula from teachers to students (through named awards in a subject) and supported by a series of professional services. Consider instead the following:

1. Knowledge development through subjects (as well as about subjects)
2. The dynamics of teaching and learning as gifting, exchange and sharing of knowledge, skills and experience and how gifting, sharing and exchanging might occur, and who with, to ensure continued and sustainable transformation
3. The social and practical application of ideas (social engagement) that build practical bridges between labour and work within the world.

As three interrelated pillars, these form a subtly different, cyclic educational model underpinned by the cooperative principles of the circular economy. While many elements of such principles are ostensibly already enshrined in 'good academic practice', the overarching infrastructure and frameworks have seen little structural innovation and are ostensibly designed to limit risk rather than to stimulate the creative and educational potential and impact of higher-order learning. In other words, and despite much rhetoric to the contrary, HEIs are increasingly challenged by the need to innovate and to take risks. Few do; instead they persist with educational infrastructures that remain broadly transactional, slow to respond, repetitive and which, ironically (given that the arguments for stasis are frequently economic), proliferate additional costs, tasks and projects to augment the student experience.

Rethinking the practices of HEIs *through* the lens and principles of the circular economy presents possibilities for a more contemporary dynamic through which curriculum content, its production, quality, application and governance are integrated in such a way as to unlock the creative and intellectual potential that resides within any university. Equally a 'circular' approach would reposition the power relations that currently exist between students, academics and professional services. Knowledge would be seen as a gift and resource to be valued and shared, rather than a commodity to be purchased and certificated (through fees). This could create an enduring and transformative experience that could unlock new opportunities for those that partake, and impact more overtly on civic and social life beyond the academy.

This is only to argue for what is already, debatably, within the gift of HEIs. It is not to suggest that there are elements of university infrastructures that should not rightly be transactional, but instead to consider what potential a 'circular' overlay could unlock about the very special nature of universities as multiple networks of learning communities.

Whatever the medium (digital or physical) of teaching, research and engagement, the interactions of the HEI community are broadly constructed by three core types of engagements. These are generally conceived as linear, distinct processes and tasks to be 'timetabled' and 'accommodated' rather than interrelated, reciprocal and mutually reinforcing activities. These activities rarely capture the true worth, impact and potential, and do not fully harness and value all members of the institution's networks.

Universities are places where human minds meet and intertwine. Contemporary learning and human-to-human encounters occur in the following ways:

1. One-to-one (tutorials, supervision, mentorship)
2. One-to-many (lectures, training, publishing)
3. Many-to-many (group activities, meetings, MOOCs (Massive Open Online Courses), social media, websites).

Examining in detail these three forms of engagement within the learning process (and despite the very best intentions and exemplars of 'good practice'), it becomes clear that knowledge, experience and creative application continually leak away or are casually or carelessly disregarded through a lack of recognition and capture. This has the effect of sapping the richness and potential from the very institutions in our society that arguably have the most to contribute to learning. Focusing more attention on the nature and potential learning in each human encounter provides a means to more fully exploit this richness, in a similar way to re-examining how we constitute and consider 'waste'.

It is the ability to sustain the perpetual dynamic interrelationships and reciprocity between these three forms that differentiates the linear (requiring continued demands for resource and proliferating new tasks), from the circular (which (re) produces and (re) develops its resources and stimulates innovation and resilience).

In addition, instead of targeting what appears to be the tangible product of higher education (certificated learning leading to employment), we focus on providing a stimulating and dynamic educational *experience*, which, to paraphrase educational reformer John Dewey, 'is not a preparation for life, but life itself'. We shift the value proposition to one that is more enduring and vital for all members of a university's communities.[7] This is a proposition that by definition brings together cognitive, affective and practical forms of learning, trusting as we must that university communities have the desire and will to engage with one another, and to continually develop their learning, research and careers in concert.

In the circular economy, as in the gift economy, the continual transference of gifts (in the context of education – knowledge, skills and experience) is an essential trope, if the gift is not to revert to a commodity, at which point it loses its human and social connection. This circular, 'cooperative' process of development, sharing/gifting, application, reflection and new knowledge and insight, is not new, and is familiar to many fields of study. But what is distinctive is that such a structure exempts no one, and no member of the community may stand outside of their 'community of practice' irrespective of their level of experience. This includes all constituencies, from entry-level students to senior management, albeit to different degrees. Put simply, in such a model, everyone has a responsibility to teach, learn, research and practise and share those experiences (good and bad) in the safety of a 'learning home' that unites the idea, the digital and built form of the contemporary university.

Such ideas draw together the 'exchange' or 'gift economy' with the pedagogies of Paolo Freire[8] of 'conscientisation or the development of a critical awareness of one's social reality' and Wenger's models of 'communities of practice'[9] in socialising the educational experience and harnessing the cooperative reflexivity of such groups and their networks as a means to test, evidence and validate what has been learnt and to articulate its multiple impacts. The other remaining challenge for any university is then how to create networks of communities. The need to develop learning *through* subjects requires the invitation of 'others' into subject communities with different kinds of knowledge and expertise. Continual and evolving dialogues can be sustained in this way to support interdisciplinary propositions without the need to establish new project structures to address each and every problem.

It might also be argued that any such request to create a new task is in fact a key indicator that an element of the infrastructure is not operating optimally, consequently placing any institution under strain in a way that is questionably no longer tenable.

Practically this is perhaps most keenly evidenced and experienced in the increased demands and burgeoning tasks that have faced 'time-poor' academics recently and have resulted in the development of a more reductive and transactional approach to higher education, dividing communities of practice that need to be brought together, instead of, as Castell suggests, embedding societal challenges (whether local or global) within curricula, such that they become the means (or the 'matter') through which to harness knowledge more overtly and position HEIs and their subject communities more centrally in contemporary discourse.

Introducing an overlay of a circular economy not only shifts the power relationships at all stages of learning, from undergraduate to PhD, but equally might charge HEIs to examine the nature and construction of the curriculum, of contemporary knowledge and subject identities and stimulate perpetual learning and civic engagement that fosters increased porosity and cooperation and in which cost and value are more equitably balanced.

The academy has always been a 'safe place' for experimentation and for questioning and challenging the nature of received knowledge, whether these debates are conducted face-to-face or digitally. While we are only too aware how significantly access to information and acquisition of knowledge have changed, we have yet to see the full impact of this realised on the role of universities as places of learning and research in the context of the world beyond the academy, which is now critically as much part of the learning environment as that of the university campus or its digital counterpart.

While it is incumbent on all universities to be business-like, as with any business it is vital to know the role, nature and purpose of the business and to understand its contribution within a wider economic ecology. Rhetorically we might then ask what really are the 'product lines' of any university as a business and are these really as explicit as they might be? The linear economy is by its nature insatiable, and the world in which we live is becoming more and more tested by its finite resources, by pressures on time and tasks – yet we seem to persist in demanding ever more evidence and measurement that serves primarily to divert resources and attention away from and not towards the very subjects of its purpose – our future generations and an unknowable labour market.

How we capture and measure experience and 'learning gain' still requires considerable work and research. Writer Jorge Luis Borges, in his short essay 'On Exactitude in Science', described well this contemporary dilemma and to some degree, like Dewey, he suggests the need to rethink the nature of such evidence and whether it efficiently and effectively answers the questions as to the role and purpose of contemporary higher education.

> In that Empire, the art of Cartography attained such Perfection that the map of a single province occupied the entirety of a City and the map of the Empire the entirety of the Province.

> The following generations were not so fond of the Study of Cartography as their forbears had been, saw that the vast map was Useless … they delivered it up to the inclemencies of the Sun and Winters.[10]

Within higher education, we are at a critical point in our history in which our resources are under ever-increasing pressure, and where, in Borges' terms, the cartographies, or the educational infrastructures, are in danger of becoming parodies of themselves; vestigial systems no longer fit-for-purpose. Adopting and adapting the principles of the circular economy in reshaping institutional learning offers opportunities to reflect, to look and think harder and beyond the current structures and systems, which appear to devour the very thing they serve to protect, resulting in our institutions 'knowing the cost of everything and the value of nothing'. I would propose that we have within our gift the opportunity to create more responsive, elegant and contemporary 'holding forms' for universities that recognise the contingent and precious nature of education as 'a gift', for life and for living, that is treasured and continually shared and refined by creating a refined institutional ecology.

Higher education will always remain positioned between the linear and circular economies, between the intrinsic power of what it is to learn and share knowledge and the global economic conditions in which we live. It is the relationship between the linear and the circular and the balance of one with and within the other that is under question. How might we consistently apply more sustainable educational practices to the structures of higher education, as a means of mediating the inevitable political dynamics of change? How might we quietly and systematically embed what are currently tactical practices into the strategic structural core of higher education?

To address these changes also forces us to reflect on what might provide the material, or 'matter' in Douglas's terms, in creating a more 'circular' education? One modest way is to reassess the degree of leakage, the material that we currently squander and invest more in capturing what we currently allow to slip away and hence render invisible in the learning cycle. But perhaps where we are most wasteful is in the time spent inventing hypothetical scenarios and problems for students, when the world has so many societal issues and challenges that we need to address and that require thought, dialogue and action. This is the 'matter' we need to work with more overtly and in which there is an imperative to invest our time. How might pedagogies of the circular economy enable us to design the curriculum delivery and our learning and research spaces, such that they foster human potential and address societal issues in such a way that future generations are not caught in the same bureaucratic loops in which we currently find ourselves?

The subjects we might tackle would change our conception of, and the nature of, our curriculum: for example, if we taught students how to teach, if all our students were assessed not on their ability to pass examinations, but on their ability to lead, educate, communicate and build empathetic relations with others. If we taught our students how to speak in a different language, how to adapt, rethink and reinvent, reuse the things we currently disregard and how to give agency to ideas through the lenses of our different subjects, and how these might be shared across traditionally opaque subject boundaries (eg arts, business, science, social science), what would our curriculum look like?

Learning outcomes and assessment for courses would look subtly different in a 'circular' pedagogic model, bringing any subject, its learning *and* application together and into relief, so reflecting on how and where subjects contribute in the world, and providing reflections, insights and pathways to future career horizons.

We frequently revert, when convenient, to higher education as separate (monastic) and distinct from the application of our subjects, and add more 'learning outcomes' to curricula to assure 'employability' and respond to government statistics. We render our applied material invisible when it is inconvenient, risky or difficult to transact, and yet it exists every day in the media. It is present in every home, street, city and landfill site and every daily encounter that frustrates our collective sense of social justice. Bringing these challenges, whether local, national or international, into the educational sphere and seeking ways to enable such dialogue have never been more of an imperative, challenging though they are to existing underpinning and risk-averse structures. If we had no campus, no capital and no professional infrastructure, the idea of a university in the circular economy is not diminished; it might even stimulate us to build a new kind of academy that sits more lightly and elegantly in the world.

In a practical context, as a manager responsible for facilitating the Brighton Waste House, these challenges were in part realised and are documented elsewhere in this book. While the Waste House did not accomplish all aspects of what is suggested above in a formal or structural sense, it went a considerable way to demonstrating what might be achieved by a relatively small group of committed, insightful creative people from across a university community (students, academics, professionals and managers), from further education, from local government, from business and from the not for profit sector (social enterprise, NGOs and community-based activities/charities etc). Its mission was simple, but its questions were and remain profound and are as yet unanswered.

It is in scale a modest building project, but its polemical challenge and scale are significant. It is a learning space in every sense, and one that was and is designed, redesigned, used and reused, scientifically monitored and analysed, researched and continuously impactful. It is in itself a gift of collective and cooperative ingenuity that required trust, but also significant energy to achieve. It brought together many different 'communities of practice', enhanced learning in many spheres and continues to inspire children and young people, students, academics and members of the public alike. But it also signalled the challenges in complex creative leadership, in the capacity required to capture and share learning and the potential learning yet to be harnessed with reference to policy, sustainable construction, planning and of course education in its broadest sense. In the true sense of any 'circular' process, the project remains 'live', one in which the learning gained must by definition be shared, and is contingent and 'in progress' and conceived as a resource or gift to be valued.

And so to conclude where I began; to teach is to know, understand and share. In any circular or gift economy, what is critical is that such gifts are continually in motion for them to remain transformational and impactful. We need to ensure that in being a part of a learning community (a university) we are responsible not only for continuing to learn and to research, but also for sharing that learning through our teaching, whether in formal or social contexts.

I have led and worked within creative higher education for 30 years and have been fortunate to learn more about what I know, don't know and need to learn from the many hundreds of students, academics and university professionals I have worked alongside. If we are to stimulate innovation and realise new ideas within higher education, we need to create and shape a more responsive educational economy. It is now more vital than ever that we establish enabling frameworks or 'holding forms' for this so as to harness the extraordinary intellectual and infrastructural support and expertise universities have at their disposal to generate new creative, professional leaders, new forms of knowledge and a renewed sense of hope for future generations.

CHAPTER 3

How are Closed-Loop Systems Relevant?

Duncan Baker-Brown

In his essay 'Why wait for the future? There could be a present without waste'[1] Herbert Kopnick dreams about the launch of the iPhone 10. Kopnick speculates that the Apple CEO Tim Cook might point towards Apple's change from a company selling products to a company selling services.

Kopnick speculates on Cook's justification for this about-turn, as far as Apple's business model is concerned, describing the new business model as a 'win-win-win situation'. 'Winner number one' is the consumer, as they will have a place to return their old Apple products instead of putting them in a drawer to deal with sometime in the future. 'Winner number two' is Apple itself, who 'only have to buy the majority of the needed raw materials a single time rather than yearly'.

The third winner, of course, is the natural environment. Kopnick points out that:

> Obtaining one tonne of gold by recycling 40 million used mobile phones is not only much easier and cheaper than getting one tonne of primary gold out of the earth; such a method is much less harmful to workers and to the environment. We have the technology to recycle over 95% of the 15 precious metals that are in a mobile phone.

Kopnick then enquires, 'Why are mobile phone companies sawing off the branch that they themselves are sitting on by using primary raw materials to produce two billion mobile phones every year?'

Why indeed?

After undertaking over a year of research into this subject, I am buoyed up by the resourcefulness, tenacity, creativity and, in most cases, the rational business sense demonstrated by many of the pioneers of the embryonic circular economy. This is not to ignore the many established cultures around the world where reuse and adaptation has been a way of life for centuries. However, my concern has been that as these cultures and communities become more affluent they tend to drop this good practice for the bad practice associated with post World War II USA and Europe – that is the throwaway consumer linear economy.

Dealing with sustainability

In the meantime I feel that the sustainability 'brand' has been difficult to sell, and even harder to adopt. It appears to have been easily undermined by its detractors, despite huge amounts of evidence proving that humankind needs to reduce its negative presence. Many people are aware of the reasons sustainability is good, but confronting the scary issues, statistics and visual evidence is often overwhelming. 'Sustainability' is a place where one feels guilty about not doing the right thing, or not doing enough of it. Professor Michael Braungart has been onto this issue for a long time, discussing the point recently in his essay 'Learning to celebrate our human footprint',[2] where he states:

> For years this has been the basic premise of the environmental movement: we can only save the world if we choose lives of thriftiness – use less, reduce consumption, and minimise our ecological footprint ... this is not at all attractive for business, politics or society. Especially for companies and entrepreneurs it is rather difficult to communicate the 'consume less' principle to their customers.

Braungart is also famous for stating that sustainability has been interpreted as 'being less bad', which can lead to silly situations such as excess waste deliberately generated in Europe to feed the proliferation of 'energy from waste' incinerators, which of course are perceived as 'less bad' than sending waste to landfill sites.

In Cradle to Cradle, Braungart constructs a world 'where everything is beneficial ... where all materials are nutrients and everything is designed to become part of an ongoing biological or technical cycle, we can celebrate abundance'. In this world, a 'circular' society would allow humankind to live in harmony with the natural world because the concept of waste would be an anathema.

So does that mean I didn't need to write this book, which appears to be all about 'being less bad'? I would argue that the vision described in Cradle to Cradle is clear. I like the way it depends upon designers rethinking their practice, manufacturers rethinking their supply chain, and chemists inventing clever materials that don't become toxic waste. Designers will save the world; I do believe that. However, where Braungart will dismiss recycling and reusing materials (especially the 'dumb' toxic materials that hang around for a very long time) as merely 'slowing down the inevitable journey into our oceans',[3] the need for writing this book was to point out that there are actually added benefits from dealing with these 'less bad' issues. Identifying ocean waste, especially forms of plastic, as a material source could help restore coastlines and seawater back to its natural clean state. Diverting waste material from building sites, industry and our homes for reuse will reduce the burden on the natural environment to accept this stuff. The 'big clean-up' of Planet Earth must happen. Mining companies need to mine the 'Anthropocene' layer of stuff dug up by their predecessors, and start closing down conventional mines.

I acknowledge that there are big challenges here, not least for the 'energy from waste' incinerators searching for fuel because they are signed into 25-year contracts to be 'less bad', when society has moved on from considering that strategy to be viable (for the record, it never was). However, I believe we need to be pragmatic, and make the best of it; design our way out of this current unsustainable situation, towards Braungart's Cradle to Cradle vision. In the meantime, more circular intelligent materials will be introduced, and more products will be designed for remanufacture. Perhaps by the time the oceans are cleaned up a fully functioning circular economy will be flourishing.

We need to be pragmatic and visionary in equal measure. We need people like

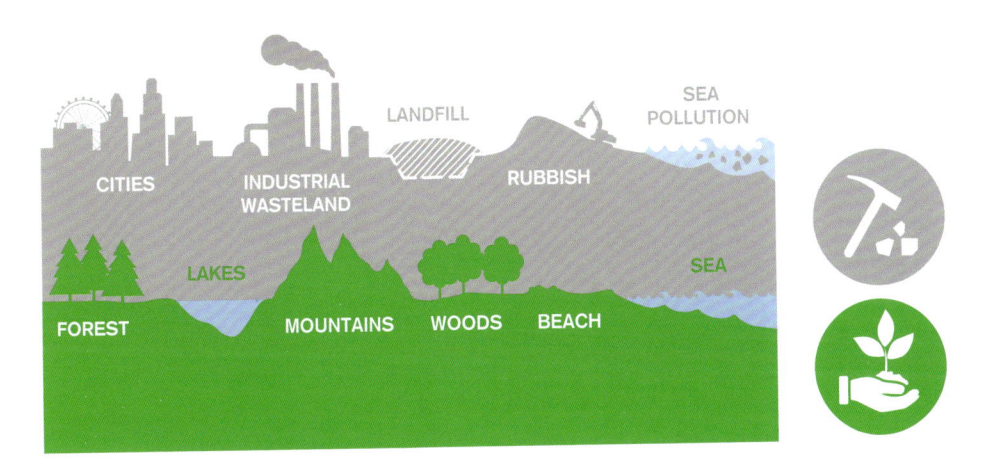

FIG. 4.1 Mining the anthropocene + Nurture natural resources

Cyrill Gutsch at Parley (see page 34) to raise awareness of the problems that face all of humanity, while simultaneously communicating a positive solution. Whether people buying jeans or training shoes made from ocean waste will be less inclined to throw them away, only time will tell. The emergent circular economy isn't dealing with virgin territories. To be successful it needs new working methods, new economies, legislation, educational techniques and systems, while dealing with the consequences of the last three linear industrial revolutions upon the natural world. Organisations such as Superuse (see page 62) and Rotor (see page 82) are having a go at experimenting with some of the new 'ways of doing', while Turntoo (see page 127) and others are imagining the new systems, procurement methods and contracts that will enable us to exist as a circular economy. In addition there are academic institutions setting up courses in the subject, supporting Masters and PhD students, while academics consider crucial issues in relation to social, economic and even the phenomenological consequences of a circular economy (phenomenology is the study of structures of consciousness as experienced from the first-person point of view. So if you work with materials and artefacts that are reused or remanufactured, then the memories or narratives associated with the previous uses or lives if you like, of these reused artefacts, have a bearing on the new use). Then there are the think tanks working hard to unravel the potentials of the circular economy; organisations such as the Ellen MacArthur Foundation[4] in the UK, Professor Braungart's EPEA[5] in Hamburg, and Professor Stahel's Product Life Institute[6] in Geneva. Doing this sort of work within the current linear economy is always going to be challenging. However, many people are more optimistic since every country in the world turned up to COP21[7] in Paris at the end of 2015. The EU Circular Economy Package[8] is a positive step as well, albeit not as big a step as many had hoped, but the EU document demonstrates the excitement about the prospect of increased wealth, employment and superior quality of life a circular economy will afford.

HOW ARE CLOSED-LOOP SYSTEMS RELEVANT?

So is it all about semantics?

The word 'economy' in the term 'circular economy' sounds familiar and tangible to business executives. I think it is more than that. The circular economy is a world where 'waste is food', where things are designed to be 'material banks for the future', using intelligent materials that don't become 'dumb' toxic waste. Sustainability is not so clear. It has become all things to everybody. Put it in front of 'economy' and you are talking about the ability to make more and more money for your shareholders. It's easily corrupted. I'm not saying that the phrase, or indeed the concept, of the circular economy won't be hacked about in the near future, with attempts to corrupt it as well. I just feel that it is a clearer concept for a mass audience to comprehend. Taking a 'linear' system and turning it into a 'circular' system is easy to visualise pretty quickly. Meanwhile, we could be arguing about sustainability and how 'less bad' we should be, while drowning in seas of plastic.

CIRCULAR SPECULATIONS

A conversation with two of the people behind Arup and BAM's Circular Building, developed with Frener & Reifer and The Built Environment Trust

To prepare for this last chapter I interviewed a diverse group of people (educators, contractors, suppliers, designers and academics) to see what they thought of the concept of the circular economy, and especially its viability. Below is an interview with two of the main protagonists behind a series of events at The Building Centre in London in September 2016: Stuart Smith, a director at Arup, and Nitesh Magdani, Director of Sustainability at BAM Construct UK. Magdani and Smith constructed a temporary pavilion that sat outside The Building Centre in Store Street, London. It was 'designed for disassembly' and called (naturally) 'The Circular Building'.

Nitesh Magdani **NM:** The way we talk about waste now is very different to before. I talk about business models and how I can add value and incentivisation, rather than talking about waste.

Stuart Smith **SS:** We are still talking about the value of waste; it represents an economic indicator, because it is a very tangible and visible thing. Just look out of the window. Any street in London has two or three skips full of waste. So people know it is there; it is a little bit of an incentive to change things.

The EU puts economic value on waste. Conversations around sustainability only really made progress once it stacked up financially; only then did it get the OK from

PART 4   LOOKING FORWARD

clients. This time around discussing the circular economy means we don't talk about the cost of waste, we talk about getting more money for what we do, including the value of residual materials and not causing us higher costs further down the road. [It's] an appreciation of whole-life costs rather than just capital cost that a lot of people are interested in, but only when the figures are put in front of them. You need early adaptors and people like us to go out and build a circular house or a waste house.

NM: When I speak to my board I don't speak about waste or 'carbon' because they don't understand it, but they know that clients respond to delivering something more efficiently. If they can sell something onto a client as a benefit then it is absolutely the right thing to do, especially if the client is saying 'I want you to add value. I want this building to perform better' or 'I want to look at operational costs and I want more cost certainty'. The circular economy is one of the things we are talking about that delivers on all of these things.

SS: I think the world has changed as well. When you look back 10 or 20 years, corporate responsibility was quite a different thing. Consumers have driven corporate responsibility and people sat in boardrooms are taking note of that. People want to shape companies to do better things.

NM: We had a discussion only the other week about 'Should it be Corporate Social Responsibility or should it be sustainability?' CSR is very inward-focused, whereas sustainability is very innovation-driven. How can you deliver products for your clients that are better? That often means trial and error. It means being innovative and trying new things. With construction you are now seeing a lot more closed-loop systems. People are taking waste from one system as material for another.

People are acknowledging that it might be cost neutral now, but in the future they have a source of material that they don't need to worry about. It's like Timberland. I don't know if you know the story of Timberland Tires?[9] Another tyre manufacturer approached Timberland asking if they could use their waste product, ie old tyres, as soles for shoes. Timberland did its own research, and made an amazing decision: now Timberland has its own tyre manufacturing business, and it supplies the shoe company with its old tyres! Timberland knows the exact make-up of the material, including the complete supply chain that supplies their shoes.

Philips Lighting have a new initiative: Philips City Farming.[10] So rather than just selling the LED technology developed for growing vegetables, they are now growing the vegetables in high-rise vertical farms in Eindhoven. Tomatoes use 90% less water than normal because of this technology.

These are good examples of how sustainability has informed businesses to make good innovative circular business models that make more money than before.

DBB: Is coming up with those ideas difficult? It feels like the circular economy could just take off quickly and in five years' time everybody could be doing it. It feels less problematic than trying to sell the idea of sustainability.

SS: Yes, because it is obvious. If you strip out all the buzzwords, and for a while sustainability was all about buzzwords, and then talk about what you are actually doing, why it makes sense, you don't even need to mention 'circular economy' or 'sustainability' or 'resource efficiency' and so on, because it is all making complete sense without needing any explanation.

DBB: You can see how big corporations and brands will act on it to make even more money. Obviously they can also have the greatest effect quickly, which in turn will encourage others to adopt circular systems. Now with regards to the Circular Building: if it was dismantled and the components went back to the suppliers for reuse, and you mapped that. So, then the project was a success, was it not?

NM: We have all learnt from the experience with both the designers and the construction supply chain. You can see 'end of life' very quickly. So we have sped up the process with the Circular Building.

DBB: Then to rebuild it as a variation: it doesn't have to be the whole building. It could be just one bay. What I was interested in is showing that if something was rebuilt, and if you gave it a different programme or site, how it would have to adapt. There is no one design that fits all scenarios. Buildings have to adapt.

SS: How Buildings Learn by Stuart Brand.[11]

At the point of going to press the Circular Building was dismantled and the components were stored, waiting to be reassembled or sent back to the suppliers for reuse.

FROM TOP

FIG. 4.2 The Circular Building being assembled

FIG. 4.3 The Circular Building complete

FIG. 4.4 The Circular Building being disassembled

PART 4   LOOKING FORWARD

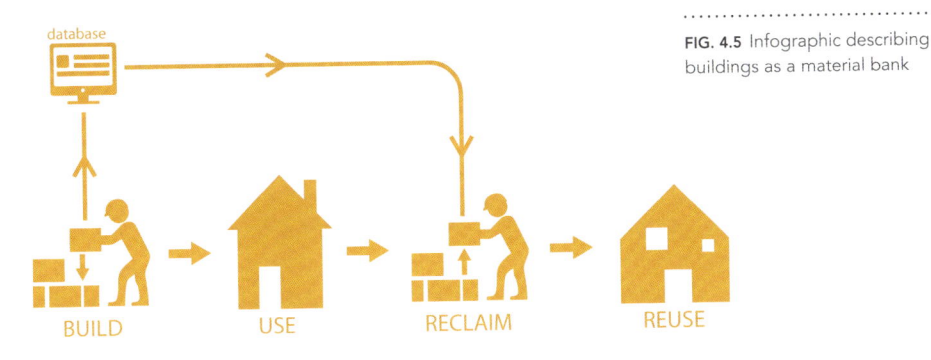

FIG. 4.5 Infographic describing buildings as a material bank

BUILD → USE → RECLAIM → REUSE

The Circular economy in practice

There are many projects I probably should have included in this book; projects that have informed many people's thinking. The Swiss Sound Box, designed by Peter Zumthor for the 2000 Hanover Expo, is a beautiful temporary pavilion, conceived as a welcoming place for Expo visitors to relax and 'just be'. Typically for Zumthor, the building was immaculately detailed, with dramatic music and light shows. The pavilion was constructed out of 144km of timber, all with a cross-section of 200x100mm, which totalled 2,800 m^3 of larch and Douglas fir. Assembled without the use of glue, nails or bolts, the timber was carefully stacked and braced with steel cables and springs. When the Expo was over, the cables were released. This in turn liberated all of the timber, which had become seasoned and stable, and allowed it to be sold for many other construction and making projects. The building went from pavilion to building supplier – the concept of 'buildings as a material store' was very simply personified.

FIG. 4.6 Peter Zumthor's Swiss Sound Box (2000) was a material store for many other buildings

HOW ARE CLOSED-LOOP SYSTEMS RELEVANT? **CHAPTER 3**

Looking forward

It is no coincidence that the circular economy is emerging at the same time that digital networks improve. Identifying and quantifying new material flows will require big data to do a lot of the networking and hard work for us. It doesn't take a visionary to imagine near future virtual networks where suppliers and contractors swap waste material online for free; a virtual market. Keeping material sources 'flowing' in useful directions, avoiding landfill or incineration, will be the objective. One day soon these techniques will be universal. Big data concepts such as BIM are already used to quantify everything about a new building design in one collaborative model. Google and others already have simple 3D CAD models of most buildings in most cities. Soon there will be BIM models, not only of new buildings, but existing ones as well… and for me that is when it gets interesting. BIM models will collect 'material passports' (see page 127) which in turn will tell anybody who is interested the exact potentials of a building, a neighbourhood or a city to provide material for future developments. At one level it sounds a bit Orwellian, the idea of big data knowing every brick, pane of glass or steel beam in a building, new and old. However for the circular economy to work, this information will be crucial, and not only for architecture. Imagine an online market that tapped into all industries and quantified new material flows as soon as they become available, avoiding the need for excessive warehouse storage. Enlightened designers and manufacturers would borrow or lease the material before returning it to the 'Material Flow Market'. I believe that we are not too far away from that vision. I also feel that designers *will* save the world. Most importantly: 'there definitely is no such thing as waste, just stuff in the wrong place'.

I thought I'd leave the last words off this book to a young architect, Bongani Muchemwa. While studying at the University of Westminster in 2013, Muchemwa proposed an 'Eternal Building School': one large closed-loop neighbourhood in a perpetual state of design, construction, inhabitation and deconstruction. I asked Muchemwa about his own thoughts on the viability of the circular economy, especially as he had now worked for a commercial practice in London for a few years. Here is part of his response.

> In China, the demolishing of buildings by hand to preserve and reuse materials is often economically feasible as labour is still cheap and technological means might be relatively expensive in terms of capital investment. However, this kind of archaeological care is not often possible in developed countries: it's often cheaper to pull down buildings using explosives and machines, rebuilding new developments with fresh materials. Perhaps recycled materials may offer some relief. However, I think a better understanding of materials and how they can be creatively put together may help architects to have some control.

> There could be some role here that BIM technology can play. Materials can be both virtually and physically tagged; this could help track and salvage key materials and components that could be reused, and this could be useful when it

comes to renovation jobs, for example. However it might be that greater emphasis should be taken at smaller scales, here practice should be more critical and build up exemplar projects that can be deployed at larger scales. Recently I was involved in a competition for a small university landscape architecture lab, in which we proposed not to demolish the existing structure (a wooden cabin) but to strip out the cladding, fix up the structure, paint and re-clad it in polycarbonate, a cheap and great material. And use some of the wood from the salvaged cladding on the lab extension, an idea we learnt from the French architects Lacaton and Vassal, who deploy this kind of design attitude at larger scales.

FIG. 4.7 The 'Eternal Building School' by Bongani Muchemwa, an architecture Masters project speculating on closed-loop systems and the idea of a city as a perpetual building site

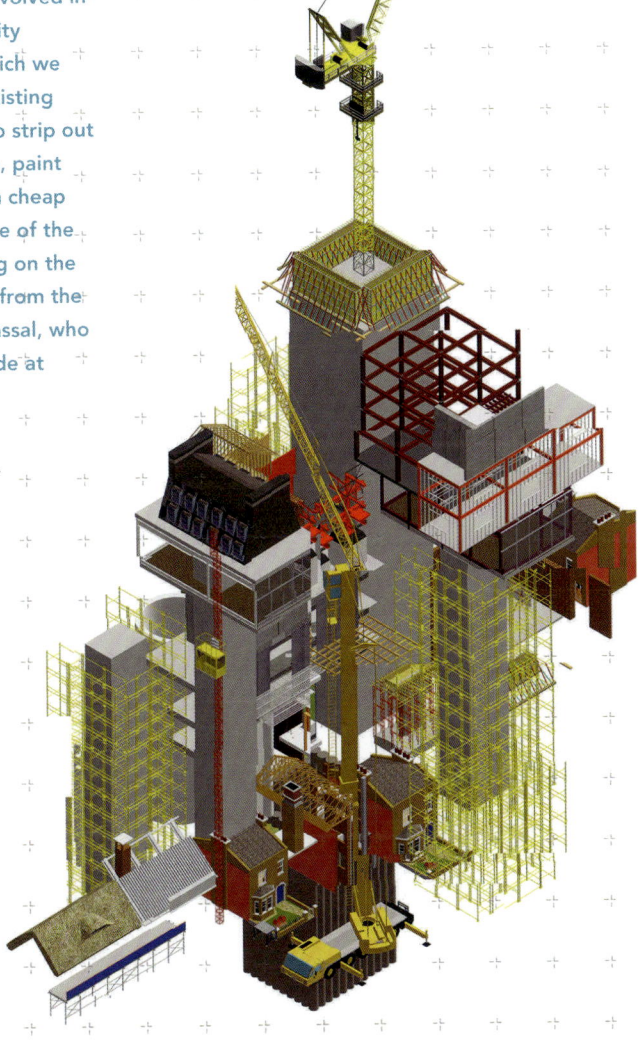

HOW ARE CLOSED-LOOP SYSTEMS RELEVANT? **CHAPTER 3**

ecobu...

OF THE 420 MILLION
TONNES CONSTRUCTION
MATERIAL USED EVERY
YEAR IN THE UK - 120
MILLION TONNES
GET WASTED

BBP

BBM
SUSTAINABLE
DESIGN

FOR EVERY 5
HOUSES BUILT, 1
HOUSE WORTH
OF MATERIALS IS
WASTED

THINK ... THE BIN ...

ENDNOTES

Foreword

1. Onions, C.T. *Shorter Oxford English Dictionary On Historical Principles.* Oxford Press. 1972 Edition. p382
2. For a good exploration of the tabula plena I recommend Roberts, Bryony (Ed). *Tabula Plena. Forms of Urban Preservation.* Lars Muller Publishers. Zurich. 2016.

Preface

1. The Bailey bridge is a type of portable, prefabricated truss bridge normally made of steel. It was developed by the British Army and saw extensive use during World War II. Some Bailey bridges are still in use today, for instance in remote areas in France.
2. Maslow, A 1943 'A theory of human motivation', *Psychological Review*
3. Ellen Franconi et al 2016 'Circular business opportunities for the built environment', in *A new dynamic 2: Effective systems in a circular economy.* Ellen MacArthur Foundation
4. Altogether, the new tunnel system consists of 152km of tunnels and produced 28.2 million tonnes of evacuated rock. Source: 'Aus dem Berg in den See und anderswohin', *Neue Zürcher Zeitung*, 24 May 2016, p7
5. http://www.clubofrome.org/a-new-club-of-rome-study-on-the-circular-economy-and-benefits-for-society/#more-1300
6. http://www.idsa.org/sites/default/files/Nemerson.pdf

....

OPPOSITE

The Waste Totem designed by BBM for EcoBuild 2013, made completely of waste timber and ply, and decorated with second-hand paint. It then became part of the Waste House

Introduction

1. McDonough, W and Braungart, M 2002 *Cradle to Cradle: Remaking the way we make things.* New York: North Point Press
2. Talk by Professor Dr Michael Braungart, 18 May 2015: 'Being Human' at The SCIN Gallery, London

Part 1: Chapter 1

1. Girardet, H 1992 *The Gaia Atlas of Cities: New directions for sustainable living.* London: Gaia Books
2. Taylor, MS 2007 *Buffalo Hunt: International trade and the virtual extinction of the North American bison.* Cambridge, Mass: NBER
3. McDonough, W and Braungart, M 2002 *Cradle to Cradle: Remaking the way we make things.* New York: North Point Press
4. Royal Society for the Encouragement of Arts, Manufactures and Commerce, founded in 1754
5. https://www.thersa.org/discover/publications-and-articles/reports/the-great-recovery-rearranging-the-furniture
6. Product-Life Factor (1982 Mitchell Prize-winning paper): http://www.product-life.org/en/major-publications/the-product-life-factor
7. https://www.ellenmacarthurfoundation.org
8. https://www.theguardian.com/sustainable-business/2016/aug/11/worlds-first-circular-economy-mba-student-graduates
9. Girling, R 2005 *Rubbish! Dirt on our hands and crisis ahead.* London: Eden Project Books
10. WRAP's vision for the UK circular economy to 2020: http://www.wrap.org.uk/content/wraps-vision-uk-circular-economy-2020
11. EU Circular Economy Package, 2015: http://ec.europa.eu/environment/circular-economy/index_en.htm

12. WRAP, 2015: http://www.wrap.org.uk/content/circular-economy-study-identifies-3-million-jobs-across-europe
13. http://bbm-architects.co.uk/portfolio/built-ecologies
14. http://bbm-architects.co.uk/portfolio/the-house-that-kevin-built
15. European Waste Statistics, Sept 2015: http://ec.europa.eu/eurostat/statistics-explained/index.php/Waste_statistics
16. UK Statistics on Waste, Government Statistical Services, Dept of Environment Food and Rural Affairs, Aug 2016, p9
17. Friends of the Earth 2009 'Over Consumption? Our use of the world's natural resources', ch 5, p21
18. *The Guardian* 29 Aug 2016 'The Anthropocene epoch: scientists declare dawn of human-influenced age': https://www.theguardian.com/environment/2016/aug/29/declare-anthropocene-epoch-experts-urge-geological-congress-human-impact-earth

Part 1: Chapter 2

1. https://en.wikipedia.org/wiki/List_of_countries_by_GDP_(PPP)
2. http://www.nytimes.com/2016/07/04/business/amazon-is-quietly-eliminating-list-prices.html
3. http://www.oecd.org/greengrowth/material%20resources,%20productivity%20and%20the%20environment_key%20findings.pdf
4. http://www.worldwatch.org/node/810
5. http://www.atlas.d-waste.com
6. http://www.worldwatch.org/node/810
7. https://www.newscientist.com/article/mg19426051.200-earths-natural-wealth-an-audit
8. https://www.theguardian.com/environment/2016/apr/19/great-barrier-reef-93-of-reefs-hit-by-coral-bleaching and http://www.abc.net.au/news/2016-06-21/reef-bleaching-could-cost-billion-in-lost-tourism/7526166
9. http://www.braungart.com
10. https://next.ft.com/content/f4b47ecc-bdf2-11e5-846f-79b0e3d20eaf
11. http://www.atlas.d-waste.com
12. http://ec.europa.eu/environment/waste/prevention/legislation.htm

13. https://www.gov.uk/government/publications/waste-prevention-programme-for-england
14. http://www.wrap.org.uk/content/innovation-waste-prevention-fund-england
15. http://www.neweconomics.org/blog/entry/the-sharing-economy-the-good-the-bad-and-the-real
16. http://www.actionforhappiness.org
17. http://www.buymeonce.com
18. http://www.wrap.org.uk/content/resource-efficient-construction
19. http://www.ssauk.com/useful-information/size-of-the-industry
20. http://www.dailymail.co.uk/news/article-2861908/Monster-sea-size-four-football-fields-world-s-largest-container-ships-sets-maiden-voyage-China.html
21. https://www.gov.uk/government/uploads/system/uploads/attachment_data/file/487916/UK_Statistics_on_Waste_statistical_notice_15_12_2015_update_f2.pdf and https://www.gov.uk/government/uploads/system/uploads/attachment_data/file/482255/Digest_of_waste_England_-_finalv3.pdf
22. http://www.wrap.org.uk/sites/files/wrap/WRAP%20contribution%20to%20economic%20growth_0.pdf
23. https://www.gov.uk/government/uploads/system/uploads/attachment_data/file/47621/1358-the-carbon-plan.pdf
24. http://www.carpetrecyclinguk.com
25. http://www.communitywoodrecycling.org.uk
26. Resource scarcity prediction: Armin Reller, University of Augsburg, Tom Graedel, Yale University, 23 May 2007 feature article in the *New Scientist*, 'Earth's Natural Wealth: An audit' by David Cohen, https://www.newscientist.com/article/mg19426051.200-earths-natural-wealth-an-audit https://www.newscientist.com/issue/2605/

Part 1: Chapter 3

1. https://www.pbs.org/weta/thewest/resources/archives/eight/trconserv.htm
2. http://europa.eu/rapid/press-release_IP-15-6203_en.htm
3. http://europa.eu/rapid/press-release_IP-15-6203_en.htm
4. http://www.wired.co.uk/article/how-to-be-creative-in-business
5. Bidgoli, H (ed) 2010 *The Handbook of Technology Management*. Hoboken, NJ: Wiley, p296

6 https://www.theguardian.com/sustainable-business/2015/mar/23/were-are-all-losers-to-gadget-industry-built-on-planned-obsolescence

7 http://www.greatrecovery.org.uk/resources/designing-for-a-circular-economy

8 http://www.theguardian.com/sustainable-business/10-things-need-to-know-circular-economy

9 http://www.ellenmacarthurfoundation.org/circular-economy/schools-of-thought/cradle2cradle

10 House of Commons Environmental Audit Committee, 'Growing a circular economy: ending the throwaway society', Third Report of Session, July 2014, http://www.publications.parliament.uk/pa/cm201415/cmselect/cmenvaud/214/214.pdf

11 European Commission, 2014, 'EU Waste Legislation'. Archived from the original on 12 March 2014

12 http://www.mrw.co.uk/opinion/merging-the-circular-economy-and-waste-hierarchy/8654179.article

13 Government waste prevention programme: 'Prevention is better than cure: the role of waste management in moving to a more resource efficient economy', (December 2013), p9

14 https://www.ellenmacarthurfoundation.org/circular-economy/overview/concept

15 'Making Things Last: Consultation on creating a more circular economy in Scotland': https://consult.scotland.gov.uk/zero-waste-delivery/making-things-last

16 http://www.green-alliance.org.uk/Opening_up_new_circular_economy_trade_opportunities.php

17 http://www.esauk.org/esa_reports/Circular_Economy_Report_FINAL_High_Res_For_Release.pdf

18 http://epi.yale.edu/epi/country-profile/united-kingdom. The EPI was created by the Yale Center for Environmental Law and Policy (YCELP) and the Center for International Earth Science Information Network (CIESIN) at Columbia University, who partnered with the World Economic Forum to develop indices for assessing environmental performance.

19 *Proceedings of the Institution of Civil Engineers – Waste and Resource Management*, volume 168, issue 1, February 2015, pp3–13: 'The circular economy: from waste to resource stewardship, part I', Julie Hill

20 http://product-life.org/en/3ecos/part1-ECCEpackage021215

21 As updated by the 'Further Alterations to the London Plan' (FALP) in March 2015

22 Sophie Thomas RSA Great Recovery – speech at RWM 2014

23 http://digital-built-britain.com/resources

24 https://soenecs-public.sharepoint.com/case-studies1

Part 2: Introduction

1 McDonough, W and Braungart, M 2002 *Cradle to Cradle: Remaking the way we make things*. New York: North Point Press

Part 2: Step 1

1 http://www.parley.tv/oceanplastic/#the-mission

2 Cyrill Gutsch, quoted in the article 'Plastic is a design flaw – this is how to fix it', 26 Sept 2016, http://www.gameplan-a.com/2016/09/plastic-is-a-design-flaw-this-is-how-to-fix-it

Part 2: Step 2

1 These issues are discussed at length in Chapman, J 2015 *Emotionally Durable Design: Objects, experiences and empathy*. Abingdon: Routledge

Part 2: Step 3

1 2012 *Druot, Lacaton & Vassal: Tour Bois-le-Prêtre*. Berlin: Ruby Press

2 Warm Homes and Energy Conservation Act, 2000 (UK)

3 www.gov.uk/government/statistics/final-uk-emissions-estimates

4 https://retrofit.innovateuk.org

5 https://www.theguardian.com/environment/2014/oct/10/uk-looks-to-dutch-model-to-make-100000-homes-carbon-neutral-by-2020

6 Chamber, NB 2011 *Urban Green: Architecture for the future*. New York: Palgrave Macmillan

Part 2: Step 4

1 http://www.c2ccertified.org

2 http://www.hebel.arch.ethz.ch/

3 Semester Schedule document 'Ressource Schweiz' published in Spring 2015. ETH Zurich D-ARCH written by Hebel et al, presented to undergraduate architecture students

4 https://www.thersa.org/discover/publications-and-articles/reports/the-great-recovery-rearranging-the-furniture

5 Ruby, Ilka und Andreas (2010), Mine the City, Re-Inventing Construction, edited by Ilka and Andreas Ruby, Ruby Press, Berlin, Germany, pp243–247

6 Graedel, Thomas, *Urban Mining, Recycling Embodied Energy,* greenbuilding.world-aluminum.org website, accessed on-line: 22.01.2014, http://greenbuilding.world-aluminium.org/facts/urban-mining

7 'Waste = Food (Cradle to Cradle)' https://vimeo.com/3237777

8 McDonough, W and Braungart, M 2002 *Cradle to Cradle: Remaking the way we make things.* New York: North Point Press

9 Hawken, P 2010 *The Ecology of Commerce: A declaration of sustainability.* New York: HarperCollins; Benyus, J 1998 *Biomimicry: Innovation inspired by nature.* New York: Morrow

10 Karl-Henrik Robèrt, *The Natural Step: a framework for achieving sustainability in our organisations*

Part 3

1 http://arts.brighton.ac.uk/business-and-community/the-house-that-kevin-built

2 Department for Environment, Food and Rural Affairs, Government Statistical Service, 'UK Statistics on Waste 2010–2012', published March 2015

3 Waste and Resource Action Plan (WRAP), published 2011: www.wrap.org.uk

4 McDonough, W and Braungart, M 2002 *Cradle to Cradle: Remaking the way we make things.* New York: North Point Press

5 An Innovate UK initiative published findings in April 2014 ('Retrofit the future: a guide to making retrofit work') clearly demonstrating that many completed buildings did not perform as expected https://retrofit.innovateuk.org/documents/1524978/2138994/Retrofit%20for%20the%20future%20-%20A%20guide%20to%20making%20retrofit%20work%20-%202014

6 http://arts.brighton.ac.uk/ease/wastehouse/thtkb-london-2008

7 www.ribaj.com/buildings/brighton-waste-house-brighton

8 Quoted at http://www.treehugger.com/urban-design/does-density-make-cities-more-affordable-alex-steffen-thinks-so.html

Part 4: Chapter 1

1 Chapman, J 2005 *Emotionally Durable Design: Objects, experiences and empathy.* London: Earthscan

2 Bakker, C, Hollander, M and van Hinte, E 2014 *Products That Last: Product design for circular business models.* The Netherlands: TU Delft Library

3 Bocock, R 1993 *Consumption.* Oxon: Routledge, p46

4 Bateson, G 1972 *Steps to an Ecology of Mind.* Chicago: University of Chicago

5 Thackara, J 2015 *How to Thrive in the Next Economy: Designing tomorrow's world today.* London: Thames & Hudson

6 Cooper, T 'Which way to turn? Product longevity and business dilemmas in the circular economy', in Chapman, J (ed) 2017 *The Routledge Handbook of Sustainable Product Design.* Oxon: Routledge

7 Sudjic, D, 2008 *The Language of Things.* London: Allen Lane

8 Tonkinwise, C 'Is design finished? Dematerialisation and changing things', *Design Philosophy Papers,* 2, 2014, p190

9 Jones, JC 'Continuous design and redesign', *Design Studies,* 4, 1983, pp53–60

10 Hunt, J 2003 'Just re-do it: Tactical formlessness and everyday consumption', in *Strangely Familiar: Design and everyday life.* Minneapolis: Walker Art Center, pp56–71

11 Redström, J 'RE:Definitions of use', *Design Studies,* 29, 2008, pp410–423

12 Ehn, P 'Participation in design things', in *Proceedings of the Tenth Anniversary Conference on Participatory Design 2008, PDC '08.* Indianapolis: Indiana University, pp92–101

13 Taylor, D 2011 *Design Art Furniture and The Boundaries of Function: Communicative objects, performative things* (PhD Thesis), University of the Arts London and Falmouth University, p227

14 Megginson, LC 'Lessons from Europe for American businesses', *The Southwestern Social Science Quarterly,* 44(1), 1963, p4

15 Robinson, M 2010 'Making adaptive resilience real', Arts Council England, p14 [Online]. Available at: http://www.thinkingpractice.co.uk/wordpress/wp-content/uploads/2012/06/making_adaptive_resilience_real.pdf

16 Packard, V 1964 *The Waste Makers.* Middlesex: Penguin

17 London, B 1932 *Ending the Depression Through Planned Obsolescence*, Pamphlet, US

18 Calkins, EE 1932 'What consumer engineering really is', in Sheldon, R and Arens, E *Consumer Engineering: A new technique for prosperity*. New York: Harper & Brothers, pp1–14

19 Slade, G 2007 *Made to Break: Technology and obsolescence in America*. Cambridge, MA: Harvard University Press

20 Chapman, J and Marmont, G 2017 'The temporal fallacy: Design, emotion and obsolescence', in Egenhoefer, RB (ed) *The Routledge Handbook of Sustainable Design*. Oxon: Routledge

21 Fry, T 2011 *Design as Politics*. New York: Berg

Part 4: Chapter 2

1 Douglas, M 1966 *Purity and Danger: An analysis of concepts of pollution and taboo*. London: Routledge & K Paul

2 http://www.treehugger.com/urban-design/does-density-make-cities-more-affordable-alex-steffen-thinks-so.html

3 Hyde, L 2006 *The Gift: How the creative spirit transforms the world*. Edinburgh: Canongate Books

4 https://www.ellenmacarthurfoundation.org

5 Castells, M 2001 'Universities as dynamic systems of contradictory functions', in Muller, J et al (eds) *Challenges of Globalisation: South African debates with Manuel Castells*. Cape Town: Maskew Miller Longman, pp206–223

6 Poritz, JA and Rees, J 2016 *Education is not an App: The future of university teaching in the Internet age*. London: Routledge

7 In his essay 'Self-Realisation as the Moral Ideal' (Early Works 4:50), Dewey writes, 'If I were asked to name the most needed of all reforms in the spirit of education, I should say: "Cease conceiving of education as mere preparation for later life, and make it the full meaning of the present life."'

8 Freire, P and Bergman Ramos, M (translator) 2000 *Pedagogy of the Oppressed: 30th anniversary edition*. New York: Bloomsbury Academic

9 Wenger, W 1998 *Communities of Practice: Learning, meaning and identity*. Cambridge: Cambridge University Press

10 Translated into English by Andrew Hurley, the original Spanish title is *Del rigor en la ciencia*. Some English translations prefer *On Rigour in Science*. The story was first published in March 1946, in the journal *Los Anales de Buenos Aires, año 1, no 3*, where it formed part of a piece called 'Museo'. It was collected later that year in the second Argentinian edition of *A Universal History of Infamy*.

Part 4: Chapter 3

1 Kopnik, H 2016 A Future without Waste? Zero Waste in Theory and Practice', edited by Christof Mauch, published by the Rachel Carson Center for Environment and Society

2 Braungart, M 2016 'Learning to Celebrate Our Human Footprint', edited by Christof Maunch, published by the Rachel Carson Center for Environment and Society

3 Talk by Professor Dr Michael Braungart, 18 May 2015: 'Being Human' at The SCIN Gallery, London

4 https://www.ellenmacarthurfoundation.org

5 http://epea-hamburg.org

6 http://www.product-life.org

7 United Nations Climate Change Conference in Paris, December 2015, http://www.cop21.gouv.fr/en

8 http://ec.europa.eu/environment/circular-economy/index_en.htm

9 https://www.timberlandtires.com

10 http://www.lighting.philips.com/main/products/horticulture/city-farming.html

11 Brand, S 1994 *How Buildings Learn: What happens after they're built*. London: Viking Press

INDEX

Note: page numbers in italics refer to illustrations.

12 Principles of Design for Environment (Eco-Design) xvii
20K Houses 59, 60

Adams, Ansel 24
Adidas 34–6, 53
adobe 114, 145
Ahearn, Kevin 42, 44
AIR (Avoid, Intercept, Redesign) 33, 51
Alliander HQ 130, 131, *132*
aluminium 88, 113
Amphibious Envelope 121
ANA Intercontinental Hotel xvi–xvii
Apple 15
Architype 122–6
Auburn University, Alabama 58

Bakker, Joost 68
BBM 11, 12–13
Billiet, Lionel 104–8
biomaterials *see* organic materials
Bionic Partition 121
Bocock, Robert 162
Boddington, Anne 14, 166–72
Boro clothing 66–7
Braungart, Michael 2, 10, 174
Brexit 26
bricks 46, 47, *114*, 118–20
Brighton Waste House 145–58, *172*
Brooker, Graeme ix–xi
Brummen Town Hall 128, *129*
BS 5906: 2005 27–8
building information management (BIM) 27, 180
building materials from waste products *see* recycling waste; reusing waste
Building Regulations 153
Built Ecologies (exhibition) 13
Bullus, Anna 37–8
Bureo Skateboards 42–4
Burkina Faso 114–17

C2C ExpoLAB 133–6

carbon emissions *see* CO₂ emissions
carpet tiles 137–42
ceramic floor tiles 83, 107
Chapman, Jonathan 161–5
China Harvest Map 77–8, 79
Circular Building 176, 178
circular economy xiii–xiv, xvi, 10, 15, 22–8, 109–42, 174–6
and BIM 27
case studies
  Alliander HQ 130, 131, *132*
  Brummen Town Hall 128, *129*
  Burkina Faso 114–17
  Enterprise Centre, UEA 122–6
  Hy-Fi organic compostable tower 118–21
  New City Hall, Venlo 133–6
pedagogic methods 110–13
definition 24, 176
extent of 23
looking forward 173–81
origins 22–3
political approaches 23–4
UK performance 24–5
Circular Economy Package (EU) 11, 21, 26
City of Fashion and Design 98, *99*
cladding 72, 73, 86, 98, *101*, 102, 131
'Client House' programme 58
climate adaptation 98
climate change agreement COP21 8, 52
Climate Take Back 138
Club of Rome study xv–xvi
CO₂ emissions 20
CO₂ reduction 12, 14, 100, 102
coffee grounds 39–41
compost from waste 41, 68, 69
concrete xvii, 98, 135–6, 150
construction waste (*see also* deconstruction waste)
EU guidelines 26
minimization 27
quantities 15, 20, 146

COP21 8, 52
corporate responsibility 15, 177
Cradle to Cradle 2, 8, 10, 174
Curface 39, 41
Cyclifier 64, 65

Dahy, Hanaa 48
deconstructing buildings xvi–xvii, 113
deconstruction waste 104–8, 110–13
EU guidelines 26
re-use 82–5, 86–8, 128, *129*, 131
Design Academy, Eindhoven 48
design for disassembly 110–13
design for reuse 27
Digital Built Britain plan 27
dismantling buildings xvi–xvii, 113
'disposable' nappies 45
Docks de Paris building 98, 99
Dordtyart Cultural Centre 65

earthen construction 114, 145
Eco-Design principles xvii
Ecovative 47, 118
education 166–72
Ellen MacArthur Foundation (EMF) 22, 24, 166
Elvis & Kresse 56–7
Empire State Building xv
employment opportunities 24, 122, 125, 126
energy efficiency 100, 102, 149
EnerPhit 102
Enterprise Centre, UEA 122–6
Environmental Audit Committee (EAC) 23
environmental performance assessment 24, 26
Environmental Performance Index (EPI) 24
Environmental Services Association 24
EPEA (Environment Protection Encouragement Agency) 86
Eternal Building School 180–1
European Union (EU)

Circular Economy Package 11, 21, 26, 175
recycling target 26
Waste Framework Directive 23
waste prevention programmes 18

Facit® 147
Fairweather, Adam 39
fire hoses 56
Fletcher, Cat 16–20, 148, 150, 152, 154
floor tiles 83, 107
Foamglas® insulation 86, 88
food and catering 68–70
Freear, Andrew 60
Freegle UK 19, 148, 152
furniture 39, 41, 70, 107

The Gaia Atlas of Cities 7
Gardener Stewart Architects (GSA) 102
Girardet, Herbert 7
glass and glazing 58, 86, 88
Google 41
Gotthard rail tunnel, Switzerland xv
Graedel, Thomas E 113
Grand Parc, Bordeaux 91, *92*
Great Recovery programme (RSA) 8–9
Green Alliance Circular Economy Taskforce 24
Greencup 39, 41
Greenfield, David 21–8
gumdrop bins 37–8
Gutsch, Cyrill 34, 49–51, 175

Handbook for Off-site Reuse 104–5
Harvest Mapping 62, 63, 64, 76–7
Hebel, Dirk 110–13
higher education 166–72
high-rise buildings xvi–xvii, 86–7, 90, 91
Hill, Julie 25
The House that Kevin Built 13–14
Hub 67 71–4

188   INDEX

Hy-Fi tower 118–21
Hy-Fi Tower by The Living, New York xii

IDSA Principles of Design for Environment (Eco-Design) xvii
inclusive business 139–40
Inside Flows 64
insulation 45, 101, 102, 131, 150
Interface 137–42

Jakob + MacFarlane 98
Japanese Boro clothing 66–7
Jongert, Jan 62, 75–9

Kéré, Francis 114–17
Kéré Architecture 114–17
Kneppers, Ben 42
Komai, Sadaharu 93–7
Kopnick, Herbert 173
Kraaijvanger Architects 133–6

La Tour Bois-le-Prêtre 90, 91
Lacaton & Vassal 89–92
leasing products 78, 127–8, 142
Lions Park playground 60, 61
local identity 13
local labour 24, 122, 125, 126
locally sourced materials 14, 114–17, 122–6, 139–40
Lock, Andrew 71–3
Lock, Diana 15
London Fire Brigade 56
London Infrastructure Plan 27
LYN Atelier 71–4

MacArthur, Ellen 10
Magdani, Nitesh 176–8
Maslow, Abraham xiv
Mason's Bend 58
material passports 73, 127, 180
McCloud, Kevin 147
McMaster, Douglas 68–70
Mears Group 150–1
metals 60, 73, 88, 113, 173 (see also steel framing)
ModCell® 147, 148
modular construction xvi, 96, 128
Muchemwa, Bongani 180–1
Museum of Modern Art (MoMA) 118–20
Mussel Choir 118
mycelium bricks 118–20
Myco Foam 47
Mycro Board 47

natural materials see organic materials
Nestlé HQ, Vevey, Switzerland xv
Net Positiva 42
Net-Works programme 139–41
Newbern Fire Station and Town Hall 59, 60

Newspaper Wood 45
Nordic Built Innovation 86
nylon waste 140–1

Olympic Delivery Authority (ODA) 71, 73
Opalis project 104
organic materials 14, 47–8, 114–17, 122–6 (see also mycelium bricks; wood products)
mycelium bricks 118–20
sheep's wool 45
thatch 123, 125
Oslo Urban Mountain 86–8

Paddington Maintenance Depot (PMD) xviii
Palais de Tokyo 89
Parley for the Oceans 33–6, 49–54
Parley Ocean School 54
partition walls 86, 121
Passivhaus standards 102, 126
Philips City Farming 177
plastic waste 33, 49–54, 140–1
political approaches 23–4, 26, 27–8
Potocnik, Janez 26
prefabricated construction xvi, 13, 48, 125, 128, 147
product certification 128, 135, 141–2
product lifespans 161–3, 165
PV panels 130, 131, 149

Rau, Thomas 127
RAU Architects 127–32
Recyclicity 65
recycling waste 33–54
Adidas training shoe 34–6, 53
building materials from waste products 45–8
Bureo skateboards 42–3
EU target 26
gumdrop bins 37–8
Re-worked 39–41
Reday, Genevieve 10
Redcup 39
reduction of material use 81–108
La Tour Bois-le-Prêtre 90, 91
Oslo Urban Mountain 86–8
Palais de Tokyo 89
Rented House Life 93–7
Retrofit 98–103
Rotor & RotorDC 82–5, 104–8
refurbishment 89–92 (see also retrofit)
refurbishment hierarchy 23
Remade South East 15
renewable energy 139 (see also PV panels)
Rented House Life 93–7
resource management hierarchy 23, 24

restaurant application 68–70
Retrofit 98–103
retrofit, energy efficiency 100–3
Retrofit the Future 100
reusing waste 55–79
Elvis & Kresse 56–7
Hub 67, by LYN Atelier 71–4
Rotor Deconstruction 104–8
Rural Studio 58–61
Silo, zero-waste restaurant 68–70
Superuse Studios 62–5, 75–9
traditional Boro clothing 66–7
Re-worked 39–41
RIBA House of the Future 11
Romney Marsh Visitor Centre 12
roof tiles 45
Rotor Deconstruction 82, 84, 104–8
RSA Great Recovery programme 8–9
Ruby, Ilka and Andreas 113
Rural Studio 58–61

Sanremo Srl 41
Schimdt Hammer Lassen Architects (SHL Architects) 86–8
Scotland 24
Sea Shepherd Conservation Society 51, 52
sheep's wool 45
Silo 68–70
skateboards 42–4
Smile Plastics Ltd 39
Smith, Stuart 176–8
social sustainability 16, 62, 139–40 (see also local labour)
Soest, Tom van 48
soil conditioner 41, 68, 69
solar energy 98, 130, 131, 149
Spink, Rosie 22
Stahel, Walter xiii–xviii, 10, 26
Stansfield, Nigel 137–42
steel framing 98, 117, 131
StoneCycling 46, 48
Superuse Studios 62–5, 75–9
supply chains 127, 139–40, 142, 152, 180
sustainable design 161–5
Swiss Sound Box 179

take-back / reuse schemes 19
tall buildings xvi–xvii, 86–7, 90, 91
thatch 123, 125
The House that Kevin Built (THTKB) iii, 13, 147–8
The Living 118–21
Thomas, Sophie 8–9, 22, 113
timber-framing 93–7, 125, 149, 153, 157 (see also wood products)
Timberland 177
Timmermans, Frans 21

Tonkinwise, Cameron 164
tower block refurbishment 90, 91–2
training shoes 34–6, 53
Turntoo 127–32

UK policy and approach 24
United Nations climate change agreement COP21 8, 52
University of Bath 13, 148
University of Brighton 145–58
University of East Anglia (UEA) 122–6
University of Stuttgart 47–8
urban mining 112–13

van de Westerlo, Bas 133
Vassal, Jean Philippe 89–92
Venlo, New City Hall 133–6

waste 146
prevention 17–18
quantities 15, 17, 20
refurbishment 27–8
storage 27
transportation 20
Waste and Resources Action Programme (WRAP) 23, 25
waste hierarchy 18, 23
Waste House 145–58, 172
Waste Management Planning Advice for New Flatted Properties 27
Watson, Paul 49–50, 52
wear of materials 82, 84
Wesling, Kresse 56
whole life costing 12, 27, 135
Wilmcote House, Southsea 101, 102
wood products 75 (see also timber-framing)
cable reels 45
in new build 128, 131
Newspaper Wood 45
salvaged timber 125, 129, 131, 149
timber panels xvi, 147
Wood Recycling Network 20
Woodard, Ryan 8
WRAP (Waste and Resources Action Programme) 11
WWF 42

zero-waste see circular economy
zero-waste restaurants 68–70, 152
Zumthor, Peter 179

INDEX **189**

PICTURE CREDITS

Adam Walker 72 centre right
Adidas Group 32
Arup 178 bottom
Barkowphoto xii, 2, 120 bottom
BBM Sustainable Design 11–13, 155 top left, centre right, bottom left, 156 top right, 178 top & centre, 182
BioMat/ITKE 47 centre
BioMat/ITKE, Photo: Boris Miklautsch 47 top
BioMat/ITKE, photo: Hannaa Dahy 47 bottom
Bongani Muchemw 181
Bosence Building Conservation (www.bosence.co.uk) 46 bottom right
Bureo Inc. 43–44
Cat Fletcher 18
Darren Carter / Morgan Sindall 123 centre & bottom, 124, 126
David Greenfield 23
Dirk Hebel 111–112
Dr. Ryan Woodard 2, 4
Druot, Lacaton & Vassal 90 centre & bottom
Elvis & Kresse 56–57
Erik-Jan Ouwerkerk 116–117
Gardner Stewart Architects 101 (all)
Greencup Coffee 41
Gum-Tec Ltd 37, 38 (all)
Henrietta Williams Photography 123 top
Hsu, A. Et Al. (2016). 2016 Environmental Performance Index. New Haven, Ct: Yale University. Available: www.epi.yale.edu. (Creative Commons License) 25
Iwan Baan 121
Jakob + MacFarlene 99 top
Jill Tate 71, 72 centre left & bottom, 74
Jim Stephenson viii
Justin Lui 119 centre bottom
Kéré Architecture 115 (all)

Kimonoboy (www.kimonoboy.com) 67
Leigh Simpson 14
Lyn Atelier 72 top
Nicolas Borel 99 bottom
Olivier Beart 83 bottom left
Parley 35 top, bottom, 36, 49, 53
Philippe Ruault 80, 90 top, 92 (both)
Photo by Interface Inc. 137
Picture by Eric Mairiaux 84
Project by Rational Feelings Pr & Marketing
    Lead Photographer: Christian Bazzo
    Assistant photographer and video maker: Tommaso Meneghin 40 centre left
Re-Worked Ltd 40 top & centre right
Rotor 83 top, centre, bottom centre & bottom right, 104
Sadaharu Komai 93–97
Schmidt Hammer Lassen Architects 87 (all)
Sea Shepherd Global 35 centre
Silo 69–70
Smile Plastics Ltd 40 bottom (left & right)
Stone Cycling 46 top & centre
Studio Cuthbert 7, 175, 179 top
Superuse Studios 63–65, 75
The Living 118–120 top
The RSA – The Great Recovery Project (2012–2016) 9
The University of Brighton 155 top right, centre left, bottom right, 156 centre right & bottom
Theo Lowenstein 156 centre left
Thomas Heye 129
Thomas Rau 129 bottom right, 130 (all), 132
Tim Hursley 59 (all), 61
Ton Desar, City of Venlo 134 (all except top left)
Walter Stahel xiv
Wikiarquitectura 179 bottom